What Makes Us Human

"How do you go from a bunch of cells to something that can think?" This question, asked by the 9-year-old son of one of the authors, speaks to a puzzle that lies at the heart of this book. How are we as humans able to explore such questions about our own origins, the workings of our mind, and more? In this fascinating volume, developmental psychologists Jeremy Carpendale and Charlie Lewis delve into how such human capacities for reflection and self-awareness pinpoint a crucial facet of human intelligence that sets us apart from closely related species and artificial intelligence.

Richly illustrated with examples, including questions and anecdotes from their own children, they bring theories and research on children's development alive. The accessible prose shepherds readers through scientific and philosophical debates, translating complex theories and concepts for psychologists and non-psychologists alike. *What Makes Us Human* is a compelling introduction to current debates about the processes through which minds are constructed within relationships.

Challenging claims that aspects of thinking are inborn, Jeremy Carpendale and Charlie Lewis provide a relationally grounded way of understanding human development by showing how the uniquely human capacities of language, thinking, and morality develop in children through social processes. They explain the emergence of communication within the rich network of relationships in which babies develop. Language is an extension of this earlier communication, gradually also becoming a tool for thinking that can be applied to understanding others and morality. Learning more about the development of what is right in front of us, such as babies' actions developing into communicative gestures, leads to both greater appreciation of the children in our lives and a grasp of what makes us human.

This book will be of interest to anyone curious about the nature of language, thinking, and morality, including students, parents, teachers, and professionals working with children.

Jeremy Carpendale is Professor of Developmental Psychology at Simon Fraser University in British Columbia, Canada, and the father of two.

Charlie Lewis is Professor of Family and Developmental Psychology at Lancaster University, UK, and the father of two.

What Makes Us Human

How Minds Develop through Social Interactions

Jeremy Carpendale and Charlie Lewis

Routledge
Taylor & Francis Group

NEW YORK AND LONDON

First published 2021
by Routledge
52 Vanderbilt Avenue, New York, NY 10017

and by Routledge
2 Park Square, Milton Park, Abingdon, Oxon OX14 4RN

Routledge is an imprint of the Taylor & Francis Group, an informa business

© 2021 Taylor & Francis

Library of Congress Cataloging-in-Publication Data
A catalog record for this title has been requested

ISBN: 978-0-367-53792-0 (hbk)
ISBN: 978-0-367-53793-7 (pbk)
ISBN: 978-1-003-12510-5 (ebk)

Typeset in Sabon
by Taylor & Francis Books

To Hannah and Max, and Deborah, plus Charlie's gang: Rosie, Tom, Camilla, Lyndsey, Laurie, William, Edward and Otto

Contents

Figures

Preface

We wanted to write this book, first, because it concerns our own research questions, regarding the development of children's thinking about the social world, their language development as well as moral development. Second, the available books on this issue tend to present one side of the story. We want to tell the other side. For example, Steven Pinker, a professor of psychology at MIT, entitled one of his books *How the Mind Works*, and the philosopher Jerry Fodor responded with a book entitled *The Mind Doesn't Work that Way*. We also disagree with Pinker but for quite different reasons, and this book is our response to the position that Pinker shares with many others. A subtitle to this book could be "how the mind *really* works." Finally, we want to answer questions posed to us by our children. Jeremy's daughter, Hannah, at 3½ asked, "Daddy, what is meaning?" and "How do I remember things?" and "What is thinking?" She happily went out to play while we spent the next years grappling with these fascinating yet complex problems. Later, as an adolescent, she quizzed her father about his position on the mind–body problem. Both Hannah and her brother Max asked how people made up words for things, which Jeremy took as asking about how language works. Max, at 9, asked, "How did things start to think?" And he said that all his other questions like do ants sleep and does the universe go on forever came down to his big question, which was, "how do you go from a bunch of cells to something that can think?" Then, at 16, he asked what Jeremy thought of the idea of a noble savage and the evolution of altruism, and can we be certain of any knowledge, and, by the way, is there any such thing as free will? Although we don't claim to resolve all these complex issues, we do want to present a view of the development of human thinking as a way to approach these questions.

This book is intended for anyone interested in the nature of the mind, language, morality, thinking and, above all, the process of human development, which drives and explains all these skills. These miraculous developments occur under our noses, in our own homes and so are taken for granted and appear less complex and mysterious than other wonders of the world. But the mind is one of the most complex things to attempt to understand, and its development is fascinating. We believe that it is possible and timely to present some of the intriguing and important debates within developmental psychology in a way that is accessible to interested readers, regardless of their background. We will not assume a background in developmental psychology because we do not think that it should take years of graduate school to be able to understand what is at stake in these continuing debates. This book will be of interest to anyone fascinated by questions concerning the nature and development of thinking and human minds. This will include parents, teachers, and readers intrigued by what it takes for a child to develop human social skills. Understanding more about the development that is happening right in front of us, such as babies' actions developing into gestures, leads to both a greater appreciation of the children in our lives and a grasp of what makes us human.

Acknowledgements

This book has been in progress for some time so too many people to name have contributed in diverse ways. These include discussions with our mentors Michael Chapman, Michael Chandler, John Shotter, and John Newson, with colleagues Ulrich Müller, Bill Turnbull, Tim Racine, and Tanya Broesch, and with friends who read chapters, including Rosie Smith, Al Walters, Rolly Lorimer, and Kay O'Connor. There are many students, too many to name but particularly Viktoria Kettner, Beau Wallbridge, Vicki Parnell, Jim Stack, Stephanie Malone, and Joanna Lunn, whose questions helped us further consider and refine our ideas. We especially want to acknowledge our children Max and Hannah and Tom and Camilla and our partners, Deborah O'Connor and Rosie, as well as all of the children in our lives, grandchildren, nephews and nieces, and great nephews and great nieces. Having so many children in our lives constantly reminds us of the primacy of relationships and cognitive development in what makes us human. These children have made us question what we take for granted, so that we can see what is in front of us afresh in every developing relationship.

Chapter 1

The problem
What is it to be human?

In which we describe human forms of thinking and discuss possible explanations.

We are what we are through our relationships with others.
—George Herbert Mead[1]

When we look at the stars and wonder about the beginning of the universe, or ponder the origins of life, we rarely pay attention to the fact that it is our human minds that allow us to ask and attempt to answer such questions. How human ways of being and thinking develop is just as wondrous and fascinating. Explaining the subtleties and complexities of this process is still beyond our complete understanding. The nature and development of the human mind is the subject of this book, and it touches our lives much more than distant galaxies or ancient fossils. Perhaps it is because human ways of living and thinking are so familiar and taken for granted that they appear less mysterious than the key processes examined by other sciences. But attempting to understand the mind and explain the development of how we interact and think is an enormously complex and fascinating field of study. As developmental psychologists, we study the miraculous development of the mind that occurs in our own homes and under our noses. How is it that humans grow from young babies who are still learning to coordinate their reaching in order to grasp objects to adults who can have a conversation as well as wonder about the stars?

What is thinking and how does it develop? How is it that you can read and understand this sentence? How is it that those curious marks on the paper somehow convey meaning? How do we understand what others say? Furthermore, how is it possible to think about and reflect on these questions? We have a tendency to overlook the fact that we can even ask and attempt to answer questions such as "How did the universe begin and will it end?" Snails, mice and deer are not concerned with such matters. Even though dogs, ravens and chimpanzees show intelligent activity, they are not troubled by questions about how it is that they can solve problems. Why is it that humans, and not other species, can worry about the future and reflect on themselves? How did humans evolve and develop the capacities for looking backwards with regret or pride and forward in hope or fear? How is it that such capacities for imagination exist in humans, and tend to be taken for granted, yet do not seem to be present in other species?

Varieties of social species

To understand what it is to be human we first consider what humans are not. We contrast ants and humans, not to draw attention to similarities, but rather to point out how achievements, which may appear similar on the surface, are achieved through radically different means. Some might suggest that what is important about being human are accomplishments such as spreading across the planet, building large structures and living in cities, as well as developing agriculture and tending livestock. But for millions of years over 11,000 ant species[2] have been hunting, gathering, farming, tending livestock, and building huge structures relative to their size, even with air conditioning, where they live in groups of millions. Indeed there are thousands of species which conduct a range of these activities. They capture or kill ants from neighboring nests—activities that could be described as taking slaves and waging war. Whereas some species of ants made the transition from hunting and gathering to agriculture 50 to 60 million years ago, humans experienced this shift not much more than ten thousand years ago. Ants have mastered the diverse environments in which they thrive, all without science, and without explicit awareness.[3]

Some ant species have even challenged human populations. In 1518 and 1519 Spanish colonists of Hispaniola were so overwhelmed by stinging ants that many families abandoned their homes. The horrified colonists, needing someone to plead with God on their behalf, used a lottery to select a patron saint, St. Saturninus, a third-century martyr, and they held a procession and feast to deter their tiny assailants.[4] Rather than attempting divine intervention, the ants used more effective strategies against the humans, but the infestation did subside over a period of years.[5]

This appeal to a saint for divine protection suggests important differences between ants and humans. Ants don't have systems of belief such as religions, or diverse forms of art from music to sculpture. Humans write books about ants, but ants don't write about us, or indeed about anything. Ants don't complain about working conditions and start unions or establish political parties. They don't sing operas, form heavy metal accordion bands, or talk about the weather and organize picnics (although they may attend them). Of course, ants don't talk at all. Ants may die doing what humans might describe as defending their nests, but they don't get medals. The idea of an ant hero sacrificing her life in the way a human may for a belief doesn't make sense in their way of life.

Humans, in contrast, live for beliefs and die in the name of causes. Aspects of human cultures from the Egyptian pyramids to Stonehenge to the carved cedar memorial poles of the Haida of Haida Gwaii don't seem to be essential for physical survival, and yet they somehow are vital for the belief systems people depend on. Status, traditions, family crests, and how others think about us are foundational aspects of being human, yet they seem to be missing in other species. Humans have diverse cultural belief systems—we live in social worlds based on justifications; we give each other reasons for our action. We are a story-telling species; we need purpose and meaning in our lives.[6] We have histories. We reflect on the past, and wonder about the future, whereas ants live only in the present. Although we can describe their activity as preparing for the winter, that form of awareness is not needed for their lives. Ants have what we might describe as brutal campaigns against their neighbors but they don't reflect on the morality of these raids, whereas we humans may. What are these differences due to?

Perhaps being human has to do with self-awareness. Jeremy's son, Max, was 8, when he asked the fascinating question: "Do animals know they are alive?" Of course, other animals *are* alive, but they do not seem to be aware of this in the way that humans are. We humans know we are alive. Can we explain how humans—a part of nature—have evolved to the point of being aware of themselves and of nature? The Dutch poet Cees Nooteboom put it in a way that has been familiar to developmental psychologists since the 1920s, and within Tibetan Buddhism:[7] "We are nature's method of thinking about itself."[8] Humans, it seems, are the only life form on this planet, the only part of the universe as far as we know, that is aware of itself.

This self-awareness means that humans are most likely the only species on the planet with the understanding that we are alive, and, therefore, can become aware of the implication of this knowledge, which is that we will die. This awareness of the future and of our death is the knowledge that got humans kicked out of the blissful ignorance of Eden.[9] Knowledge of others' view of ourselves is shown in the biblical story of the Garden of Eden, with its roots in *The Epic of Gilgamesh*,[10] a

4000 year-old poem from ancient Mesopotamia. This serves as a metaphor for the implications of our self-awareness and of humans' eternal quest to avoid death. Our ability to imagine the future can potentially fuel our search for purpose and meaning in life. Humans are a species with the ability to ask questions about where we come from, and we need stories to provide a secure, comfortable place for us in the otherwise inhospitable and overwhelmingly vast universe.[11]

We argue that an understanding of the "self" develops within social relations through becoming aware of others' view of ourselves. This makes us so vitally concerned with how other people think about us—others' respect is important for our sense of who we are. We live in webs of interpersonal commitment to each other based on trust. Our friendships and relationships are fundamental to our lives. We construct identities around how others view us. We have selves in the sense that we can reflect on ourselves from others' perspectives. Pet owners might claim that their animals also have selves, but although they may *be* selves in the sense of having particular ways of acting and interacting—a personality, in a way—they don't *have* selves in the sense of being self-aware. This, we argue, develops through taking others' perspectives. We develop as persons because we grow up being treated as *someone* rather than *something*.[12]

We focus on the differences in the ways in which ants and humans learn to live within radically differing environments because to understand what it is to be human, to recognize the human mind, it is vital to notice the crucially different ways in which ant societies and those of other species work compared to human social groups.

We both come from a school of developmental psychology which holds that human social interaction is the key to what makes us human. We contend that the differences between our species and ants are a consequence of the nature of our social relations. The ability to master these social processes leads each of us as individuals to develop a human mind. You might think that other species also interact with each other, but there is an important difference. Ants follow trails marked by pheromones, chemical signals, left by other individuals, but laying a trail does not require understanding how others respond to the chemicals left behind. This simple form of communication has made possible the incredibly complex organization in the societies of social insects. Although we can also see this form of unintentional communication in human interaction, most human communication works in a crucially different way. We are aware of the meaning that our actions or words have for other people. Of course, misunderstandings do occur, requiring *repairs* to achieve mutual understanding. Such awareness of how others understand us is *not* necessary, or at all in evidence, for the forms of communication used by ants and many other species. It is difficult to convey the importance of this difference and its far-reaching consequences.

It is this awareness of others' view of us that we are concerned with in this book. We focus on how such awareness originates, and we are interested in what humans can do with this form of communication that arises first, and gradually, in social interaction.[13]

Many other animal species are skilled at engaging with their world in flexible and intelligent ways. Ravens, chimpanzees and many other animals can be very adept in that sense. Humans, however, are able to engage in *reflective* thought. This adds an additional level of complexity through which to engage with the world. Thinking and language are so much a part of our everyday experience that we are apt to overlook what they are and how we use them to acquire such a sophisticated system of self-reflection and communication. Indeed we only reflect on this when scientists (or children) ask difficult questions. Our ways of thinking and interacting with each other are so natural that they are difficult to notice. One skill of novelists and artists is to reveal the significance of those everyday experiences—the importance of aspects of our world that are right before our eyes. We take it that it is the role of scientists to bring to our attention what was always there, but overlooked. The neglected issue that we are bringing forward is the nature of the human mind and its capacity for perceiving and reflecting on the world. We focus particularly on the significance of the everyday interactions between babies and their caregivers for the development of human communication and thinking. In Gregory Bateson's words:

> It is as if the stuff of which we are made were totally transparent and therefore imperceptible and as if the only appearances of which we can be aware are cracks and planes of fracture in that transparent matrix.[14]

Once we are aware of the problems, it is no small task to explain the human mind. As Alexander Pope[15] asked:

> Could he, whose rules the rapid Comet bind,
> Describe or fix one movement of his Mind?
> Who saw its fires here rise, and there descend,
> Explain his own beginning, or his end?
>   ("Essay on Man," Epistle II)

The level of self-awareness achieved by humans has many consequences for how we understand our lives, but the task we take on in this book is to explain how this awareness develops. If we are right that crucial human forms of thinking develop within our relationships with others then there are many parts to the story that we have to provide. As developmental psychologists we have to document closely how children acquire these skills. What are the conditions, the ingredients, and processes which make this possible? We will describe the developmental niche, the biological, social, and emotional cradle, in which human babies grow up.[16] In order to do so we must be clear about the foundations on which our approach is built.

Assessing our assumptions

> The end may hang on the beginning.
>
> —Beryl Markham[17]

Beryl Markham was actually referring to the dangers of flying fabric covered biplanes across Africa in the early part of the twentieth century, but the same lesson also applies to doing good science. It is essential to be careful regarding the unexamined assumptions on which theories are built. In attempting to explain human thinking, theorists often fail to notice the assumptions they start from, yet these preconceptions already set up the problems and even constrain the possible answers. The unnoticed assumptions that are part of the fabric of contemporary debate are an awkward obstacle that we must overcome in presenting our view of the nature of human forms of life and thinking. Although psychology prides itself on being an empirical science, the starting points for theories are, in fact, sets of preconceptions or philosophical assumptions; there is nothing empirical about them. These are sometimes termed *worldviews* because they represent particular perspectives. We see these as the first step and the one that we don't even notice.[18] But it is that step which sets us on a particular path and commits us to the end point.

Attempts to explain human thinking can be grouped into two contrasting types of approaches that are based on different worldviews. One of these frameworks begins with the individual mind as taken for granted. If it is assumed that the mind is there to begin with then, from this perspective, it is thought that children must face the problem of figuring out that other people that they see as bodies also have minds. In philosophy this is called "the problem of other minds." It is thought to involve somehow overcoming the gap between the individual and others. We focus on this perspective in Chapter 5.

Individualistic approaches assume that individual minds are the starting point, which are required in order for social relations to be possible. And, therefore, the problem babies face is to learn how to communicate with others. This way of thinking can be seen in *The Confessions of Saint Augustine*, first published in 379 AD, and a best seller for over fifteen hundred years! This view is evident in Augustine's description of what he believed his life was like as an infant:

> Gradually I became aware of my surroundings, and wished to express my demands to those who could comply with them; but I could not, since the demands were inside me, and outside were their fulfillers, who had no faculty for entering my mind. So I worked my limbs and voice energetically, trying to signal out something like my demands, to the best of my little (and little availing) ability.[19]

Of course, Saint Augustine, just like the rest of us, would not actually be able to remember his early life as an infant. Instead, his attempt to reconstruct his experience must be based on his adult assumptions about infant development. Augustine's account presupposes an adult way of thinking. It is as if he imagined that as an infant he had language and thinking skills, but had somehow ended up in a foreign country and could not yet speak the local language.[20] This was how he perceived his difficulty making himself understood.

There is a tendency for adults to take their own experience for granted and assume that babies are just like us. Adults have the experience of having a mind that seems to be private and it feels that it must have always been this way. So, we assume that babies are like this too—they must be born that way. This tendency to project our adult way of experiencing the world onto babies has been termed *adultocentric*,[21] and this way of thinking is surprisingly common in theories. It would equate babies with adults, isolated in separate prison cells attempting to find some code with which to communicate between cells, such as tapping on the bars. This is the analogy used by the American philosopher, George Herbert Mead[22] to point out the problem with this way of thinking. Adultocentric explanations are based on the workings of individuals' minds (and so can also be referred to as internalist or mentalist). They begin with what Willis Overton calls a "split" between the mind and the world, in which the infant's mind works so that he or she can already reflect upon that world.[23] But if the mind is assumed to start with, then a problem with this perspective is that it does not explain how the mind develops.[24] And this is our task in this book.

In contrast, the second framework, which we endorse, does not begin with the individual mind, but instead with social processes. It, thus, explains the emergence of mind through this interaction. From this perspective, for interaction to begin it is not necessary that babies understand others as having minds. This can develop through social experience. This perspective is referred to as a *relational* or *developmental systems* approach. These contrasting frameworks emerge in the various areas covered in this book including views of knowledge, language, social development in infancy and childhood, as well as evolution.

As a clear example of this systems way of thinking, consider Donald Winnicott, the English pediatrician and psychoanalyst, who famously asserted that, "there is no such thing as a baby." But we can see babies! So why did he make this baffling remark? Winnicott went on to clarify that, "if you set out to describe a baby, you will find you are describing a *baby and someone.*"[25] He intended to draw our attention to the interconnectedness of infants and caregivers—the fact that babies are totally dependent upon, and necessarily develop within, a few key relationships. This means that we must study the whole system in which the baby functions and develops—the pattern changes as the infant becomes more skilled.

Not only do the patterns of interaction between babies and their parents or caregivers gradually change, infants learn about how their parents respond in particular contexts. From this simple beginning, forms of communication between babies and parents gradually become refined, leading to the complex exchanges we experience as adults.

The relational argument, in contrast to Saint Augustine's view, is that human minds emerge through interaction with other people. It explains mind and intelligence as the developmental outcome of these social processes that are rooted in the natural world of biological and physiological features—we should not lose sight of the fact that humans are bodies in time and space.

The quotation from George Herbert Mead that we started this chapter with, that "we are what we are through our relationships with others,"[26] is not just some new age intuition. It is a tradition in philosophy and psychology that converges with recent work in developmental biology, neuroscience, cultural studies and feminist relational approaches, as well as some forms of cognitive science.[27]

If persons acquire the ability to engage in human forms of thinking within this social environment, then we also need to explain how this social-cultural niche evolved. This is a reciprocal (infant and caregiver contribute to the interaction) and bi-directional (both parties influence the other) developmental (both adapt to the other and change as a result) and evolutionary process (we return to just what has evolved in Chapters 2 and 8). We explain human thinking as an emergent product of typical activity patterns. We believe that developing awareness of ourselves requires taking others' perspectives toward our self. In this way we become aware of ourselves because of others' reactions to us. That is, having a self depends on communication with others. This idea can be traced back to the philosophy of Socrates and other Greek thinkers, and to other cultures. For example, the Zulu expression "Umuntu, Ngumuntu, Ngabantu" ("a person is a person through other persons") pervades African traditional thinking about human nature and formed the basis of the philosophy of Nelson Mandela. Umuntu is the practice of human interaction and this is related closely to "Ubuntu," which is the sense of being or identity that emerges from social relatedness. Desmond Tutu explains that:

> Africans have this thing called UBUNTU. It is about the essence of being human, it is part of the gift that Africa will give the world. It embraces hospitality, caring about others, being able to go the extra mile for the sake of others. We believe that a person is a person through another person, that my humanity is caught up, bound up, inextricably, with yours. When I dehumanize you, I inexorably dehumanize myself. The solitary human being is a contradiction in terms and therefore you seek to work for the common good because your humanity comes into its own in belonging.[28]

Similar ideas about dependence on other people for becoming a person can be found in other cultures. For example, the Japanese kanji symbol for a person is a representation of one person being supported by another person, accentuating the idea of personhood in relation to others. And kanji symbols are derived from Chinese characters. This sort of a relational perspective is typical in indigenous cultures such as Canadian First Nations, and this extends to approaching justice through rebuilding healthy relationships.[29] Even though individualism is often dominant in Western scholarship there is also a theme concerning communities and social networks.[30] A relational perspective can be found in some sciences. Ecology, for example, is focused on relations, and current biology and genetics are now relational, as we will discuss in Chapter 8. In fact, it could be argued that when we look closely enough at anything we see interrelationships.

An obstacle to explaining relational approaches is that they are sometimes not on readers' conceptual maps. Perhaps this is because there are generally assumed to be two alternatives in explaining development:

either to focus on the individual and biological characteristics or, if that is questioned, to consider how the person is shaped by social forces. According to this second position it is "society," as represented by parents and teachers, which shapes young children. It is classically known as the socialization approach of social learning theory put forward in an extreme form by B. F. Skinner and in a more nuanced way by Albert Bandura. But it starts from the same problematic assumption as individualism, as both theories assume a split between self and other that we describe above—either Augustine's self as an adult in an infant's body or learning theory's stress on external shapers of human skills. For them the question is which pre-existing part—the individual or the environment—is more important.

But, of course, everyone assumes interaction is essential so isn't that the same as relationism? No, not quite. Relationism takes interaction a step further. It is a third option that holds that we must focus on the whole system consisting of babies and parents who look after them. This is a matrix in which biological characteristics and social relations are inextricably interwoven and mutually create each other. The action is in the relations between babies and their parents, and this shift to emphasize the developmental process makes a crucial difference. If we focus on such relations we see how they create the social and emotional world in which babies develop. Persons are developmental outcomes of this process.

We have a tendency to see just objects, instead of the relations between them. For instance, we see the airplane and the ground, but not the airflow around the wing. So, it is hard to understand how something as big as a Boeing 747—the size of an apartment building—can fly. To see relations takes imagination, or a wind tunnel and smoke, in order to make the airflow around the wing visible. These general approaches are applied at all levels to all topics from neuroscience and evolution to meaning, language, and culture. And they result in very different answers to our question about the development of human thinking.

In presenting a relational account there is the danger that critics will jump to the conclusion that we disregard the importance of biology and evolution. Nothing could be further from the truth! In thinking about how human intelligence emerges from the social process we must think about genetics and neuroscience, as well as the evolved characteristics of infants and parents[31] that make this process possible. Doing so means that it is essential to take development seriously. Filling in the evolutionary side to our story requires explaining how the social process starts. If human minds depend on particular forms of communication (not the other way around), then we have to explain how social interaction develops. There is an evolutionary side to this story. From this perspective, what has evolved are biological characteristics of the infant that influence his or her social environment, and set the social process going in which communication and then mind and thinking can emerge. In part, the environment nurtures development and is social because babies need to be cared for. It is this essential point that we emphasize throughout this book.[32]

Taking development seriously

We think that the tendency in recent cognitive science to take the adult mind as the model to be explained leads to dead ends. Instead it is necessary to approach the problem differently. As developmental psychologists, we observe the process of abilities being put together over developmental history. In the eloquent words of the psychologist Elizabeth Bates:

> Looking at the adult end of that development, we can be overwhelmed (narcissists that we are) at the complexity and perfection of a symbol-using mind. But if we trace this marvel to its beginning in human infancy, we will see that this particular work of art is a collage, put together out of a series of old parts that developed quite independently. This does not make the achievement any less wonderful. But it does begin to make it more understandable.[33]

It is this understanding that we are after. We resist the tendency to look at the polished end product of the symbol using human mind, and instead we observe how these abilities gradually develop, how these skills are put together within interaction.

Bates goes on to remind us that if we are thinking about the evolution of a trait we do not have to assume that this is encoded in the genome.

> Nature is a miser. She clothes her children in hand-me-downs, builds new machinery in makeshift fashion from sundry old parts, and saves genetic expenditures whenever she can by relying on high-probability world events to insure and stabilize outcomes. Looking at the beauty of her finished products, we often fail to see that they are held together with tape and safety pins.[34]

There may be expectable aspects of the environment that play a role in the development of a diverse range of human skills. One of these "high probability events" in infants' lives is other people. Not only is the environment that babies develop in vital for their survival, it is necessarily social and serves as a wonderful medium in which they learn to become human.

Biology and development

What is it that produces such differences between humans and other species? Can human thinking be explained simply as determined by our genes? This is a continuing hot topic in the popular press. In a sense, genes must feature in any explanation. But they are only one factor among many others. DNA is a relatively inert molecule, not an active agent that can determine outcomes. Through complex cellular processes involving various forms of RNA (single strands of repeated amino acids), genes are an essential part of the process in the first step in constructing proteins. But they do not even provide the complete story in folding proteins and it is still a very long way from such molecules to thinking (see Chapter 8). Genes are a crucial factor in a cascade of additional levels of interacting factors that are involved in human development, but neither genes alone nor the chemistry involved in the firing of neurons will provide a complete story regarding the nature of a promise or why Charlie is a Tottenham Hotspur fan. What is also essential for the development of humans—a critical part of the complex developmental system leading to human forms of thinking—is other people. It is this developmental story that we will spell out in this book.

Could it be that our large brains account for the differences between humans and other animals? This is what we are often told in the popular press. Certainly, having a large and complex human brain is an essential and necessary ingredient in being human. But is this really the whole story? Can we understand the human mind by studying the brain alone? No, we don't think so. Although it's important to understand how neurons work, this alone won't give us insight into what is essential about human experiences like the ability to make promises. This should be clear from a thought experiment that several developmental psychologists and philosophers have dwelt on, of having a baby grow up on a desert island. To make survival easier let's imagine such an island where all the material needs are miraculously available, but there is no human contact. Unlike Robinson Crusoe, marooned when he was already an adult with the ability to talk and think, we (and many others) would contend that a baby growing up without other people would not develop human forms of thinking. Just why we subscribe to this view will be inferred from the topics and issues that we discuss throughout this book. At this stage we can conclude that a focus solely on the brain as an explanation for thinking overlooks how neural connections must be shaped through our interactions with the world of objects as well as other people. The development of an individual's thinking must be socially based.

One common fashion in cognitive science is to explain forms of thinking by claiming that they are innate or "hard-wired." Yet, this approach simply puts development in a "black box"—something left to others to explain.[35] It assumes that any explanation can be deferred—an IOU. To make sense and help us it would need to explain how DNA molecules propel us into forms of thinking. They simply pass the buck, from psychology to biology, and a simplistic interpretation of the latter. It is someone else's problem, not our department. Although the idea of innate knowledge might seem new, it is actually an ancient notion with roots in philosophy.[36] Decades ago, the Canadian psychologist, Donald O. Hebb, known for his work on how neurons form connections, chastised authors who made such claims.[37] Hebb and his colleagues argued that anyone asserting that thinking is innate should feel an obligation, at the very least, to indicate how such a promissory note might be cashed in. The conclusion he reached is that claiming that something is "hard-wired" may acquire some cachet as it appears to be a biological explanation. In fact, it is not. Furthermore, recent work in neuroscience does not support these claims. A biologically grounded explanation should try to begin uncovering the complex developmental story leading to human forms of thinking (see Chapter 8).

There are many forms of explanation. We argue that a developmental approach is vital. This is a detailed description of the emergence of forms of interaction. There are many levels of interacting factors in the developmental process going from molecules to minds (e.g., see Chapter 8).[38] We wish to direct attention to the overlooked role of interacting with others in this process. So, for example, we will describe in Chapter 4 the gradual emergence of forms of gestural communication in infancy.[39]

Given that our argument is that a system of meaning on which thinking is based must necessarily arise in everyday interpersonal interactions, it follows from this that we must take a different approach to explaining how the mind evolved. Instead of resorting to explanations based on claims about getting from genes to neural circuits, we must broaden the scope of factors considered in the developmental system that facilitates or creates the human mind. Other people are vital in this process, because thinking is first social before becoming individual. Contemporary accounts of the constructive role of experience in neuroscience[40] and the ways in which genes interact in the environment[41] converge with our position.

For example, in a recent summary of the subtle interplay between genes (the "genotype") and the individual's experience (the "phenotype") the geneticist Michael Meaney states that:

> All cellular processes derive from a constant dialogue between the genome and environmental signals. Thus, genotype–phenotype relations are defined by the context within which the genome operates. Likewise, the consequences for Gene-Environment interactions at the level of function are defined by the broader context, including the demands of the prevailing environment.[42]

The environment that humans experience is uniquely complex and social. From this perspective, we have to look at the necessary conditions in which human babies grow up that make the development of human forms of thinking possible. The way that humans' particular embodiment might lead to reasoning has been the source of discussion for centuries. In a verse from the *Progress of the Mind*, Erasmus Darwin, the grandfather of Charles Darwin, speculated on this topic.

> Proud man alone in wailing weakness born,
> No horns protect him, and no plumes adorn;
> No finer powers of nostril, ear, or eye,
> Teach the young Reasoner to pursue or fly.—
> Nerved with fine touch above the bestial throngs,
> The hand, first gift of Heaven! to man belongs;
> Untipt with claws the circling fingers close,
> With rival points the bending thumbs oppose,
> Trace the nice lines of Form with sense refined,
> And clear ideas charm the thinking mind,
> Whence the fine organs of the touch impart
> Ideal figure, source of every art;
> Time, motion, number, sunshine or the storm,
> But mark varieties in Nature's *form*.[43]

In this verse, Erasmus Darwin, a physician as well as a poet, so beautifully described the way in which our biological foundations (our physical structure and basic behavioral repertoires) provide fundamental clues to human "being." He suggested that it is the hand, the "first gift of Heaven," that leads to "the thinking mind" and is "the source of every art." This idea began before Erasmus Darwin penned these words, and speculation about the role of the hand in thinking has continued to the present.[44] Our manual dexterity enables us to manipulate objects. But, to extend Erasmus Darwin's thinking, the same movements of finger and wrist also allow us to engage in early human communicative gestures such as showing or pointing. Other aspects of our embodiment (we orient our bodies towards objects and others, for example) are important for a complete explanation of human thought, but there is another phrase in the poem that we should reflect upon.

It is even more important to explain how it is that "man alone in wailing weakness born" develops the form of intelligence we see in humans but not other species. In fact, we believe that it is this very "wailing weakness" which sets up conditions for the development of communication, then language, and then a grasp of the mind and thinking. The helplessness of human infants guarantees a social niche for development, a protective and supportive social environment formed by parents or caregivers. Their care in response to babies' wailing provides the seed from which communication can develop. Crying means something to parents—the baby is uncomfortable in some way—and the response is to comfort and interact with the infant. The meaning of such parenting gestures is conveyed even though at first infants are not aware of their cries being the impetus for this interaction.

We should be clear that not all linguists, neuroscientists, and cognitive scientists would agree with what we have to say. Some cognitive scientists are happy with the claim that the computer makes a good model for understanding the mind, and that thinking is like computation or information processing. But science works through debate, and we will discuss flaws in the assumptions on which other approaches are based and how our view differs from others. In contrast to our view of what it is to be human and how human forms of thinking develop, other approaches to explaining the nature of human thinking begin from the individual. We examine and respond to such theories in Chapters 8–9.

Minds as machinery: Thinking as computation

One currently popular account of thinking is known as the computational theory of mind. This idea is that thinking is similar to what a computer does and involves the manipulation of mental symbols that refer to the world. We focus on it here, because it permeates popular discussion so much that many researchers take its assumptions as unquestioned truths. This view is most widely accessible to a general audience through books such as Steven Pinker's provocatively entitled *How the Mind Works*.[45] Pinker, a professor of psychology at Harvard University, exemplifies the view that thinking is computation, and furthermore that the mind is made up of a series of devices that perform computation. He takes this a step further in claiming that these computational devices are specified by our genes and have evolved over evolutionary time to solve the problems our ancestors faced when surviving with a hunting and gathering way of life.

We disagree with Pinker's claims about "how the mind works." We don't think it works that way, and this book is alternative to Pinker's views. Although a biological and evolutionary side to the story is clearly required, we believe that the assumptions explicit in this position regarding the nature of human thinking are flawed and we provide alternatives. The core assumption that we reject is that thinking is computation or information processing. The further claims about evolution then follow from that point, although these claims are not so widely held. Evolution must clearly be an important part of any story, but the position exemplified in Pinker's writing is only one possible application of evolutionary theory. Moreover, this application only follows if the assumptions he starts with regarding the nature of the mind are accepted. If we are right that these assumptions are fundamentally flawed, then the implications based on them collapse. Again, we do not question the importance of evolutionary theory and neuroscience; rather, we question the result of linking these approaches to the assumption that the mind works like a computer—the computational view of the mind.

Why do we object to the claim that "the brain processes information, and thinking is a kind of computation"? This might appear to be a simple and straightforward statement. However, there is an immediate problem because it conflates two quite different meanings of "information." It could be correct to say that light hitting the lens of a camera and being recorded as an image carries information. However, the word information is also used in a second sense to talk about a person seeing something and knowing about it. The problem is that the camera doesn't know anything whereas the person does. It is the person knowing something that we have to explain.[46] This problem tends to be overlooked due to the sleight of hand in using the same word—information—but in two radically different ways. Doing this glosses over the very real problem that requires an explanation.

Computers, or books, can be used to store massive amounts of information, in one sense of the word, but they still don't know anything. They require a person to make sense of this information, to interpret and to understand this "information." The person using the computer provides meaning to the input and the output. The computer itself doesn't know or understand anything. So, if the computer is to serve as a model or metaphor for the mind then we also need to include the person providing the meaning because otherwise the computations are meaningless and they cannot be linked to the world—the thinking cannot be about the world. But this step would get us further into trouble because no one wants a model of the mind that has to include a person—traditionally called a homunculus—to attribute meaning. And the problems would just snowball because that small person would also need a small person in his or her mind, and so on and so on.[47]

Another way to present this problem with the computer metaphor has to do with how symbols acquire meaning. The core idea in the computational theory of mind is that thinking is like computation, involving the manipulation of symbols. Thinking is about the world and so accordingly these symbols must be about the world. But the problem is how? The "symbol-grounding problem" is the fatal flaw for the computational theory of mind. We deal with more problems with the view of meaning in Chapter 3, and we propose that meaning is, instead, rooted in social relations. In Chapter 9 we return to evaluate the idea that thinking is computation, involving representations of the world, given that this metaphor is used so widely.

If this way of explaining human thought and grounding meaning doesn't work, what is the alternative? If our thinking is about the world we need some system of meaning, some way that our thoughts are linked to the world so that we can think about the world even if it is not present. This is "one of Nature's most interesting achievements—the construction of the capacity for symbols."[48] If human forms of thinking are based on the use of symbols then understanding the development of this capacity to use symbols is essential. This is what our book is about.

What is ahead

We considered using the kanji symbol for person, described above, on the cover of our book superimposed on top of a brain scan. We would juxtapose this representation of the dependence of a person on others with a brain scan for several reasons. First, because the fMRI scan is beautiful and attractive, and second, because anything to do with the brain seems to be very popular in the media. Perhaps neuroscience sells newspapers these days, or at least that seems to be the opinion of journalists and editors. In any case, readers are treated to new findings from neuroscience most weeks. In fact, some recent research has found that when general readers examined an article with a brain scan, even though it did not add additional information, they rated the scientific reasoning as much more convincing than the same article with only a bar graph or no figure at all.[49] So a picture of a brain scan has been labeled "that fast-acting solvent of critical faculties."[50] Subsequent research suggests that the effect is due to neuroscience information, even if it is irrelevant.[51]

We are not trying to take advantage of this "brain scan effect" so that you will be more convinced by our argument. In fact, the motivation for our book is to move against the current tide to focus solely on the brain as an explanation for what it means to be human. Central to our argument are the ideas that beautiful images of brains lead us to assume that we were born with those areas of the brain already specialized for forms of thinking. The fact that brains develop and that functions become located in particular regions of the brain tends to be overlooked, as do the social bases of the neural processes that are identified in such scans. Brain scans may seem like hard evidence, that you can't argue with a picture, and there is something actually there that is not just words. Fortunately, neuroscience experts are usually more cautious, but in the popular press images of brains are transformed into magically "seeing thoughts." In fact, the images produced by an fMRI machine are related to blood flow in areas of the brain that have been especially active, but these patterns follow a great deal of "cleaning" away background firing of cells that happens all the time. We still have some distance to go to get from the activity of neurons to an explanation of our human experience of self-awareness, to what it is to be human.

With a title like *What Makes Us Human*, we need to be clear about what aspects of this vast topic we will *not* be covering. Clearly we can't do it all. Many other books cover additional aspects of development.[52] We address the problem of how thinking becomes possible, but not the many problems that may occur once human forms of thinking have developed. In this book we will not talk about matters such as family problems and their causes and solutions, nor the diversity of personalities, and interpersonal relationships, or the complexity of historical events. Rather, we will talk about the development of human forms of thinking and interaction that make such complexities possible in the first place. Butterflies don't have family problems and dogs don't lie. Why not? It is not just that dogs are too honest.[53] We are concerned with how human forms of thinking develop within the social cradle of human infancy, and how differences in human forms of life make history and the diversity of cultures possible.

Through this book we will trace out the full and profound implications of the idea from Mead that being human arises through our relationships with other people.[54] If the stark differences between humans and ants have their roots in the different ways the two species interact, resulting in different forms of communication, language, human forms of thinking and mind, then we need to look closely at the nature of human language and the forms of interaction on which it is based. Of course, the human nervous system is also required to support the complexity of this interaction and neural pathways develop within such experience.

The first step in this voyage begins in Chapter 2 with describing the human developmental system, the social and emotional niche in which human babies develop, facilitated by their helplessness. We examine factors that set up the conditions in which human thinking develops. In Chapter 3 we discuss the nature and development of human communication. We extend this discussion in Chapter 4 with an examination of how infants learn how to communication by using gestures such as pointing. All of these are aspects of children's understanding of other people. This topic of social understanding is further delved into in Chapter 5 with a focus on children's understanding of the psychological world of beliefs, desires, intentions and so on. The mastery of the social world is further explored in Chapter 6 with the topic of moral development. This also the topic of Chapter 7 with a discussion of recent theory and research on moral development.

Chapters 2–7 present the view of human development we have started to introduce here. We acknowledge that this is a controversial area and that not everyone will agree with the account we have presented in Chapters 2–7. In the next two chapters, 8 and 9, we will consider two competing explanations for human thinking. We introduce representative approaches and review some difficulties with them. It is an aspect of scholarly work to set one's discussion within a context of other existing approaches. In work aimed strictly for a purely academic audience the usual way to do this is at the beginning, which then opens space to consider the view proposed. In this case, however, we intend our presentation to be broadly accessible to a wide audience. Therefore, we present our positive position to begin with and then, in Chapters 8 and 9, we consider competing approaches. In Chapter 8 we review ideas about the role of biology in the development of thinking. In Chapter 9 we critically the claim that computers make a good model for human minds. Some of our colleagues may wish to first read Chapters 8 and 9 in order to understand why we argue that our approach is needed in the field.

Finally, in Chapter 10, in drawing conclusions we very briefly discuss further implications of the view of human development we have presented. Because persons develop within cultures and also change those cultures in a bidirectional manner, it is important to discuss the role of culture in human development.

We start, in Chapter 2, by discussing the social context in which babies develop. In beginning to coordinate their action with their caregivers, infants first learn to communicate with gestures and then language, on which human thinking is based. This brings out how human thinking emerges within the interaction children experience that is simultaneously social, emotional, and cultural. One of our hopes is that through this discussion you will gain further appreciation for children, leading to even more enjoyment of the children in your life.

Notes

1 Mead (1934, p. 379).
2 For an engaging analysis see Sleigh (2003).
3 Hölldobler and Wilson (1994, 2011). Although a typical worker ant is less than one-millionth the size of a human, the total population of ants has been conservatively estimated at about ten thousand trillion, so the collectively biomass of all the ants on the planet probably equals that of the approximate 7 billion humans.
4 Mann (2011).
5 Hölldobler and Wilson, (1994, p. 64).
6 Becker (1973).
7 Aldwin (2014).
8 Explaining this is the problem of the origin and development of knowledge, which was the central goal for Jean Piaget, throughout his long career. The quote is from an interview on CBC radio with Eleanor Wachtel, January 2009.
9 Canfield (2007).
   Other cultural stories likely make a similar point, e.g., the Haida story of how the Raven stole the light and released it, allowing people to see each other.
10 Wright (2004, p. 65).
11 Becker (1973).
12 Spaemann (2006).
13 We contrast ants and humans to make the point clearly, but, of course, when we look at more closely related species we see far more continuity, as we would expect in taking an evolutionary perspective. We take Darwin seriously and so we don't expect any complete and abrupt gap between species. It is important to look for continuity between closely related species, but for what we want to do in this book it is also important to highlight the differences between humans and other species, which we are attempting to explain.
14 Bateson (1979, p. 15).
15 Pope (1967, p. 139).
16 Hobson (2002).
17 Markham (1983, p. 168).
18 Wittgenstein (1968).
19 Augustine (2001, p. 39). In an earlier translation (Augustine, 1923) the Latin was translated as "my soul" whereas in the 2001 translation this was interpreted as "my mind."

20 Wittgenstein (1968).
21 Schaffer (1977).
22 Mead (1934).
23 This book fits with a re-emerging movement within developmental psychology dedicated to studying the role of social interaction in social understanding (e.g., Carpendale & Lewis, 2004, 2006, 2015; Hobson, 2002; Reddy, 2008). We place these under a banner of "relational approaches" (Overton, 2006, 2010, 2013).
24 This may be termed *individualism*. This approach has been influential in cognitive science, but is now declining in popularity (Hutto, 2013).
25 Winnicott (1964, p. 88, emphasis in original).
26 Mead (1934, p. 379).
27 In order to take development seriously it is necessary to consider its contexts and, in particular, the role of social experience. Thinking about this aspect of development has a long history. A century ago, while George Herbert Mead was working on how human thought develops, there were also various other scholars around the world engaged with similar ideas concerning children's abilities. The Russian psychologist, Lev Vygotsky, was also writing in the 1920s about the origin of the mind in social relations. In fact, this convergence of ideas may have been partly due to a common influence from Pierre Janet in Paris and James Mark Baldwin who had left North America for Paris. In North America, philosophers such as Charles Sanders Peirce and John Dewey were from a similar tradition. We are concerned with the perspective that these authors promoted but are not attempting a historical analysis. We focus on current research on young children to examine the nature and development of human thinking. All to easily theory has continued to neglect this perspective. Although we have to deal with complex philosophical issues, we do so by watching how babies learn to communicate and this brings our thinking in line with the relational theories of a hundred years ago.
28 This quotation was taken from www.tutfoundationuk.org in 2013 but has since been taken down. For the quotation and discussion see www.beingbetterhumans.com/ubuntu.
29 Ross (2006).
30 Sprintzen (2009).
31 We use the word "parent" here to refer to all those who care for babies, not "biological" parents.
32 We build on from a point made twenty years ago by Michael Tomasello et al. (1993) that socio-cultural processes are vital in ratcheting up our biological endowment to produce attributes that we identify as being truly human. Without these we are lost—the desert island baby would not be fully human. We return to this point in Chapter 10.
33 Bates (1979, p. 1).
34 Bates (1979, p. 1).
35 For example, Tancredi (2005).
36 See Bickhard's (2009) discussion of Parmenides.
37 Hebb, Lambert, and Tucker (1971).
38 Gottlieb (1991).
39 This is an historical or developmental explanation (Hendriks-Jansen, 1996).
40 Mareschal, Johnson, Sirois, Spratling, Thomas, and Westermann (2007).

41 Meaney (2010).
42 Meaney (2010, p. 67).
43 Darwin (1978, pp. 91–93).
44 Tallis (2011).
45 Pinker (1997).
46 Müller et al. (1998a, 1998b).
47 The computational view has a number of supporters who have attempted to defend it from this criticism. One attempt is that instead of one intelligent homunculus there could be armies of stupid homunculi. But this does not solve the fundamental problem; instead it just pushes the problem further down. But even a stupid homunculus who only had to operate one switch would still need some knowledge to know when to pull the switch.
48 Bates (1979, p. 1).
49 McCabe and Castel (2008).
50 Crawford (2008, p. 65).
51 Weisberg, Keil, Goodstein, Rawson, and Gray (2008); Weisberg, Taylor, and Hopkins (2015). This research, which shows mixed effects, is discussed in Cumming (2013).
52 For example, Carpendale, Lewis, and Müller (2018).
53 Wittgenstein (1968).
54 Mead (1934, p. 379).

Chapter 2

The baby in the social cradle

In which we discuss the unique social and emotional cradle in which human babies develop.

Proud man alone in wailing weakness born.

—Erasmus Darwin[1]

The evolution of infancy created a niche for the interactive emergence of specific human cognitive capacities.

—P. E. Griffiths and K. Stotz[2]

Wildebeest born on the Serengeti are ready to get up and run for their lives away from cheetahs, but human infants take years to be able to fend for themselves and have to be cared for until they can master their environments. When we look at human potential and the great intellectual achievements that children reach, like language, or reading, how is it possible that babies are so helpless when they are born? To resolve this apparent paradox we have to consider human development within its evolutionary context. The environment babies develop in, and their helplessness, actually contribute to the development of skills that serve a role in their survival. Babies require parents who care for them and we as adults respond to their signals, particularly their cries. We need to examine infant development in order to solve the puzzle of how the "wailing weakness" in which "man alone" is born results in the development of the human mind.

Worlds of experience: A stroll through the worlds of babies

In 1934 the theoretical biologist Jakob von Uexküll enticed his readers to understand the radically differing experiences of various animals. In his essay "A stroll through the worlds of animals and men: A picture book of invisible worlds," he invites us to consider a sunny day in

> a flower-strewn meadow, humming with insects, fluttering with butterflies. Here we may glimpse the worlds of the lowly dwellers of the meadow. To do so, we must first blow, in fancy, a soap bubble around each creature to represent its own world, filled with the perceptions which it alone knows. When we ourselves then step into one of these bubbles, the familiar meadow is transformed. Many of its colorful features disappear, others no longer belong together but appear in new relationships. A new world comes into being. Through the bubble we see the world of the burrowing worm, of the butterfly, or of the field mouse; the world as it appears to the animals themselves, not as it appears to us. This we may call the *phenomenal world* or the *self-world* of the animal.[3]

Von Uexküll gives the example of the world experienced by a tick. With basic photosensitive receptors, the deaf and blind female tick can, after mating, climb to the tip of a twig on a bush. There she waits until she detects butyric acid, produced by mammals, and then lets go and falls from her resting place. This often results in making contact with a mammal. The tick can sense temperature, which indicates if it has successfully landed on prey. In this way, what the organism is sensitive to results in the environment it experiences.[4] Her movements are prompted simply by particular changes in light, odor and touch, and then her reactions influence the location and nature of her "bubble" of experience as she moves to the next stage of the life course.

It may seem odd to say that organisms influence their environment because we usually presume that this is fixed and pre-existing. We tend to think of the environment as setting the problems that the organism must overcome. But this is where we must exercise imagination equivalent to von Uexküll's and consider the relations between organisms and their world of experience. The world a species experiences depends on what it can detect and interact with. For example, for an organism with the right digestive tract grass becomes a food, whereas it is not food for those animals lacking such a capacity. For other animals grass might be an obstacle, or perhaps a building material for nests, and so on.

The evolutionary biologist, Richard Lewontin, argued that we cannot define the environment apart from the organism. Stones are salient for thrushes because they use them to break things. But, "these same stones are not part of the environment of juncos who will pass by them in their search for dry grass with which to make their nests."[5] Lewontin goes on to argue that:

Organisms do not adapt to their environments; they construct them out of the bits and pieces of the external worlds. Organisms determine what is relevant. While stones are part of a thrush's environment, tree bark is part of a woodpecker's, and the undersides of leaves part of a warbler's. It is the life activities of these birds that determines which parts of the world, physically accessible to all of them, are actually parts of their environments.[6]

Even for animals living in the same location, their relevant environment will be different. For example, a dearth of discarded shells would be a significant problem for a population of hermit crabs, because it would leave them exposed to predators. But this problem for a hermit crab would be completely invisible to other species such as blue-swimmer crabs, which do not use shells for protection.[7] If organisms play a role in shaping their surroundings,[8] how do human babies influence their environments in which they develop? What is the bubble that human infants experience? What is their "social cradle"?[9]

From carrying to communication

Various biological characteristics can influence the type of social environment in which human infants develop. Think, for example, about the way humans typically carry their babies compared to chimpanzees and bonobos. The American psychologist and primatologist Sue Savage-Rumbaugh pointed out a subtle difference in how infants are carried that may have important implications for development. Infant bonobos are able to hold onto their mothers and support themselves. This makes it is possible for their mothers to carry their infants as they travel on all fours. Their infants must cling on to their mothers and so at this stage saw "only the rushing panoply of green as they traversed the forest."[10] In contrast, when Sue Savage-Rumbaugh was raising the infant bonobo named Kanzi, she and the other care-givers held Kanzi upright in their arms in the way human infants are typically carried. This simple difference resulted in a very different sort of environment for Kanzi because he could then look around and touch things, and he would lean and reach toward objects he was interested in. This meant that his interest and desires were obvious to the person carrying him due to his shifting weight and extended arms. His caregiver could respond to his interest and this provided a reactive social environment in which it is possible to develop requests.[11] This simple difference has the potential to result in a socially responsive environment—a situation in which an infant could learn how to manipulate his or her social environment.

Bonobo infants grasp their mother's fur with all four limbs, but human infants, lacking sufficient muscle power and prehensile[12] feet, must be carried in some other way such as in their parent's arms. The human foot is adapted for support and leverage—for walking. Its arches provide a rigid lever and shock absorber that makes the bipedal gait possible. An essential bone in making this change possible is the fourth metatarsal. There has been a longstanding debate about when this feature of human feet evolved. When the 3.2-million-year-old fossil *Australopithecus afarensis*, best known as Lucy, was discovered in 1974, the bones from the feet were not found and so this question could not be resolved. Recently, however, the fourth metatarsal from the species Lucy belonged to was found at Hadar, Ethiopia, indicating that Lucy and her species walked in the way that modern humans do.[13] This also means that Lucy's feet would not have been good for grasping and climbing trees, so by at least 3.2 million years ago *Australopithecus afarensis* had lost prehensile feet. Therefore, infant *Australopithecus afarensis* could not hold onto their mothers in the way Bonobos do, and thus would have to be carried in a different way. This is one example of a small difference in species related to ours, which does not appear to be related to thinking at all, but has the potential to lead to a different sort of social interaction experienced by infants, creating an environment in which human forms of communication might begin to develop.

Of course, we do not know what sort of communication developed in *Australopithecus afarensis*. Furthermore, ways of carrying babies vary across cultures, especially if they must be held for long periods or transported over rough terrain. This leads to fascinating questions about how such differences may be related to infant development. This speculation about the way human infants are carried and its possible role in human development needs further investigation and the idea may need to be modified. This possibility, however, is an example of how a small change in the baby's environment that has nothing to do with social cognition could result in different sorts of social experience—a different developmental niche with the potential for the development of forms of communication and cognition. We should be clear, however, that this alone would be far from sufficient to explain what makes us human. Many other biological characteristics are, no doubt, also important and we turn next to biological characteristics which are more obviously social.

That humans cannot cling onto their mothers is in one sense a disadvantage, as our ancestors had to derive less efficient means of protecting their young which took them away from foraging or escaping danger. At the same time our frailty, or "wailing weakness," can also be helpful in human development. The human niche results in a particular problem space, a social environment, which responds to a helpless infant's attitudes in ways the physical environment does not. Before we begin to examine this frailty, let's consider an infant who can hold his weight while on all fours. The floor will not assist him achieve his goals but his mother or father may help by supporting or aiding his movement. For example, when an infant at 6½ months was obviously trying to crawl. His mother described him as finally getting up on all fours and "revved up," but he ended up going in the wrong direction, backing up under a table, much to his frustration. The physical environment did not help him, but if he was attempting to grasp an out-of-reach object, his caregivers might help him achieve his goal. This shows the potential for the highly social and responsive environment that human infants develop within.

"In wailing weakness born": The advantages of helplessness

> Man is the only one that knows nothing, that can learn nothing without being taught. He can neither speak nor walk nor eat, and in short he can do nothing at the prompting of nature only, but weep.
> —Pliny, *Natural History* (ca. 70 AD)[14]

In Chapter 1 we quoted part of a poem by Erasmus Darwin that focused on how the human hand may determine some key differences between humans and other animals. Humans have developed grasping skills in one limb (the hand) while losing them in another (the foot). This is certainly part of the story, and it is essential to consider the nature of human embodiment—we are bodies engaged in physical and social space. But we need to reflect upon the context in which babies develop, particularly how this is determined by their own characteristics and sensitivities. The key question in accounting for human learning is how social interaction begins. If minds emerge within an interactive social process, how does this get going and how did the conditions for social relations evolve? What has to be explained are the origin of the social interaction skills, and then how the development of forms of communication, language, and mind follows.

Human infancy consists of a particular problem space in which babies have desires that become manifest in their attitudes towards things, and this is evident in their actions such as leaning and reaching. As we see in the example above of one baby's attempts at crawling and reaching, young infants may not be able to achieve their goals. This is where the fact that they are necessarily cared for becomes important, because they develop within a network of people who can respond to their desires as manifest in their actions. Infants' caregivers may respond to their attempts to reach something, for example. The effect of a different problem space can be seen in comparing chimpanzees in two settings. In the wild, chimpanzees do not seem to develop gestures such as pointing. However, in captivity when cared for by humans, many chimpanzees do spontaneously start pointing to request food that is outside their cage when a caregiver is nearby.[15] These captive chimpanzees experience a problem space that is similar to the experience of relatively helpless human infants.

Since Erasmus Darwin's description of the "wailing weakness" in which "man alone" is born, a number of other scholars have also commented on the significance of the extended period of helplessness in human infancy.[16] Freud, in 1895, argued that helplessness in infancy was the root of communication.[17] Human infants are at first incapable of getting what they need, but their crying helps others understand or guess these needs. So, he argued that "the original helplessness of human beings is thus the primal source of all moral motives."[18] Unfortunately, Freud did not follow up on this intriguing remark. Ian Suttie,[19] in critiquing Freud, argued that the infant is totally dependent on the parent and must maintain this relationship. Babies are adapted to their environment of helplessness and dependence on their caregivers. Love is an essential factor in this relationship. The infant's strong emotional bond is necessary for maintaining the infant parent interaction. Suttie explored the potential long-term effects of this highly charged emotional relationship.[20]

The puzzle of human infancy was approached from a biological perspective by the Swiss zoologist, Adolf Portmann. In his classic book *A Zoologist looks at Humankind*, Portmann pointed out that we are born about one year early relative to similar species.[21] What he termed secondary *altriciality* refers to a shortening of the gestation period. This results in human infants being born in a relatively helpless state. A factor in this adaption may be that in order to be bipedal, the human birth canal cannot be too large, and therefore babies have to be born earlier so that they are smaller.[22] The cost is that newborns are helpless and must be cared for if they are to survive. But humans are also born with relatively developed senses. This is termed *precocial*, and this ensures that early development takes place in a social environment during the year that in other species would be within the womb.[23] Because infants develop in interaction with others their brains are shaped within this complex social experience involving sequences of conversational turn taking.[24]

Evolution has resulted in a social, emotional, and cultural niche of dependency in which human infants develop.[25] This social cradle is sustained through emotional engagement. It is important that parents and babies enjoy engaging with each other. Babies are cute—their lives depend on it. Writing in the post war sexist language of 1950s Britain, John Bowlby noted that, "It is fortunate for their survival that babies are so designed by Nature that they beguile and enslave mothers."[26] Emotions are an essential glue for parent–infant dyads, structuring the social world of the baby and parents. Therefore, emotional reactivity is crucial for the baby in order to respond to caregivers' interaction, but at birth infants differ in their characteristic emotional reactivity. If babies are not reactive enough to a parent's engagement this is not helpful for getting the social process going. On the other hand, if babies are overly reactive and find the parent's emotional engagement with them to be too stimulating, then they may turn away to decrease the stimulation. This is a problem if it removes them from the very social processes that are so essential in typical human development. Within their interaction with caregivers, infants develop further skills in regulating their emotions, and these emerging abilities depend on their caregivers' ways of engaging with them.[27]

With further development, emotions begin to play additional roles. As babies become able to move about more easily, the danger of getting too far from a parent begins to become important. Infants need to be able to stay close to the safely of a parent. This way of thinking about parent and child interaction is similar to issues that arise in the study of animal behavior, the area known as ethology. John Bowlby started combining ideas from psychoanalysis with insights from ethology, but he was sidelined by the psychoanalytic community for questioning the orthodoxy. However, his theory of attachment has been highly influential, resulting in a great deal of important research and policy decisions about when and how we should intervene to support children. For Bowlby, the infant-caregiver attachment system is both a strong emotional bond and a means of ensuring that babies stay close enough to their parent who is caring for them, often their mother. An attachment starts to form at around 4 months, but grows in intensity from 6 to 24 months—this is known as the attachment stage. Originally Bowlby assumed that this was the mother, but two of his colleagues, Rudolph Schaffer and Peggy Emerson showed soon afterwards that the infant could have two or more "attachment figures" and these need not be biological relatives.[28] This form of relationship is based on the history of interaction with their caregiver, particularly on how the adult interacts with them.

In very early infancy crying makes babies' needs manifest to parents. But it is not that young babies cry in a conscious attempt to signal their distress. To begin with, they are not aware that they are communicating. Consider this sort of behavior in another species. Rat pups cry when they are out of the nest, and their mother responds by returning them to it. Their crying functions as a signal, but it is not that the pup is calling out that he wants to be rescued and returned to the nest. The high-pitched vocalizations the pup makes when out of the nest are involuntary and are the result of the cold which causes the pup's heart to slow down, and this in turn leads to compression of the abdomen in order to increase the rate at which blood returns to the heart, and the result of this process is a high-pitched vocalization.[29] In other words, rat pups cry when they are cold, and this results in their mother returning them to the nest. In this way, they influence their immediate environment, but without awareness that they are doing so.

Human babies may be a bit like rats initially, in that they cry when hungry, cold or uncomfortable with no sense of communicating their discomfort. Parents and other caregivers, on the other hand, act in very different way. They attempt to interpret the baby's behaviors and to invest meaning in them. The pediatrician Hanus Papoušek and his wife Mechthild, a psychiatrist, noted over forty years ago that parents act as a "biological mirror" (copying infant facial expressions), and a "biological echo" (mimicking infant sounds) to their newborns' actions.[30] We have known for a similar length of time that skin conductance measures show a stress reaction in response (autonomic arousal and a rise in diastolic blood pressure) to hearing babies' cries.[31] Such sounds arouse in us a need to reduce them.

Babies soon take advantage of the attention that their caregivers pay to them. We turn now to discussing a range of skills that begin as mere behavioral responses to an internal stimulus like hunger or cold or an external event, like a loud bang. Early in the first year, a child will respond to a smile with a similar expression and this soon becomes meaningful to her or him. There is a myth about clams being happy but this doesn't mean that they can smile, let alone grasp the significance of this gesture. If clams could smile they might be able create a different sort of environment and they might not get eaten so often.[32]

The significance of smiling

Smiling is a common human activity that is part of our everyday lives and we take it for granted (unless you live in Yorkshire, where Bill Bryson claimed that this is a rare social gesture![33]). Yet it is easy to overlook its significance for human development. Ever since Charles Darwin's claim that some human expressions are universal,[34] it has been assumed that this is a prime case of behavior that appears to be innate— all human babies smile, except those with considerable damage to their brain; only humans smile; and it seems to have universal meaning. Although other great apes such as chimpanzees do occasionally raise the corners of their lips, this expression does not seem to serve as a social signal because other chimpanzees do not respond to in a social way. Smiling is present to some extent in newborn infants, even those born congenitally blind[35], so its production seems to require no experience or learning.

Let's take a closer and more detailed look at the development of smiling to reflect on whether it is simply a biologically given ability. In fact, these early facial expressions are not the same as mature forms. The smile of a newborn infant is not yet a social action because infants first make this facial expression when they are asleep, and later only when they are drowsy.[36] At the age of 4 to 6 weeks infants begin smiling when they are awake, and these smiles are in response to a range of events, from parents to a curtain blown by the wind. It seems that a common characteristic of stimuli that lead to a smile is a rapid change in the baby's state of arousal.[37]

Although smiling may begin as a physiological reaction to arousal, parents usually respond to their infants' smiles by smiling themselves. Within weeks, typically developing babies coordinate smiling with looking at a parent.[38] Various aspects of this social skill emerge at different ages. By 4 to 6 months of age some infants already seem to smile when they expect interaction from their parents. This can be seen in an experiment called the "still-face procedure." In this situation, mothers[39] are asked to interact with their 4- to 6-month-old baby for one minute and then they are told to hold their face still for one minute, that is, to stop interacting and just look at their baby. This is actually very difficult for parents to do because they know their baby is expecting the interaction to continue. Those babies who had come to expect a response, smiled at their mothers during this still face phase, apparently in an attempt to get the normal enjoyable interaction going again.[40]

Smiles that could be described as "coy" can be seen as early as 2 months of age. In Figure 2.1 a baby gazes at herself in a mirror (far left photo), starts to smile (center left), widens her eyes and turns away (center right and right). Vasudevi Reddy[41] describes this as an "embarrassment-like" reaction. Although this is a fascinating step in social development, it is important to keep in mind that babies still have a long way to go in order to reach a level of understanding that is like ours. It does not necessarily reveal a grasp of others viewing the self that would be involved in you or I being self conscious. At this age the infant is only starting to get used to the nature of social interaction and is unlikely to be able to grapple with this type of reflexivity. Infants only gradually develop expectations about what happens within interpersonal relationships—and so they can anticipate the others' reactions within particular settings. The baby in Figure 2.1 may well have averted her gaze because the "infant" in the mirror's smile became too threatening. In any case, it is very cute! And this serves to draw adults into engagement with infants.

Another form of smiling emerges between 8 to 10 months of age. When playing with toys and turning to look at their mothers, 8-month-old babies tend to smile at the toys and at their mothers, but do not smile when turning from the toys to their mothers, as they will do a few months later in analogous situations. But by 10 months of age when playing with toys babies begin smiling as they turn to look at their mothers.[42] It is perhaps not surprising that they coordinate these actions when they have mastered postural control, such as sitting upright. Smiling in this position involves the development of a number of other motor actions like coordinating perceiving the toys and accurate reaching for and grasping them, as well as regulating their levels of arousal. All these skills and their coordination are gradually constructed through babies' action on their world.[43]

This is only a rough sketch of a complex developmental story through which babies acquire this important social ability. But even a brief outline is enough to show that the development of smiling is more complicated than simply claiming that human expressions that we take for granted are simply "innate." There is a complex history of this emerging social skill that is gradually mastered by babies within their developmental niche, and this context for development in which infants are embedded is also constantly changing as they develop further skills. As babies become more proficient at using forms of communication such as smiling, they will likely receive more complex reactions from other people, leading to further development. It will take several years for the child to be able to keep a

Figure 2.1 An "embarrassment-like" reaction in small babies studied by Vasudevi Reddy

"poker face" while telling a joke or smiling while hiding very different feelings, and even adults slip up in these actions.

As humans we tend to like smiles; perhaps we feel that dolphins and beluga whales are cute because it looks like they are cheerful. As babies' abilities change they become able to engage in more complex actions, which in turn influence their social environment in new ways. This developmental story is far more interesting than the simplistic assumption that each human capability is inborn. Instead, development of any skills in all species occurs through a process of interaction with several aspects of the environment. Indeed, some have long argued that the word "transaction" is a better depiction of a mutual sequence of influences between individual and environment.[44] This goes beyond a simple unfolding of pre-existing characteristics. Abilities such as smiling develop within particular developmental contexts, and such skills maintain as well as extend social and emotional niches. Beyond infancy and childhood, smiling becomes increasingly complex and can convey many different meanings across social situations and cultures. To experience an inkling of this complexity try paying attention to when you smile and what you experience when others smile at you. It is surprising how someone smiling at us can influence how we are feeling, and how many different forms of this expression there are—from uncontrolled delight to schadenfreude[45] (taking pleasure at another's misfortune).

The eyes as windows

The expression that "the eyes are the windows to the soul" reflects the common feeling that they reveal something about a person's mental life, about their thoughts and feelings. This is why some poker players resort to wearing dark glasses if they have not perfected their "poker face" to conceal that they have a good hand or bluff that they have one. The eyes are critically important in infant social development in a number of ways. Being able to follow the direction of other people's gaze is an essential social skill that is important for sharing attention, learning words and being competent in social interaction in general. So, what does being able to follow gaze indicate about a child's level of social understanding? Andrew Meltzoff and Rechele Brooks claim that when children follow the gaze of others it

> entails the ascription of a mental life to a viewer. We follow where another person looks because we want to see what they are seeing. When we see people direct their gaze somewhere, we wonder what object is catching their attention.[46]

In other words, if a child follows someone else's direction of gaze it is assumed that he or she is interested in what the person is looking at. Although this makes sense if we are talking about adults or children, it is not so obvious that the same would hold for very young babies because it assumes a great deal of understanding on their part. Some other species can also follow gaze direction. It has been observed in many other primates. In fact, chimpanzees are actually quite good at gaze following. For example, with a chimpanzee kept in a cage, if a person stares at the back of the cage and the chimpanzee looks there but can't see what the person is looking at the chimp will check again to identify the direction of the person's gaze. It seems that some dogs can also follow gaze in some situations, and even domestic goats follow the gaze direction of other goats.[47] Although looking where other goats are looking may be very useful in finding food, it is probably going too far to say that they consciously wonder what the others in the herd are looking at.[48]

Another reason to be cautious about strong claims regarding the meaning of gaze following is that we see a variety of forms, from very rudimentary sensitivity to eyes in newborns to far more sophisticated gaze following at 18 months involving checking that the other is looking where you want them to. One dilemma concerns deciding which is the "real" gaze following. Even babies at only 2 to 5 days old have some sensitivity to gaze. Indeed they are reported to show intense looking at faces just after they are born. They prefer looking at faces with eyes open versus closed, and with eyes looking at them compared to averted gaze.[49] This is far from the skill achieved by 1- or 2-year-old children, but it is a necessary foundation on which to build further social abilities. This tendency to look at eyes draws babies into paying attention to important parts of their social world.

Just as with smiling, it is not necessary to assume that babies are born with innate social knowledge about eyes. Rather, something about the combination of their visual system and their typical environment facilitates a gradually emerging understanding of what gaze implies.[50] For example, consider the role of mutual gaze between infant and caregiver. What are the underlying processes that are responsible for maintaining this face-to-face interaction? Babies can focus best at about 30–38 cm., so the face of a parent holding the infant will be the aspect of the environment that is most in focus.[51] Thus, the baby's capabilities exploit the environment that he or she experiences. Eyes may be particularly attractive to look at because, compared to other primate species, the human eye is unique in having a large area of white sclera around the darker-colored iris, which makes it easier to see movement, and therefore easier for others to see where someone is looking.[52] It has been suggested that this facilitates cooperative social interaction.[53] From our perspective, these biological characteristics may have evolved because they can also facilitate the social process through which infants develop human skills in social interaction, and on which thinking is then based.

Furthermore, an infant looking at her parent's face may sustain the adult's interest, perhaps because reciprocal gaze may be experienced as showing the infant's interest. In the first month parents tend to place themselves in front of their babies at about 42 centimeters, and aspects of newborn infants' visual systems may be well suited to support this face-to-face interaction. Fairly rapidly, over the first two months this distance extends to about 72 cm, presumably as infants become more proficient.[54] So we should be cautious about thinking of the infant simply as "immature." The infant's visual system appears well suited to its social environment, because humans carry their offspring.[55] This sparks a chain of events. For example, at about 4 months when infants start to disengage from mutual gaze, their parents interpret the direction of their look and any actions (voluntary and involuntary) to be about objects in that direction.[56]

Studying gaze

In order to explore the potential for gaze direction to influence young babies, Vincent Reid and Tricia Striano conducted an intriguing study in which they showed 3-month-olds a picture of an adult looking at one of two objects (Figure 2.2). They then showed the infant a photograph of only the two toys shown in the previous picture (Figure 2.3).

In this study the babies looked longer at the lighter object when presented with the objects. The researchers interpret this as showing that babies had already looked at the dark object because they were influenced by the direction of gaze in the picture above.[57] And this suggests that already at three months babies are making use of social cues from others' gaze direction.

The most common way to assess whether babies can follow others' gaze direction was first used by Michael Scaife and Jerome Bruner in the early 1970s. In this research procedure a baby is seated on his or her mother's lap across a table from an adult who makes eye contact with the baby and then turns to look at an object on her left or right (there is an object on each side). The question is at what age does the infant follow the adult's line of gaze to look at the correct object? Scaife and Bruner found that 30% of 2–4-month-old babies made at least one turn in the correct direction out of two trials.[58] By 11 to 14 months of age all of the babies were doing this. In research following up on this early

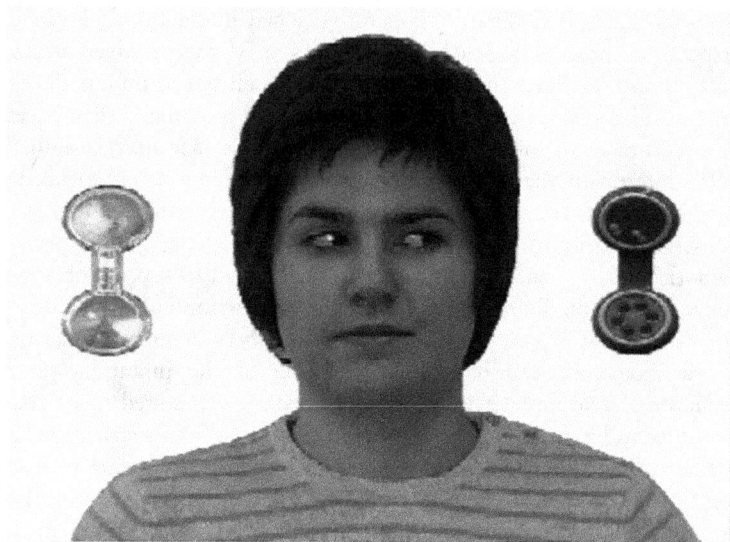

Figure 2.2 An early demonstration of joint attention by Vincent Reid and Tricia Striano: infants are first shown this photograph of an adult looking at two objects

Figure 2.3 The infants are then shown this photograph of just the objects

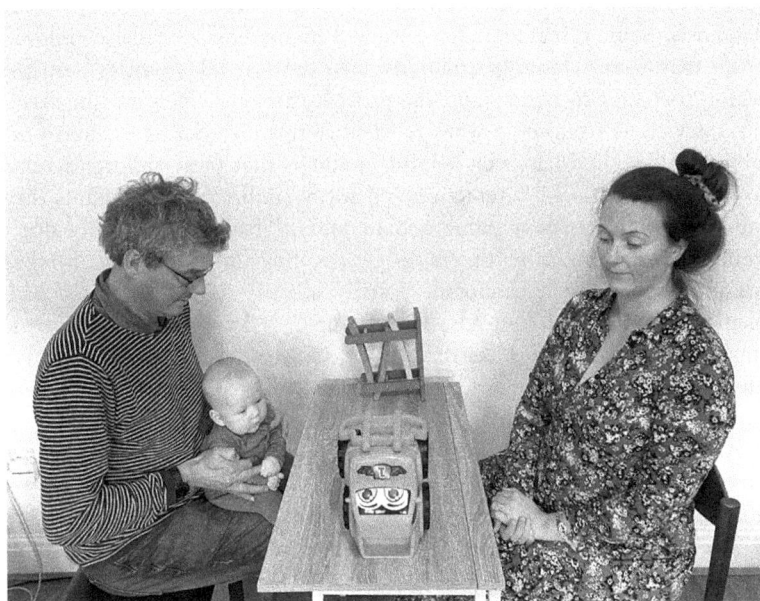

Figure 2.4 To test for the emergence of gaze following researchers explore when infants look to where an adult has turned

study there have been many variations on the procedure, and there is evidence that babies as young as 3 months tend to look in the right direction if the object is in their visual field, that is, in their peripheral vision without moving their eyes.

By 6 months babies are getting better at looking in the right direction but they tend to stop at the first object they see even if it is not the one the experimenter is looking at. At 12 months they can find the correct target that the experimenter is looking at even if it is the second object. These sorts of experiments, however, are done in laboratories that are not full of the usual household clutter, so actually following gaze in less perfect conditions might be more challenging. By 18 months infants are getting really good at following other people's direction of looking and they can even follow gaze to objects behind them. There are also other studies in which someone else looks at something behind an obstacle, like a wall. In such situations 12- to 18-month-olds will crawl or walk around it to see what they are looking at.[59]

A further source of evidence that sensitivity to other people's eyes is important for social development is that children who are later diagnosed with autism have problems with sensitivity to gaze. Autism is not typically diagnosed until children are at least 3 years old, and so it is very difficult to study the differences in these children that led up to the diagnosis. Some researchers have studied home movies of these children when they were infants (particularly their first birthday parties[60]) in the search for clues to understand the process through which autism develops, as well as to develop ways to identify this disorder as early as possible. This method has been helpful. It shows that these children tended to have reduced social interaction and social smiling, and as infants they fail to respond to their name and to faces. They also generally don't point in order to show things to others. But this approach also has drawbacks because it cannot necessarily identify the cause of the problem or even how it unfolds. For example, it has been noted several times that the problems faced by individuals with autism may involve motivation rather than, or in addition to, an inability to read social signals.[61]

An approach taken to deal with this difficulty is to study the younger brothers and sisters of children with autism because these siblings have a much higher chance of developing this disorder themselves because there is a genetic influence—about 9% of siblings are diagnosed compared to less than 1% for other children. In one study like this Lonnie Zwaigenbaum and her colleagues[62] studied 150 siblings of children with autism and 65 of these children were followed until they were 2 years old. At 6 months those babies who were later diagnosed with autism were more passive and less responsive to attempts to engage their attention. At 12 months their eye contact was poor as was their visual tracking, and they showed less social smiling, lower social interest and did not seem to express happiness in the way other babies do. They also seemed to fixate on non-social aspects of the environment and this was combined with reduced responses to other people's attempts to engage them socially. Unlike typically developing children, 2-year-olds with autism do not prefer what looks like biological motion in a display of lights.[63] Also, in contrast to their typically developing peers, babies who were later diagnosed with autism decreased rather than increased in looking at others' eyes between 2 and 6 months.[64] All of these response patterns likely result in far less engagement in the social world, and this reduction may make them miss vital parts in the developmental process of coming to understand our social world as second nature.

Following gaze direction to know where others are looking is an essential social skill for coordinating attention with others, and it is a key factor in further social development. Following other people's gaze is essential in knowing what they are paying attention to. For example, in order to learn words for objects babies have to know what other people are talking about. We have so far focused on coordinating *visual* attention because this is the most common means of coordinating attention, but babies born blind still need to learn how to share attention with others. They do so in different ways using other senses like touch and hearing. Because this is more difficult and can take longer, these children may be somewhat delayed in developing social understanding.[65]

Gaze following is an early form of infants' knowledge about other people. It is a practical form of social knowledge. That is, following where someone is looking usually leads to an interesting sight. Others' head turns thus convey meaning to the baby, and this is a form of social understanding. This could begin just as a signal, much as smoke indicates fire. But with further development the interaction around a head turn can become much more complicated. The social expectations or understandings of particular situations that infants are exposed to are gradually combined to form more complex social understanding.

Conclusion: Creating and being created by the social world

Babies influence their environment even though they are born helpless. The very fact of the "wailing weakness" in which they are born requires a social environment so that they are cared for and, thus, human infants grow up in a social world. It is essential that babies have a means of signaling when they are in need of something. Of course, very young infants have no conscious awareness of asking for something; their crying is simply a natural response to discomfort. But even in their crying, babies also have a role in influencing this social environment and gradually coming to understand it through learning from the responses they receive.

In this chapter we have discussed examples of how infants develop skills like sharing mutual gaze and attention, as well as smiling within social relations. Acquiring each of these social skills then changes infants' interaction and how others react to them:

> It is true, of course, that once mind has arisen in the social process it makes possible the development of that process into much more complex forms of social interaction among the component individuals than was possible before it had arisen. But there is nothing odd about a product of a given process contributing to, or becoming an essential factor in, the further development of that process. The social process, then, does not depend for its origin or initial existence upon the existence and interactions of selves; though it does depend upon the latter for the higher stages of complexity and organization which it reaches after selves have arisen within it.[66]

Child development is a cumulative, back and forth process with each stage of a developing ability building on the previous stage and also opening up new possibilities for further development. Many theorists use the term constructivism to describe this process. Imagine, for example, the further possibilities or potential for action that opens up when a child learns to walk. This is an early indicator that "travel broadens the mind."[67] But skills already learned may need to be reconstructed. Karen Adolph and her colleagues have conducted studies in which new walkers either crawl or walk to a sudden drop. If they crawl, they very gingerly test whether they can reach the lower level, are very good at estimating this in the first place and react to a parent's encouragement according to their judgement. But if they have just learned to walk the very same children hurl themselves off a ledge because they have no experience of making height judgements from a walking position and they gradually learn how to do this.[68] This is a clear example of how children react to their present situation in terms of their history of development within a specific area. Each new situation is different, and adjustment in response relies upon a complex history of experience. Thus we see a gradual process of development of more complex ways of interacting with their worlds—their physical and social worlds. We use the term "relational perspective" to refer to our approach to explaining how social understanding emerges. The focus is on the relations between the child and her world, and the individual's contribution to those relations should not be overlooked.

Individuals vary in their characteristics and this contributes to their relations with others. A child's usual way of responding to events has been referred to as his or her *temperament*. This was a term originally used to describe the tuning of a piano or harpsichord. It is now used to identify differences among infants in their character, their typical ways of responding to events. The general point is that babies are different. For parents with more than one child this is well known, and siblings know about differences among each other. We have argued in the first two chapters that it is not possible to separate such differences into a part explained by genes and a part explained by the environment. In spite of this babies do begin with differences. Among other influences, they have experienced differences in the womb and they have different family structures. Parents also differ and the relations between infant or child and parents will depend on how parents and children interact.

In the process of unpacking the developmental niche in which babies grow up we have touched on the forms of interaction that emerge between parents and babies. This already shows the beginning of communication, a crucial aspect of what makes human development possible. In the next chapter we turn to more directly grapple with the problem of how human communication works and develops in more complex ways. To do this requires that we think about the nature of this complexity and much depends on how children learn the meaning of utterances and gestures. Instead of just following philosophers' debates it is possible to also watch babies in order to see how they master skills in communication.

Suggested further reading

Griffiths, P. E., & Stotz, K. (2000). How the mind grows: A developmental perspective on the biology of cognition. *Synthese*, 122, 29–51.
Kaye, K. (1982). *The mental and social life of babies*. Hemel Hempstead: Harvester Wheatsheaf.

Notes

1 Darwin (1978, pp. 91).
2 Griffiths and Stotz (2000, p. 45).
3 Von Uexküll (1934, p. 5).
4 "The organism in a real sense is determinative of its environment" (Mead, 1934, p. 215). Contemporary theorists suggest that there are problems in thinking about the environment as a stable obstacle that the organism has to

deal with (West & King, 2008). Throughout this book we repeatedly encounter approaches that assume splits or dichotomies, and we argue that the study of action allows us access to key relations. In this chapter we consider the split between organism and environment, and suggest that a more fruitful approach involves the two in relation to one another.

5 Lewontin (2001, p. 64).
6 Lewontin (2001, p. 64).
7 Griffiths & Gray, 2004).
8 "All organisms consume resources by taking up minerals, by eating. But they may also create the resources for their own consumption, as when ants make fungus farms" (Lewontin, 2001, p. 64). Beavers raise water levels to make the environment better suited to them. But, in contrast, some trees may produce shade that prevents their own seedlings from growing. "Ecological succession is precisely the history of self-destruction of species by alternations of their own environment" (Lewontin, 2001, p. 64).
9 Hobson (2002).
10 Savage-Rumbaugh, Fields, Segerdahl, & Rumbaugh (2005, p. 16).
11 Savage-Rumbaugh and Fields (2011).
12 Prehensility is the ability to grasp onto or hold something. While the human feet have some prehensility this is not enough to hold our weight.
13 Ward, Kimbel, and Johanson (2011).
14 Cited in Kaye (1982, p. 54).
15 Leavens (2011); Krause et al. (2018).
16 Freud (1954); Mead (1934); Suttie (1935); Portmann (1990); Gould (1977); Bruner (1972).
17 Freud (1954).
18 Freud (1954, p. 379).
19 Suttie (1935).
20 Earlier, Hume also speculated on the implications of infancy: "The long and helpless infancy of man requires the combination of parents for the subsistence of their young; and that combination requires the virtue of chastity or fidelity to the marriage bed" (*Political Society*, section IV, paragraph 5).
21 Gould (1977); Portmann (1990).
22 Gould (1977); but see Zeveloff & Boyce, (1982).
23 Bowlby, (1958, p. 367); Bruner, (1972); Suttie (1935).
24 Mareschal et al. (2007).
25 Odling-Smee, Laland, and Feldman (2003).
26 Bowlby (1958, p. 367).
27 Shanker (2004).
28 Schaffer and Emerson (1964).
29 Jones (2008).
30 Papoušek and Papoušek (1977).
31 Frodi et al. (1978).
32 Pet dogs or cats can experience a social world, and experience it as different from the physical world, as well as brings this world forth by their actions.
33 Bill Bryson's *Notes on a Small Island* (Bryson, 1996) presents an excellent account of taciturn Yorkshire folk. In his book *The Road to Little Dribbling: More Notes from A Small Island* (Bryson, 2015) he writes "I love Yorkshire and Yorkshire people. I admire them for their bluntness ... if you want to know your shortcomings, you won't find more helpful people anywhere."

34 Darwin (1872).
35 Darwin (1872) discusses smiling in a deaf blind girl, Laura Bridgeman, as evidence of the innate propensity of this gesture. Research since has shown that smiling in blind newborns is more fleeting and takes longer to become a shared social gesture. See, for example, Freedman (1964).
36 Jones (2008).
37 Jones (2008).
38 Jones (2008).
39 In all the studies that we know of it is the mother who is asked to perform in the still face procedure. It would be interesting to do this with fathers in cultures (e.g., the UK and USA) where men engage in more jokey interaction with their children, as a still face might be perceived differently with fathers. See, for example, Lewis and Lamb (2003).
40 Mcquaid, Bibok, and Carpendale (2009).
41 Reddy (2008).
42 Jones (2008).
43 Jones (2008); Messinger and Fogel (2007).
44 Sameroff and Chandler (1975).
45 Epicaricy is the rarely used equivalent word in English.
46 Meltzoff and Brooks (2007, p. 232).
47 Kaminski et al. (2004).
48 Carpendale and Lewis (2006).
49 Farroni et al. (2004); Rigato et al. (2011).
50 Turkewitz and Kenny (1982).
51 Huurneman and Boonstra (2016).
52 Kobayashi and Kohshima (1997, 2001).
53 Tomasello, Hare, Lehmann, and Call (2007).
54 Jayaraman et al. (2017).
55 Savage-Rumbaugh & Fields, (2011).
56 Hendriks-Jansen (1996, p. 273).
57 Reid and Striano (2005) employ some interesting controls to demonstrate this effect. In one condition the adult looks straight ahead and when presented with the two toys the baby does not look longer at one of them when presented only with the two toys.
58 Scaife and Bruner (1975).
59 Moll and Tomasello (2004); Carpendale and Lewis (2006, 2010).
60 Osterling and Dawson (1994).
61 Koegel and Mentis (1985); Jaswal and Akhtar (2019).
62 Zwaigenbaum, Bryson, Rogers, Roberts, Brian, and Szatmari (2005).
63 Klin et al. (2009).
64 Jones and Klin (2013).
65 Bigelow (2003).
66 Mead (1934, p. 226). With human infants, their life world changes as they develop, as they acquire increased abilities. Once selves have arisen out of the social process, these selves can then maintain as well as change that social process, increasing its complexity, thus changing the environment in which selves develop and evolve. Once the mind emerges it makes more complex interaction with others possible. So the product of the social process—the mind—is an essential factor in contributing to that process and makes it more complex.

67 Campos et al. (2000).
68 Several of Adolph's studies are worth mentioning here. Her early research showed that infants in different postural positions react differently to height cues (e.g., Adolph, 2000). Her more recent research illustrates how walking infants draw attention to more distant objects when signalling to caregivers (Karasik et al., 2011).

Chapter 3

Wittgenstein's baby
How do words work?

In which we consider the mundane miracle of how words work to communicate with others.

> The study of language is one mode of contemplating a mystery.
> —Ian Robinson[1]

> As a feature of life on earth, language is one of science's great remaining mysteries.
> —Chris Knight, Michael Studdert-Kennedy, and James Hurford[2]

Language is central to being human. It's closely linked to our intelligence, and this is why it has been so central in many of the repeated debates over human versus primate skills. Most people become immersed in regular conversations on a daily basis, so it may seem that human communication is straightforward—toddlers pick up their native tongue without explicit instruction and at a speed that is breathtaking. In fact, many children learn two or more languages. Over the past century humans have moved effortlessly through the ages of the radio, television, the internet and Twitter. Each form takes on a slightly different communication style. Yet understanding the very building blocks of language is, paradoxically, so difficult that some have argued that it is the hardest problem in science.[3]

How does language work? How do words work to convey meaning? Although these might seem like very straightforward questions, the topic of meaning is the elephant in the room, rarely engaged with in psychology. To be clear, we are not talking about the meaning of life or whether something is meaningful in the sense of having a purpose. Rather, in order to discuss such questions it is necessary to have a language, and what we are concerned with is how human languages work—how we communicate and understand each other. This is usually through language—with words—but this process begins much earlier with babies' gestures, and there are many resources for conveying meaning in conversation beyond words.[4] Some scholars treat meaning as a noun, as fixed, but we follow a tradition that sees it as a verb, a process not a static entity.[5]

In order to understand the development of human minds, it is essential to understand language, how it works and how it differs from communication systems used by other animals. We believe that this is because this system of meaning generated in language is what human forms of thought are based on. To address this issue we need to examine different views of how language works. Although one common opinion is that all speech does is to convey thoughts from one mind to another, we hope to demonstrate instead that meaning is grounded in the process of social interaction. And we will show how these skills emerge in infancy and childhood.

The meaning of meaning

When Jeremy's daughter, Hannah, was 3½ years old she asked, "Daddy, what is meaning?" As he struggled to come up with a coherent answer she gave up waiting for his response and happily ran out to play. We have now been grappling with this complex problem for many years. Although the nature of meaning has been the central issue in philosophy for much of the last century, psychologists rarely seem to be concerned with it. At best, they assume that we each have a "mental lexicon" (a sort of dictionary) containing information about individual words. But this neglects both the philosophical assumptions and how such a presumed mental lexicon would actually work. It gives a name to this ability, but a name is not the same as an explanation. When it comes to meaning, psychologists appear to feel that difficult questions like this can be safely left to philosophers (or children). But it is important to grasp this nettle because theories in psychology are built on assumptions about meaning, even if these assumptions are not explicitly spelled out. But just as it is important to inspect the foundation before purchasing a house and check the odometer before buying a car it is also essential to consider the assumptions on which theories are based. It is necessary to check these philosophical presuppositions in order to avoid adopting a theory based on a flawed conception of meaning.

What is the usual view of meaning assumed in psychology? The philosopher Ludwig Wittgenstein used Saint Augustine as an example of the commonly accepted understanding of meaning. Augustine gives us a particular view of the essence of human language. It is this: the individual words in language name objects—sentences are combinations of such names.—In this picture of language we find the roots of the following idea: Every word has a meaning. This meaning is correlated with the word. It is the object for which the word stands.[6]

The same idea about meaning is common in research on language development and leads to the metaphor of the child increasing their vocabulary by "mapping" the new words onto objects. We get a similar view of meaning as being fixed to words from a range of writers from the English philosopher John Locke to the more recent example of Steven Pinker in his book *The Language Instinct*.[7]

This view of meaning as fixed to words leads to a view of how language works to communicate. It is often referred to as code model or message model. In the words of the philosopher John Canfield:

> The underlying picture is that the job of language is to communicate ideas. I cannot reveal my thoughts to you directly, so I let words or other tokens stand for those thoughts, and then present you with the tokens, whereupon you correlate them with corresponding thoughts in your mind. The mind is private, speech communal; speech bridges the gap between one privacy and another. Of course this picture needs to be dressed up a bit before it can be taken out in public. But simplistic as it is, the picture lies behind and gives force to the many more sophisticated variants of it found in the literature.[8]

According to this code model, language works through a speaker encoding meaning into words that are transmitted to others who then decode the words to arrive at the original meaning. This can only work if meaning is actually fixed to words, a claim we now analyze.

What is wrong with the idea that meaning is fixed to words or gestures?

Critics have long pointed out serious problems with this view of how language works. In writing about meaning, Susanne Langer suggests that "It is better, perhaps, to say: 'Meaning is not a quality, but a *function* of a term.'"[9] For example, even simple sounds may have complex meanings:

> A shot may mean the beginning of a race, the rise of the sun, the sighting of danger, the commencement of a parade. As for bells, the

world is mad with their messages. Somebody at the front door, the back door, the side door, the telephone—toast is ready—typewriter line is ended—school begins, work begins, church begins, church is over—street car starts—cashbox registers—knife grinder passes—time for dinner, time to get up—fire in town![10]

The view of meaning as being fixed to words so that they are like labels for objects has been around since at least Saint Augustine, and it has also criticized for some time. In Jonathon Swift's novel *Gulliver's Travels* (1726, pt 3, ch. 5), Gulliver meets some scholars who have figured out that because words are just names for things they could save their breath, and therefore be healthier, by just carrying around a bag of things that they want to talk about, and they could have a conversation simply by bringing the objects out of the bag. A drawback was that if they wanted to have a wide-ranging conversation they would have to carry a very large bag. So, the scholars were weighed down under these bags, unless they could afford one or two servants to help carry them. (The women in the town refused to be involved in this silliness.)

It might be thought that this idea of carrying objects could be improved upon with new technology. Instead of large bags, smart phones can contain a large number of pictures. In fact, something like this did happen to Jeremy. A friend had asked him to buy a particular type of hairbrush while he was in Paris. Since his French was rather limited, he had a picture of the hairbrush on his phone, which he showed to people working in stores. This was effective in communicating, and they would either point him in the right direction, or shake their head indicating that they didn't have hairbrushes. However, it only worked due to the shared understanding regarding what we do in stores—we buy things. If he had stopped people passing by on the street and showed them the picture, they might have looked at him strangely and perhaps have him locked up. So, communicating depends on shared routines in particular social situations.

This view of language was satirized by that noted philosopher (and cartoonist) Gary Larsen in a cartoon in which a man has painted words on objects such as "house," "tree," "dog," "cat," and "shirt." The caption for the cartoon declares: "Now, that should clear up a few things around here!" Of course, Larsen's brilliant sense of humor pinpoints that this will not help at all and doesn't clear up anything because that is not what people do with language.

Larsen continues making fun of this view of language in a cartoon in which a pilot having spotted a shipwrecked sailor standing on a desert island beside a partially written message on the beach (HELF) desperately waving toward to the pilot, says into his radio, "Wait! Wait! Cancel that, I guess it says 'helf'." The pilot seems to be leaving the scene even though the situation makes it so clear what is actually meant. This gives us a hint toward a more complete account of how meaning is not simply the interpretation of individual words, but is rooted in common social situations on which shared understanding is based.

To continue grappling with the idea of meaning as fixed, consider further criticism from Gary Larsen. The illustrative cartoon is entitled "Where the worlds of boating and herpetology converge." The speakers in both panels are saying, 'She's a beaut, Norm. What is she, a 24-footer?'" but they are referring to a boat in one panel and to a snake in the other. This is an example of *indexicality*. That is, the same utterance can be used to convey different meaning in different settings. But if meaning is just attached to words in the way the code model suggests, how can the model explain the flexibility of language demonstrated by Langer and Larsen?

The *indexical* nature of meaning is the idea that what an utterance means depends on the context within a sequence of interaction. It is not fixed; it is not attached to a word, representation or gesture, and so on. Instead, words, phrases or images can be used to convey various meanings depending on the social situations in which they are used. For example, in certain situations compliments can be insulting, while in other situations insults can be endearing. The statement, "I will come to see you at midnight," would be a promise if Romeo said this to Juliet, but a threat if a vampire said it to his next potential victim.[11]

To articulate these difficulties further, with the idea that meaning is attached to words, consider what has been called the "whatjamicallit effect."[12] How can others understand us when we say things like, "where is the thingamibob," or "pass me the thingimajig"? How can we even call "whatjamicallit" a word? In fact, its meaning is constantly changing, or more correctly, people use it to convey different meaning. Yet in many settings people seem to have no difficulty at all in understanding such utterances. And if there is some problem it can often be quickly sorted out.[13]

Studying the ways in which utterances are used in different contexts to convey different meanings is an aspect of the study of language known as *pragmatics*. It is well known that we can use utterances sarcastically, ironically, or metaphorically to convey different meaning. For example, when Charlie said "That's excellent" to a group of students who did very well in his statistics exam they understood what he meant, but when he said exactly the same thing to the same students a week later who did poorly in their exam in child development, they also understood him (Charlie's friends and colleagues also gradually come to understand him, with enough experience).

The same sort of communication occurs in children's everyday experiences, like classic literature. When Eeyore says to Winnie the Pooh, "you're a fine friend," he, in fact, means just the opposite. But this is actually a difficult aspect of language to master. Hannah at 3½ years old noticed there was something odd when Jeremy said, "thanks, Max" to Max, at 12 months old, for wiping his nose on Jeremy's sweater. Even though she didn't understand the sarcasm she did notice that there was something different about the meaning he was conveying and she asked why he said "thanks." Until recently, many scholars held that sarcasm and irony were late developments in the child's grasp of language, emerging in the elementary school years.[14] However, recent studies suggest that children at the age of five can pick up on these utterances,[15] and our research suggests that even 3-year-olds can understand irony, at least in simple situations. For example, Maki Rooksby and Charlie enacted a scene in which one doll ruined a cake mix by adding too much salt when trying to help the cook. The 3-year-olds could quite easily understand the cook's statement, "That's great; you've really helped me." In order to clearly demonstrate this understanding they also responded correctly to many questions that were designed to control for children getting the answer to the test question right for all the wrong reasons.

Patterns of intonation can also result in conveying different meaning. Lev Vygotsky[16] used an example from Dostoevsky's *The Diary of a Writer* in which a conversation between six young drunken workmen is accomplished with only one unprintable word. But with different intonation and location in the interaction it conveyed different meaning, and they understood each other!

There are many other ways in which subtleties in the ways in which we use language demonstrate its indexicality. For example, usually if we say something like, "can you pass the salad" we are not actually asking if the person is physically capable of completing this task. Rather than asking a question, this utterance serves to make a request in a polite manner. (If the word *"can"* in this utterance is stressed it may well be taken to be a criticism of the listener. Try it at the dinner table, but ensure you are at a good distance.)

Pausing for thought: How we convey meaning

In addition to words, there are other ways in which we convey meaning. For example, both of our wives have asked us if we liked their new glasses, and each of us hesitated a moment before answering, "They look great!" (Don't try this at home). Even though we are both convinced that we paused in order to make a balanced judgement, we both received the same reaction: Those fatal pauses meant that neither of us could convince our partner that we really liked her glasses. Do pauses have a meaning? It is clear that they do, but not a specific one. So when we asked our children, getting their coats on to visit friends, "Have you done your homework?" a pause almost always meant No.

Here are some other examples collected by Bill Turnbull[17] showing how even pauses in conversation can convey meaning.

Exchange between husband and wife:

A: I'm getting fat.
B: (3 second pause)
A: Do you really think so?

In this brief exchange we can clearly see that a pause does convey meaning from the way the other person responds to it. Here the first person took the pause to mean "yes." So does a pause mean yes? Well, not necessarily, it depends on the situation. Consider the following example.

Overheard in an art gallery:

C: I really like that.
D: (3 second pause)
C: Well, I mean, I think it's the type of work that kinda grows on you.

Here the pause is taken to mean disagreement. So its meaning depends on the interactional sequence in which it is embedded. It could mean agreement, disagreement or a variety of other feelings like "you're thinking about the soccer game that you missed by visiting the gallery."[18]

It is common knowledge that facial expressions also convey meaning. For example, in writing his acknowledgements for his masterful book on Ludwig Wittgenstein, *Experience and Expression*, Joachim Schulte lists and thanks philosophers who have helped him understand and write clearly about Wittgenstein. Schulte ends by saying that, "Of especial help was a certain frown Eva Picardi gave me. Many thanks."[19] We can only wonder about how this "certain frown" was so much help in understanding the complexities of Wittgenstein's writing (we have come up with several possibilities), but the statement illustrates elegantly that even a facial expression can convey many different meanings. Of course, frowns, smiles, grimaces and so on abound in everyday life, and can be far simpler than the rather esoteric example we have used. We imagine, however, that this particular frown if seen by someone else might not have been quite so informative about Wittgenstein. That is, we must always look at the sequence of interaction when understanding how meaning is conveyed.

Different meanings can be conveyed with simple gestures even without words. For example, while on a long drive Jeremy's daughter ate a cracker. He then held out his hand and she gave him one. Later she ate an olive, and again he held out his hand, and this time she gave him an olive. That is, she understood that the same gesture in different contexts meant something different. As we will show in the following chapters, the gesture of holding out one's hand has roots that can be traced back to infancy; in this context it was a request. However, when an extended arm is obviously a request (for example, when the hand is cupped open with the "cup" upwards) it still doesn't specify what is being asked for. That depends on the situation, on what has just happened, as well as shared history. In this case, it depended on what Jeremy's daughter had just eaten, but this example could be further complicated if his daughter believed that he hates olives or that he was a cracker addict.

Charlie's father was a surgeon who operated with the same assistants over several years. He described how, with experienced teams, a hand-out gesture could be made at a point in an operation and the assistant would understand just what the surgeon needed without there being any immediate pragmatic cues to identify it—everything depends on the long history of working and communicating together.

These examples show how meaning is conveyed within interaction even without the use of words. This clashes with the common intuition that meaning is attached to words, just like the definitions in a dictionary, that we started the chapter with. But this is actually an obstacle to our understanding, and dictionaries generally list many meanings for each word, and they are constantly being revised when new words are added. Although meaning is thought of as attached to words, humor or friendliness are not considered attached to words or sentences. Whether jokes are funny or not depends on their use in a sequence of interaction, and crucially upon the timing of the punch line. This is easy to discover if a joke is told in the wrong context, or if the audience either already knows it or comes from another culture.

We now turn to an alternative view of meaning that avoids the problems we have reviewed.

Wittgenstein changes his mind: Communication through shared experience

We have mentioned before one of the most influential philosophers of the twentieth century, Ludwig Wittgenstein. He is important for the topic of this book because of his work on language, meaning, and understanding, even though most of this work remained unpublished during his lifetime. It may be helpful to know something about Wittgenstein's unusual life in order to understand his ideas. Born in 1889, the youngest of eight children, he grew up in a palatial home in Vienna full of music and culture, with seven grand pianos, and music evenings with composers such as Brahms and Mahler. His brothers were musical geniuses, but three of the four committed suicide, perhaps because of pressure from their father to take on his extensive steel business. Ludwig's remaining brother, Paul, had a career as a concert pianist, in spite of losing his right arm in the First World War. In fact, Ravel's Concerto for the Piano for the left hand was written especially for him. Although music was always central to Wittgenstein's life, he went on to study aeronautical engineering in Manchester, England, where he did research on kites and propellers. Designing propellers led him to the foundations of mathematics and then to philosophy, studying with Bertrand Russell at Cambridge.[20] Wittgenstein published only one short book on philosophy during his lifetime, the *Tractatus Logico-Philosphicus*, which was based on his work on logic and in reaction to Bertrand Russell (he also published a brief student review and an article in 1929). Wittgenstein finished this book while he was a soldier in the Austrian army on the Russian Front, volunteering for the most dangerous work, and also in an Italian prisoner of war camp, which he refused to leave until the last of his men were released.

In the *Tractatus*, which became a classic in philosophy, Wittgenstein put forward a theory in which language is viewed as a calculus—a set of abstract statements which when decoded, provide access to their truth value. In this book he felt that he had solved all the problems of philosophy, so he left the discipline and went to teach in a poor rural Austrian village school. During this time he produced a spelling dictionary for school children, the only other book he published in his lifetime. Teaching didn't last long, however, due to clashes with parents regarding Wittgenstein's discipline and his expectation that the students would go on in education, which clashed with their parents' wishes that they stay on the farm.[21]

Although Wittgenstein had inherited a huge fortune from his father, making him one of the wealthiest men in Europe, he gave it away to his family, and to poets and artists. Just before the Second World War he had to negotiate on his sisters' behalf with the Nazi government because there was some doubt about how many of their grandparents were Jewish. Getting his sisters re-classified as of German blood cost 1.7 tonnes of gold from the family fortune.[22] During the bombing of Britain in the Second World, Wittgenstein found it intolerable to teach philosophy in Cambridge. To be of use during the London Blitz, Wittgenstein went to work as a porter and then a pharmacy technician at Guy's Hospital in London (where, by coincidence, he worked with Charlie's father, then a medical student).

While teaching in Austria, Wittgenstein had continued occasionally to discuss philosophy with his friends, but it was not until the late 1920s that he started thinking that there was more to be done in philosophy, and he then returned to Cambridge and to philosophy. John Maynard Keynes, the great macro-economist, wrote to his wife about Wittgenstein's arrival: "Well, God has arrived. I met him on the 5.15 train."[23] When Wittgenstein was reconsidering his conclusions about philosophy, his conversations with the Italian economist, Piero Sraffa, were an important influence. For example, Wittgenstein had previously insisted that meaning requires that a proposition and what it refers to have the same logical form. Sraffa responded by brushing his chin with his fingertips—making a Neapolitan gesture for an insult—and asked, "what is the logical form of *that*?" Recognizing that such a gesture conveys meaning requires understanding it as part of an ongoing stream of life, as based on social interaction.[24] Sraffa's criticism forced Wittgenstein to recognize flaws in his earlier work and pushed him to revise his whole perspective. Thus, Wittgenstein is famous for having changed his mind, and it is this later work that we build on in this book.

Although Wittgenstein worked intensively on meaning, language, understanding and the philosophy of psychology, he did not feel ready to publish another book, even though he did complete a manuscript in German, entitled *Philosophical Investigations*, which he distributed to his friends. When Wittgenstein died in 1951 this manuscript was translated into English and published 2 years later. Since that time, Wittgenstein's literary executors have published many volumes compiled from his manuscripts and notes. Wittgenstein's influence has been extensive, although there continues to be much debate about how his work should be understood.

When Wittgenstein presents Saint Augustine's view of how language works, as mentioned in the beginning of this chapter, he considers whether it would be possible for a primitive language to actually work in this way. That is, could language work if words are like names for things and language encodes such names and accompanying actions? For example, we could imagine that tables and chairs all have labels attached to them, like the Gary Larsen cartoon.

As part of his argument, Wittgenstein tried to base a language on this theory. He described a simple language that might be used between a builder and a helper to coordinate their activity. The words would be like names for the various types of building material such as "slabs," "blocks," and "pillars." And there would have to be numbers, say up to five. The builder and helper could then use this simple language to coordinate their activity. So a typical example of an utterance might be "five slabs." But we immediately run into problems because what does this actually mean? It might be an order from the builder to the helper to bring five slabs, but it could also be a report from the helper to the builder that there are five slabs left, or that five slabs have already been placed, or that five slabs are needed to complete the job, and so on. It could also be an exclamation or a curse, and we could imagine more complex uses of this utterance in negotiations about buying more building supplies. We could imagine a group of builders and assistants in which this same utterance could mean go and destroy five slabs,[25] or that his sandwiches look a bit thick today. The point is that this utterance could have many possible meanings.

Even such an apparently straightforward utterance cannot simply be determined with mechanical rules. We could not program a computer to go through a series of steps to derive the meaning. Instead, we must know the situation of its use, the history of interaction between the speaker and hearer, and the sequence of activities in which it is embedded in order to see what social act is being performed. As part of a cooperative activity such an utterance can certainly be used to coordinate interaction and convey meaning. Thus, language does not work in the way Saint Augustine assumed. It does not work as a series of names for things that are used to convey meaning from one person to another. Rather, it is a part of human activity, and understanding others is built on shared experiences within similar settings. We see that language is used as part of various activities, like requesting, commanding, reporting, complimenting, expressing affection or disgust, or a host of other emotions.

Our colleague, Bill Turnbull, argues that it is important to work from recordings of actual interaction and not from imagined examples such as Wittgenstein's story of builders and slabs. So, consider an example, not imagined by a philosopher but encountered in everyday life. Jeremy's wife, arriving home as he was reading Wittgenstein, announced, "I have five bags in the car." What did this mean? Or, rather, what did she intend to convey with this utterance? Was this a simple statement of fact, or a report regarding the size of her shopping trip? If Jeremy had just asked her how much she had purchased it could have been an answer to his question. Or it could have been a request for help, or a command, in which he would play the role of helper in Wittgenstein's example above. (He went to get the bags.)

Wittgenstein's ideas are in sharp contrast to the view of meaning we criticize in this chapter. He considered his work as therapeutic in the sense of pointing out how we all tend to go wrong, to make mistakes, about meaning, language, and mind. He was not doing child psychology but rather working on meaning and language. For our goal, however, this is highly relevant and so we draw on his arguments.[26]

To address how meaning works, Wittgenstein[27] considered a picture of a man on a hill. What does this picture mean? What is it meant to convey? Is it a man climbing up, or a man sliding back down the hill? We can't tell until we see the picture in a sequence of other pictures. In another example Wittgenstein[28] asks us to consider a picture of a boxer. What does it mean? Is it the way one should stand when boxing? Or the way one shouldn't stand? Or, perhaps, it indicates a particularly famous boxer? It could be used to represent various meanings, such as to stand in for a 5-dollar bet in a game of poker.[29]

These arguments show that there are many possible interpretations of any representation, image, word, utterance, or gesture. Thus, a fixed meaning is not simply attached to a representation. Instead we have to look elsewhere for how meaning is conveyed.

There is a tendency to assume that meaning is located within us, in each of our heads, and we may wish to transmit it to others; we try to "get our meaning across." If we fail and the other person obviously misunderstands us then we try again. This feeling seems to fit with our personal experience. It may be the source of the code model introduced above. However, we have now seen the problems that we encounter when we try to think carefully through the implications of such a view. Any sense that we may have of language as a code that is transmitted is illusory: it is caused by the fact that our communications are so grounded on repeated practices that we intuitively misread meaning as activity into meaning as fact.

To understand this illusion, it is helpful to think developmentally in terms of how infants and children get into the loop of successful communication. Through this way of thinking, we can see that our human experience is a developmental accomplishment. Our adult experience of meaning and our attempts to convey meaning are the outcome of an extended developmental process. To understand this development we have to look at the forms of interpersonal engagement in which babies and children grow up: the focus of the next chapter concerns how young children can become proficient communicators from a very slow start.

Meaning is a process, a function, not a content. By using it as a verb, rather than as a noun, we remind ourselves that it is not attached to representations (another slippery term that is used too often in psychology). So why do we think meaning is attached to words? Why do dictionaries work? These documents record a shared history of conventional uses of words. But dictionaries have constantly to be updated, and words are still used in creative ways, ways that cannot be found in a dictionary. That is why mastering additional languages cannot be done solely through reading dictionaries. The result of attempting this can be the source of much humor. The anthropologist Evans Pritchard lived among the Azande for several months thinking that they were very keen bird watchers. It took him a long time to realize (or be told) that their references to swallows usually were about people who indulged in sexual infidelity (swallows dart around).

Finding meaning in shared experience

How do we as humans come to understand words, given that they are so flexible in terms of what is meant? Successfully conveying meaning must be based on a history of shared interaction involving similar experience with routine patterns of action. For example, waving goodbye to the owner of a Greek restaurant after a wonderful meal and saying, "*kalamári*" may serve to mean good day, even though *kalamári* actually means squid and the speaker meant to say, "*kalí méra.*" It is the prior shared practice of saying goodbye or good day that makes this utterance meaningful. Indeed in the evening "*kalí spéra*" (good evening) would have been more appropriate. The fact that this is a common routine experience shared by most others allows us to convey meaning, and to have others understand us, even if the word is not used in the usual dictionary sense. We all know about saying goodbye and good evening, and the owner of the restaurant had no difficulty in understanding the intended meaning. It is a shared routine, what Wittgenstein called "a form of life" or a "fact of living."[30] This is a pattern of activity that we all know about. This sort of routine starts in infancy and we come to know what to expect.[31] If meaning is rooted in such patterns of activity then we need to learn about how these routine forms of interaction develop.

Children learn patterns of interaction that form the foundation for language. They become able to make requests and engage in routines of responding, refusing, and greeting. We believe that many common routines may be found in all human societies,[32] although how particular social acts are accomplished will vary, and some may be specific to certain cultures. Children then learn language to go with particular activity patterns like making a request. John Canfield describes some of these early language games or patterns of interaction on which language is later based. Refusing and making requests appear early, whereas the game of naming objects such as ball and flower actually appears later and may not be universal across cultures.[33] The natural reactions on which requests and refusals are based become gestures as children learn how their parents typically respond. This represents two forms of human interaction. Requests may develop from reaching, which is a natural reaction (see Chapter 4). Humans reach for objects because our hands are adapted to grasping—as we suggested in Chapter 1, our interactions and thoughts are embodied, they are based on our natural human ways of acting.

Other forms of human interaction may also be universally based on natural human reactions, such as the examples in Carl Sandburg's poem "Choose":

> The single clenched fist lifted and ready,
> Or the open asking hand held out and waiting.
> Choose:
> For we meet by one or the other.[34]

In this poem Carl Sandburg draws on our common knowledge that a raised clenched fist is a natural human reaction associated with anger and preparation to fight, whereas, in contrast, an open extended hand is a natural part of a request or offer of help. These two contrasting actions are aspects of common human forms of interaction that form the basis for shared understanding, for meaning. A raised fist has been used by dozens of political groups to indicate power, strength, or solidarity, while an open hand is often proffered for a handshake, a gesture of openness and acceptance.

We began this chapter with the problem of language and how it works. We have examined this incredibly complex aspect of human life because language is an essential aspect of human forms of thinking, and, therefore, we need to understand the key issue of how meaning is conveyed. Any theory of language must be based on assumptions about its nature, and we have seen that the common view of meaning being attached to representations has many difficulties; that is, it does not appear to be credible! Therefore, we have started to approach an alternative view of meaning as based on everyday experiences of shared understanding, joint routines or patterns of interaction in which a child comes to understand what usually happens next. In the next chapter we discuss the specifics of how meaning emerges by exploring how infants develop the ability to use gestures.

Our goal is to explain the development of human forms of thinking. Some scholars would object to our approach, claiming that syntax (the grammar or the structure of utterances) is the essence of language, but we want to know how it is that words have meaning to begin with. We acknowledge that explaining the development of syntax is also a very difficult task, one that goes far beyond want we can do in this book.[35] However, we believe that an adequate account of syntax must rest on a workable view of the process through which meaning emerges in human development. We need to have something to talk about before we can construct sentences. The complexity of syntax distracts us from the more basic issue of how words have meaning. And the same issue of meaning already emerges with gestures even before babies start using words. Similarly, the incredible complexity of a Boeing 787 could distract us from the basic principles of lift that make flight possible and apply equally to a sparrow, a Golden Eagle, or an F-14 Tomcat. Of course, an Airbus A380 is orders of magnitude greater in complexity than the Wright brothers' aircraft but the basic principles of lift that make it possible for both to fly are the same. To conceptualize language properly, it is the nature of meaning that we have to be concerned with because it this that makes the rest of the complexity possible. This is what enables language to get off the ground. It makes language possible, and it is an understanding of the process through which meaning is conveyed that is needed in order to understand human thinking. Therefore, we have to explain this foundational form of interaction in which meaning arises.

The fact that words have meaning is perhaps so obvious that it rarely occurs to us to ask about how this works. Yet it is an everyday, mundane miracle, something that we live immersed in so that we overlook it too easily. For Wittgenstein, the trick is to pay attention to what was always right in front of us.

> What we are supplying are really remarks on the natural history of human beings; not curiosities, however, but facts that no one has doubted, which have escaped notice only because they are always before our eyes.[36]

To do so it makes sense to look first for the simplest examples of meaning being conveyed. That is, to look at how babies start to use gestures, which we turn to in the next chapter.

Suggested further reading

Goldberg, B. (1991). Mechanism and meaning. In J. Hyman (Ed.), *Investigating psychology: Sciences of the mind after Wittgenstein* (pp. 48–66). New York: Routledge.
Jones, S. (2008). Nature and nurture in the development of social smiling. *Philosophical Psychology*, 21, 349–357.

Notes

1 Robinson (1975, p. ix).
2 Knight, Studdert-Kennedy, and Hurford (2000, p. 1).
3 For example, Christiansen and Kirby (2003).
4 Turnbull (2003).
5 This is a point made and discussed by John Shotter in *Social accountability and selfhood* (Shotter, 1984).
6 Wittgenstein (1968, §1).
7 Steven Pinker's bestselling book, "The Language Instinct," states that humans belong to "a species with a remarkable ability: we can shape events in each other's brains with exquisite precision. I am not referring to telepathy or mind control or the other obsessions of fringe science; even in the depictions of believers these are blunt instruments compared to an ability that is uncontroversially present in every one of us. That ability is language. Simply by making noises with our mouths, we can reliably cause precise new combinations of ideas to arise in each other's minds" (Pinker, 1994, p. 15). Although Pinker emphasizes that this view is different from telepathy, his description suggests considerable similarity between the two. His view, clearly articulated, is that in language meaning is transmitted from one head to another—or that my utterance evokes the same representations in your mind–brain system. He presents the common belief that we encode meaning in words and then transmit these words to others who decode the words and derive the meaning. This might appear to make sense because it sounds just like the way a telephone works. This view, known as a code model of how language works to transmit meaning can be traced back at least as far as the 17th century when the English philosopher John Locke wrote, "To make words serviceable to the end of communication, it is necessary, as has been said, that they excite in the hearer exactly the same idea they stand for in the mind of the speaker" (*Essay*, III, ix, 6). John Locke assumed that the only way that words could work to communicate is if they have fixed meaning, allowing encoding, transmission and decoding, in order to transmit the same meaning from one mind to another. This idea is at the heart of the computational view of the mind that we described in Chapters 1 and 3.
8 Canfield (1995, p. 201).
9 Langer (1942, p. 56).
10 Langer (1942, p. 60).
11 Itkonen (2008, p. 284).
12 Levinson (1995).
13 Of course, there are many words that work this way, such as "this," "that," "it," "she," and so on. Philosophers, linguists, and psychologists who focus

on language, are, of course, well aware that utterances can be ambiguous. However, they tend to focus on rare utterances that have two possible meanings. For example, "avoid boring professors" could mean that students should avoid professors who are boring, or that they should avoid making professors bored, or indeed that all professors are, by definition, deadly dull! It has been assumed that this problem can be patched up. But the ubiquity of ambiguity in speech is more than a minor difficulty that can be glossed over. Instead it is built into the very way that language functions. This issue is well known in linguistics and philosophy. It is because of ambiguity that Noam Chomsky and Jerry Fodor are convinced that there must be some "deep structure" that maps the meaning directly onto what they call a "wave form." That is, although we are pointing out ambiguity as a problem for the view of meaning as fixed and attached to some representation, Fodor and others take this problem to indicate that meaning must be buried further down in the mind or the brain. They didn't question the nature of meaning but rather they just added a deeper layer. But proposing some deeper level does not solve the fundamental problem; it just pushes it further down. The same problem of meaning would reappear no matter how many levels are added: we are pointing out ambiguity as a problem for the fixed view of meaning as attached to something. Instead, an alternative is needed. We argue that the process of meaning is to be found in the history of social interaction. The linguist Noam Chomsky and philosopher Jerry Fodor recognized that there are problems with this view of meaning that their approach rests on but they hold onto the hope that it can be patched up. Chomsky (2007) is still waiting for progress in semantic theory to fix the problem, and Fodor didn't think there was any other option available, so bizarre as he acknowledged his view to be, he believed it is the only option (see also Goldberg, 1991). We think there is an alternative.

14 Filippova and Astington (2008).
15 In their follow up study Filippova and Astington (2010) found that while developments took place in the primary school years, 5-year-olds showed some understanding.
16 Vygotsky (1986, p. 241).
17 Turnbull (2003).
18 Turnbull (2003).
19 Schulte (1996, vii).
20 Monk (1990).
21 After this experience he worked as a gardener for a monastery, and then he took on designing and supervising the construction of a new house in Vienna for one of his sisters.
22 Edmonds and Eidinow (2001).
23 Monk (1990).
24 Monk (1990).
25 Canfield (2007).
26 Wittgenstein (1983); see Canfield (2007); Goldberg (1991); McDonough (1989, 2004).
27 Wittgenstein (1968, §139).
28 Wittgenstein (2009).
29 Goldberg (1991).
30 Wittgenstein (1991).

31 Canfield (2007).
32 Canfield (1999).
33 For example, Canfield (2007).
34 Sandburg (1916).
35 See, for example, Tomasello (2003).
36 Wittgenstein (1968, §415).

Chapter 4

A brief history of babies

How do babies get the point?

In which we examine the way babies learn how to communicate with gestures.

> A speck of behavior, a fleck of culture, and—voila!—a gesture.
> —Clifford Geertz[1]

When Max, Jeremy's son, woke up a week before his first birthday, he immediately pointed to one of his books. It was a request for Jeremy to "read" it to him. This was clear because Max persisted until he was understood and Jeremy opened the book. At 12 months of age Max was using pointing gestures to makes requests, but at other times he pointed with his index finger just to indicate things he was interested in, like birds, trees or an airplane. When Jeremy picked Max from his babysitter Max pointed out the door, and then he pointed to all of the things on the shelf to be brought home. It was his way of commenting on going home and what was needed. Max could also combine gestures. For example, he pointed to something he wanted on a shelf and then he pointed to Jeremy, asking him to get it. Similarly, Charlie warned his daughter-in-law Lyndsey that her son William, aged 9 months and 3 weeks, would start to point at about 10 months. A week later William duly obliged, pointing to everything he saw and uttering an "ooo" sound as he did it. By the middle of his 11th month he would point at his large toy giraffe if asked "Where's Doug," much to Lyndsey's surprise. Pointing remained his main communicative gesture even after his first birthday and, just after 13 months, he started to look at the person he was pointing for just before gesturing.

These are examples of communication before language. Being human is tied up with our ability to communicate with each other. To understand this extraordinary skill we have to explain how babies learn to communicate intentionally—in terms of Chapter 3 how meaning is conveyed and grasped. This happens so easily and naturally that we barely notice it. Parents just welcome the fact that it gets easier to understand their child. To study how babies develop gestures it is not necessary to build massive particle accelerators, gigantic radio telescopes, or expensive fMRI machines. Yet in spite of this there is still little agreement on exactly how infants actually learn to use gestures.[2] In the face of this lack of consensus, one would think that this is happening on the dark side of the moon rather than in our own homes in front of our eyes. For example, how does an extended index finger become a meaningful gesture? We can use our index finger to check if a cake is cooked or paint is dry, but we can also use the same hand configuration for any number of social acts such as pointing out an unusual sight, indicating one's choice of ice cream, or accusing someone of a crime. How do we explain the change from a meaningless extended index finger, to a meaningful social gesture? And this same hand configuration can be used to convey many different meanings. Shortly after their first birthday babies use this gesture to make requests, direction attention, and ask or answer questions. Older children can also use the gesture in other ways. For example, Mackenzie, at age 4, held her index finger up and said, "one," and then added, "up there," moving her hand upward to indicate a place on the deck of the sailboat.

Even before babies begin using and understanding their first words they become well practiced at engaging in miraculous moments of face-to-face interaction and sharing attention with others. Despite the fact that babies at 14 months are novices when it comes to language, they already possess sophisticated interaction repertoires that differ from adults of other species. These draw together the skills that we focused on in the first two chapters—the sharing of a smile in the early months of life. They also need to be understood within the more general, philosophical, question of how communication is possible. To examine how meaning works and develops we will watch it in action. Let's see how these skills are put together by tracing the development of meaning as babies learn to communicate. This is a natural history—a detailed description of the social process through which babies master skills in communicating.[3] Instead of the usual approach in philosophy and cognitive science of taking adults as the model to be explained, we suggest that it is better look at how nature puts together the symbol-using mind, how this ability develops in infancy.[4] It is all too easy to assume that newborn infants encounter the same problem of making themselves understood as adults may experience when interacting in an unfamiliar language. Adopting a different perspective, we explore how the ability to communicate with gestures develops in infancy.

Learning to gesture: A trivial matter?

We have already noted that how babies learn to communicate using gestures is of "cosmic importance," according to the developmental psychologist Elizabeth Bates.[5] This is because these skills act as a basis not only for language and thinking, but also for becoming a member of a culture. Although the development of gestures may be overlooked by busy parents because it just makes understanding the child's needs easier, such gestures reflect a critical transition on the way to mastering human ways of communicating. Early actions such as pointing may be neglected, because we usually think of the roots of communication in terms of producing new words and forming sentences, but all of this highly visible part of language learning must be based on the previously formed foundation of competence in social interaction and the ability to coordinate attention with others.[6] In fact, the reason gestures may be neglected is that they are such a natural way of communicating in human ways of living that we just take them for granted. The rest of children's understanding of the social world, according to Michael Tomasello,[7] is just "icing on the cake" compared to the importance of this early step in babies' understanding their social world. Although there is general agreement about the importance of this development, there is still a great deal of controversy concerning just how babies learn how to communicate and coordinate attention with others. Two of the world's experts on the subject, Ulf Liszkowski and Michael Tomasello, acknowledge that, "little is known about the origins of the pointing gesture."[8]

The importance of this form of interaction is also evident in the fact that, in sharp contrast to typical development, children with autism tend to have problems in this domain, especially in using pointing just to share attention with another person. This is perhaps not surprising given that autism is a disorder in which children have difficulty in typical social interaction. The fact that these children have difficulty with pointing to share information is an early indicator of their later difficulties in social interaction. Their problems underline the importance of developing the use of gestures in infancy.

From reaching to requesting: "In the beginning was the deed"

When Lydia was 5 months old she, like other babies her age, reached and leaned toward objects she was interested in. She even raised her arms up toward her approaching mother. In this way, her interests and desires were expressed in her natural reactions. It was clear to adults, and particularly her mother, that she wanted to be picked up. Her actions had meaning for her care-givers, even though it is highly unlikely that she was aware that she was communicating. Extending an arm in an attempt to grasp something indicated to Lydia's parents that she wanted the object, although at this age we assume that she was not aware of the significance her action had for her parents.[9] That is, Lydia still had to learn that she was, in fact, communicating.

In learning to communicate, infants first get involved in routine everyday activities such as being fed and exchanging objects. Once they become familiar with such typical social routines around the home, they can then learn gestures or words to elicit these shared patterns of interaction. Instead of beginning with words, we follow Wittgenstein's lead in taking Goethe seriously with the idea that "in the beginning was the deed."[10] It is the shared understanding of routine activities that communication is based on. It is not that infants first learn names for objects and only then can they learn how to use the words to make requests. As adults we may do this when learning a second language. For example, if we already know English and we want to order some food while we are visiting Iceland, we have to learn some new words—we have dictionaries and phrase books to help us. Young children cannot make such direct translations from what is already known. They first learn the action of making a request, beginning with using a gesture and later with words.

In Chapters 1 and 2 we described how the newborn's activities are intertwined and increasingly coordinated with others (hence Donald Winnicott's claim "there is no such thing as a baby": see Chapter 1). To begin with there is no need for the young infant to be aware that they are communicating. For example, an infant, Grey, at 4 months communicated unintentionally by crying (his "wailing weakness," to use Erasmus Darwin's words: see Chapter 2). This was informative to adults because it was expressive—we could tell that he definitely didn't like being in his car seat! And parents may be able to infer that their infant is crying in different ways that indicate particular states, but to begin with it is unlikely that in crying in different ways babies are trying to communicate specific meanings. This is like a dog wagging its tail, which is an aspect of emotional expression, but not an intentional communicative signal. This awareness of communicating develops later in human infancy, but perhaps not at all in dogs (pet owners may dispute this but we'd need to see the evidence before we could agree with you!). An older child can come to understand the meaning that crying has for others and she may cry with the intention of attracting attention. This is a different form of communication.

How, then, does a baby learn to make a request? As in the case of Lydia, above, a reach toward an object is meaningful to parents, who quickly infer the infant's intent. Her goal is manifest in her action. However, to begin with the baby has not yet picked up on how others respond to her action. Gradually, she will learn that her parents often complete her goal by giving her the object, and then she becomes aware of the meaning for others. In this way her action can become a request. She can soon learn how to ask for something and can anticipate how her parents will respond.

At 6 months of age Grey was gaining better control of his actions. When he was being carried by someone and he wanted to be held by his mother he extended his arms and leaned toward her. For him was this a request? Well, it functioned as one even if he may not yet have been fully aware of how it worked. He was learning to interact successfully with the most responsive part of his environment. In reaching toward some-one his desire to be held by that person was evident. In doing so he was learning to control his immediate environment, but was his action social? Well, for him there was not yet any clear line between social and non-social experiences. Did he anticipate what would happen? Probably not to begin with but he would complain until he was happy. This pattern of interaction is built on expressing his desire. His social environment—his parents—responded to his expression, so he gradually became aware of how other people responded to his actions.

William did the same thing. At about 10 months he would reach to his mother if upset, while being held by someone else. If Charlie said "Oh come on" to him he would stop and seemed content. Charlie's strategy no longer worked by his first birthday and there were occasions on which only his mother would do. He had learned that he could satisfy his desires with a little more emphasis on his part and at the same time the closeness of his attachment to his mother intensified. There are sev-eral ways in which this social understanding emerges out of such every-day activities. For example, most infants learn an "arms up" gesture early on in development.[11] They learn what to expect when they extend their arms toward their parent—they get picked up. This is a form of interaction in which later patterns of meaning can emerge.

Asking for objects may be a slightly more complex form of request. At about 9 months Grey also learned a means of getting food from his mother if he saw her eating something that looked good. He would lean forward and open his mouth. His desire was clearly understood by others. This could even work with other adults on the street, although we don't recommend this for ordering food in a restaurant, unless you lack a language in common with the waiter and you are very hungry.

Other natural actions that may develop into a gesture for requesting are reaching and grasping. For example, Madeline at 13 months was eating bread and jam and she raised her arm and opened and closed her hand while looking at her mother. Her mother said, "Oh, you want some more?" Madeline had learned to use this hand movement as a request. It is likely that this developed from her attempt to grasp something that was responded to by her parents, who understood the action as a request.

The social foundation of communication

We have just illustrated a possibility for how babies acquire the skills to get what they want in simple situations. The development of their early gestures shows how meaning emerges in interaction with parents. Our approach to how this happens is based on ideas developed over 100 years ago, by George Herbert Mead. In this way we follow Darwin rather than Descartes. That is, we look for continuity across evolution and development, rather than absolute divisions between species. We trace a natural history of more complex forms of communication, rooted in patterns of interaction that become increasingly complex. For Mead there is nothing mysterious about meaning; it is already there in the structure of social act.[12] We are misled when we reflect on our adult experience of communicating. We feel as if we have something in our head, some meaning that we attempt to get across to others. We may have the subjective experience that an idea pops up in our heads and all we have to do is to transmit this to others. But we forget that our adult experience is the end point of a long process of development. In previous chapters we have already seen the problems with this common, and apparently commonsense, view of meaning. Instead it is best to look at other species and human babies in order to see the process unfold more clearly.

Mead did not get into the complicated matter of infants' changing skills in the way developmental psychologists must in order to uncover the origin of meaning in human interaction. The problem, then, is to fill in the messy details of how this actually works in development. Mead's focus was on how it was both possible and necessary to take the perspective of others in order to acquire a sense of the self. There is the potential for reciprocal interaction between Mead's theorizing and current research on the roots of social interaction and language in the development of joint attention in infancy. Analysis of contemporary developmental psychology can give concrete detail to his ideas, and his approach can provide a way of making sense of current debates on the emergence of communication in infancy.

According to Mead, meaning arises through interaction with the environment, before individuals become conscious of it. In its simplest form, it is the significance of some aspect of the environment for an animal. As suggested in Chapter 1, grass is "meaningful" for a cow as food, and an orphaned lamb, like a newborn human, quickly learns the significance of a milk bottle.[13] So meaning arises in the relations between the animal and the environment.

In many other species animals will acquire information from others who do not intend to communicate it.[14] For example, when an animal senses danger and runs from it, this functions to alert others in a herd of a threat and perhaps the direction of safety, even though it is highly unlikely that the initiator intended to convey this meaning. A dog wagging his tail (or crouching or snarling) communicates something to other dogs. This is part of an evolved bodily means for expressing emotions because dogs are social animals, but there is no evidence that the dog intends to communicate and is aware of doing so. A person who is embarrassed may turn red, and this functions to communicate even though there is no intention to do so—indeed knowing that you are signaling simply exacerbates the problem.

We still have several steps to take before reaching the type of meaning that human languages are based on. The elementary form can be seen in the social process of interaction. One dog's snarl has some meaning for a second dog. The second dog responds to the growl. In a fencing match one person responds to the other's thrust with a parry.[15] Here we see that the significance of an individual's act is in relation to the other's response to it. We don't need to assume that meaning is in an individual's head. Instead it is objectively there in the responses made during the sequence of interaction. Nor is it something mental or mysteriously added to the physical act. We can see this in the mother hen's cluck and her chick's response.[16] The chick's response to the hen's cluck shows the significance of the cluck for the chick. When a cedar waxwing returns to her nest and perches on the edge, her chicks, if they are hungry, will respond by opening their mouths, and the parent, in turn, will respond by feeding them. Mead referred to the actions of the animals interacting as gestures and the interaction as a *conversation of gestures*.

The point for Mead is that meaning is there in patterns of interaction before individuals become aware of it. These actions are responded to by observers even though the individual making them does not need to be aware of this meaning for others. Dancing honeybees do not need to anticipate how the other bees will respond to them in order for the complex processes of communication within the hive to operate. With their dances bees can convey the direction and distance of new sources of nectar they have found even miles away.[17] The meaning of a bee's dance is objectively there in the process, but the dancing bee does not need to understand this fact in the way that humans usually understand the meaning they are conveying to others. The incredibly complex structures of social insects such as ants, termites and bees, that we raised in Chapter 1, are built on the myriad of interactions between individuals, but the meanings present in these exchanges are not conscious for the individual organisms, and this is not necessary for the functioning of the hive.

What we have described so far is the form of interaction in which communication arises.[18] Meaning is there before babies become aware that they are communicating. What we become aware of later on in development has its roots in these social processes; it is there in the interactive social world. This is an essential requirement before an individual can start to understand on another's intention.[19]

Comprehending another's action is grounded in the embodied social process, but, when it comes to human communication and thinking there is another, more complex, form of communication that we need to take into consideration, that is, self-conscious meaning, or intentional communication. At this point the child making the gesture is aware of the meaning it has for others. This is like the distinction between smoke providing information that something is burning, and smoke signals conveying meaning in a different way. That is, someone is intentionally using the smoke to convey a particular message.

Pathways to pointing

Two weeks before her first birthday, Ella was being held by her grandmother and she seemed to be reaching toward Jeremy. But then it became clear that she was looking past his shoulder at her uncle's shiny new motorcycle parked outside the kitchen window. She appeared to be trying to indicate this, to point it out to others, because she kept stretching out her arm and making a sound until someone mentioned the motorcycle, and then she stopped. It seemed that she had achieved what she had been trying to accomplish—she had successfully communicated! It seems that Ella simply wanted to share attention with others about the motorcycle; it was not that she wanted to touch it or have a ride on it.[20] How do we explain the development, around their first birthday, of these sorts of skills in communicating that babies come to display?

We started the chapter with some examples of pointing. This apparently simple gesture has been the subject of a great deal of interest and research because it is an instance of early communication, and the same movement of the finger can be used in so many different ways. We might assume that some way to coordinate attention would be needed across cultures, but the particular way to do this may vary. Pointing with an extended index finger is common across many cultures but in some settings and in some cultures pointing with an index finger is considered rude and it can be accomplished with other body parts. Pointing with one's head or lips is also common across cultures. A less common way to point is with the nose, used by the Yupno, living in a remote region in the Finisterre Range in Papua New Guinea.[21] In cultures in which adults do not point with an index finger it is still an open question regarding whether babies start gesturing in this way and then are reprimanded and instructed to stop, or if they never begin to use this gesture.

Among the many ways in which pointing can be used, two main functions have been described by Elizabeth Bates.[22] One is to make a request for something—meaning something like "get that for me," and a second is to direct others' attention—that is, meaning, "look at that!" A third use, demonstrated experimentally more recently, is to point in order to inform others. In the research paradigm used to demonstrate this, an infant is put into a position in which he or she could inform an experimenter about the location of something they are looking for. A series of studies shows that infants will spontaneously point to locate an object, such as a stapler, that the adult had previously been using, even though the child had no experience of playing with that stapler.[23] They also point again if the adult turns to a dull nearby object like a "Post-it" sticker, when the infant is trying to draw the adult's attention to an interesting toy beyond the board with the Post-it.[24]

How do babies start to use their extended index finger meaningfully in interaction? To see this contrast between meaningful and meaningless uses of one's index finger, consider two examples. In Figure 4.1 an infant at about 4 months of age is lying between her brother and her grandmother with her arm over her head and her index finger extended. This is the hand

Figure 4.1 A pointless point
Photograph by Sheelagh Carpendale, used with permission.

configuration for pointing, but is this really a socially meaningful pointing gesture or is it a "pointless point"? It does look somewhat like she wants to say, "I know the answer!" or perhaps she is trying to order a gin and tonic, but this seems unlikely given her tender age. Infants as young as 9 to 15 weeks have been observed randomly making a "pointing" hand configuration in the flow their activity, although these are not social acts, and the babies were not expecting any response.[25]

Now, in contrast, look at Figure 4.2, showing Max at 18 months standing at the water's edge pointing. The picture is ambiguous because

Figure 4.2 Pointing

it does not contain any other people, so we cannot be sure that is a social act—he might simply be extending his index finger. We do not know what he is gesturing towards, and any reasons why we consider this as a declaration to someone are wrapped up in our knowledge and experience of pointing and our own desires to treat infants' gestures as meaningful. In spite of these caveats, his action looks very much like a socially meaningful act of pointing.

Attempting to interpret these pictures shows how important the sequence of interaction is. Now look at a third picture taken in 1913 of Jeremy's aunt when she was about 11 months old (Figure 4.3). Here she

Figure 4.3 Jeremy's aunt at around 11 months of age in 1913

is pointing but also looking at someone, suggesting even more strongly that this is a social act. Looking at others when pointing is of great interest to researchers because it appears to show that the infant is checking to see that the other person is actually looking the right way and sharing the focus of attention. It is important to examine what happens before and after a gesture to understand the intent of the person pointing, the understanding of the viewer and to hint at the shared understanding between the two.

In the 1970s Cathy Murphy and David Messer pioneered a means of systematically observing where infants are looking while using pointing gestures. They studied 10- to 14-month-olds and found that at around their first birthdays toddlers start to point in earnest, but at this age they do so without checking whether they first have another person's attention or whether the point was successful in directing the other person's gaze. This suggests that when infants start using gestures they are not yet very good at sharing an event with someone.[26] Fabia Franco and George Butterworth did some of the most systematic research on infant looking and pointing. They found developmental shifts: at 12 months infants looked mainly at their mother *after* pointing, at 14 months this checking occurred *during* the pointing, then at 16 months checking most usually happened *before* the point was made.[27]

So how important is checking to see if the other person is looking when making a gesture? Consider an infant, about 12 months old, sitting on his mother's lap, both of them are looking outward at a passing train. The infant extends his arm and index finger—we might say, he points at the train. But he does this without looking at his mother to see if she is already sharing the experience. What do we make of this observation? Is this a social act? That the baby did not check might mean that he safely assumed that she was attending because they were sitting together and the train was a striking attraction. His gesture was social in some sense because they were in contact and were both looking in roughly the same direction. The infant's pointing gesture was, of course, meaningful for the mother, who easily understood that he was interested in the train. The unknown part of the equation is how aware was the infant of this meaning for his mother. The question is when in development do infants become aware of the meaning they are conveying?

This raises a number of problems concerning how we know what infants understand. We can't interview them to find out what they mean. They can't tell us because they can't talk. Parents just tend to assume that pointing is a social act, and that babies would gesture for the same reasons adults do. Well, why do we point? Taking a moment to observe how people gesture in everyday life, and in particular how they point, shows that the gesture is widely used for many functions such as to direct others' attention, and to indicate things for others. And this is only the beginning of the many uses of such gestures. We can use pointing to make requests or commands, to ask or answer questions, or to inform others. So, we tend to assume that when infants use the same hand configuration the same possible motives underlie it. However, this might not be the case, particularly when infants first use it.

Getting the point

How do babies learn to understand pointing? Over the past 40 years developmental psychologists have come up with some interesting ways of exploring the ages at which infants reach key milestones in their communicative development such as the use and understanding of gestures like pointing. A procedure is used to test how infants and toddlers respond in novel settings to a point by an adult. In the usual set up the infant and adult are surrounded by interesting toys placed in a circle around the child and an experimenter. The aim is to see whether the infant looks at the actual object pointed at by the adult. They develop this skill in the second year, following points to close objects before those to more distant objects.

Is the problem with pointing just looking in the right direction? No. Getting the point behind a pointing gesture is not just about ending up looking at the same thing. To understand this issue, consider the following anecdote: Jeremy and Caroline were picking things up after a picnic on the beach with friends. Caroline pointed to a friend's bag and looked at Jeremy. Being older than 12 months, he competently followed the pointing gesture and ended up looking at the bag, but he didn't understand what she meant. It turned out that Caroline meant that he should carry the bag because it was heavy. What is required to understand this? Just being able to look at the right object is not enough; what is required is some shared history of interaction to make sense of that gesture. It seems that women hearing this story think that the meaning should have been obvious, and perhaps it should have been. What is interesting is that this example shows the shared experience needed for understanding communication, in this case about picking up after a picnic, and perhaps some gendered expectations.

To illustrate further what is missing in simply looking in the right direction, let's do a study. We don't need an expensive fMRI machine; this will work as a thought experiment. Imagine we are sitting in a coffee shop and I point at a chair beside us. What happens? You look at where I am pointing, so we have coordinated our lines of vision; we both focus on the chair. Have we achieved joint attention? Well, we are both jointly attending to the same object, and we both know this. However, we do not have shared understanding. You are likely looking from the chair to me in a perplexed manner, perhaps attempting to derive some meaning from this apparently nonsensical gesture. That is, there has to be some understanding of why attention is being directed. Do I want you to sit on the chair, move it, place your bag on it, admire it, or am I answering your question regarding what I have just purchased? Indeed there are any number of other possibilities. Charlie has the annoying habit of making such gestures to make his wife Rosie guess what he's on about. Fortunately she is very tolerant of this non-verbal language play. Simply pointing to a chair could be one of any number of acts; it could be a request, a declarative, or an answer, depending on the sequence of interaction we have been engaged in and on our shared history.

There has been a great deal of interest in how infants start to share attention with others, referred to as *joint attention*. However, joint attention is not just coordinating lines of sight. If a person directs another's gaze toward something there must be some way to understand why—usually drawing on past history, shared practices in which they have done something similar. In some cases a person might point to something like a rat or a spider, or to something that someone had dropped, and when the second person sees it they would understand why the first person had directed their attention there. That is, most people might want to move away (rather quickly) from a rat or a spider, or towards a dropped possession. But this is still based on shared background and expectations. In different situations the outcome and understanding might be quite different. If it was known that the second person was an entomologist interested in collecting spiders, then the intended meaning could be quite different. Or if the two people were trapped on a desert island with no food the meaning of pointing to a rat might be quite different—perhaps, "lunch"!

How do babies start pointing?

Now that we have unpacked some of the complexities surrounding the simple act of pointing, we need to go on to see how young babies master this social skill. How do they do this? We have already acknowledged that even though babies are learning to point under our very noses we still don't know how it happens. Telescopes or microscopes or brain scans are not needed, yet there is still no agreement on how this miraculous development occurs. In attempting to sort this out we need to review the theories that have been proposed. These theories tend to fall into two groups. One view is that babies start pointing because they already understand that other people have attention that can be directed. This type of approach is sometimes referred to as "rich" because it assumes that infants start their gesturing careers with a fair amount of understanding. A contrasting approach is that babies begin using their extended index finger in the hand configuration we call pointing for other reasons, and they gradually learn how people respond to them. That is, they learn the meaning the gesture has for other people. This approach attributes less to babies early on in their development, and so is sometimes referred to as "lean." This is the type of approach we have illustrated when we have described how babies develop requests, and it is consistent with G. H. Mead's view of how meaning is conveyed. As early as 1900, Milicent Shinn noted in her detailed diary of a baby's development that her infant niece used her forefinger tip to explore objects within reach and that this become linked to her habit of reaching out her arm toward objects she was interested in. This is one possible origin for pointing gestures, and it is the approach we endorse.

One of the current researchers in this field is Michael Tomasello, who directed the Max Planck Institute for Evolutionary Anthropology in Leipzig, Germany, along with a group of outstanding research colleagues.[28] They are the main proponents of the first view mentioned. However, he also acknowledges that it is simply not known how babies learn to point, and that babies may go through either pathway, and may follow the latter especially if they acquire the gesture early on in development.

How should we study the development of pointing?

So how do we find out how babies learn to point? One way would be to watch them as they master this skill. This was the approach taken in a series of classic diary studies from over a hundred years ago including Charles Darwin's diary of his son's development.[29] An important diary study was conducted in the 1970s by Elizabeth Bates and her colleagues, but this method has become far less popular.

To test these perspectives, we suggest studying the development of pointing by making a series of detailed observations over time of interaction within parent–infant dyads.[30] We will begin with one case study and then follow it up with other dyads. In a case study of an infant, Grey from 6 to 14 months of age based on diary observations recorded by his mother, we found that his initial use of an extended index finger was for touching things of interest, and this gradually developed into social pointing.[31] At 6 months and 3 weeks Grey did make the pointing hand configuration but it was while he was sleeping, so it clearly was not a social act. This fits with research mentioned above showing that even at 9 to 15 weeks infants occasionally form a pointing hand configuration, although it is clearly not communicative.[32] We infer this because such "pointing" is not accompanied at that age by any other confirmatory evidence such as the baby persisting in trying to get what he or she wanted.

Then at 7 months Grey began using his extended index finger to explore things like dark patterns on the carpet, polka dots on sheets, or his mother's freckles, which he was very interested in. He even tried to pick them up. At 9 months, his mother came into his bedroom and saw him lying on his bed with his arm and extended index finger directed upwards. Grey was apparently pointing up at the ceiling. But this was not yet a social act because he was doing it by himself in the room and he stopped as soon as she came in. At this stage, his action seemed to be associated with his own interest. It seemed to be linked to what he was paying attention to. At 11 months, Grey would point toward something and then lean or walk toward it. For example, riding in an elevator he pointed toward the patterns of embossed steel on the walls and then walked over to touch them. There was no indication that he was expecting a response from others. He didn't look toward his mother, let alone persist in trying to get a response. Rather, the action seemed be an aspect of his own orientation to the world. But, of course, he was usually with his parents and so his action was "social" in a certain sense even though he may not yet have realized it. His parents did respond because his actions indicated his attention and so they would naturally talk about what he appeared to be interested in. It seems plausible that it is through learning about the social effect of his actions that he gradually came to use pointing socially and to expect a response. At 13 and 14 months he was clearly using pointing gestures while vocalizing in order both to make requests and to point things out to his parents.

The results from this brief case study are similar to what was reported in other diary observations, for example, from Milicent Shinn over 100 years ago[33] and from Elizabeth Bates and her colleagues more recently.[34] However, we should still extend this sort of research to explore development in other children. We followed up this research with multiple case studies of other mothers and their babies. These babies seemed to master pointing in a way that was similar to Grey's pathway. That is, they first used their forefinger to touch things before that hand configuration was used socially to direct others' attention.[35]

It might be thought that imitation would play a role in learning how to point. In fact, one of the babies in the study started using this hand configuration through copying other children. He had twin older sisters who he adored and he loved watching them. One evening when they were both pointing at the dinner table, he copied them with his hand and the whole family laughed. However, he had no clear idea what they, or he, were doing or why they were reacting in that way. He still had to learn how to use the gesture in a socially meaningful way. In the month before the observation, this infant was using his extended index finger to explore objects by touching them, so he was learning how to use the gesture in the same way that the other infants were.

The same process applies in becoming skilled with the conventional hand gesture of waving goodbye. Infants may imitate the physical movement, to varying degrees of accuracy, but they still take some time to learn how to use the movement meaningfully in appropriate social situations.

The many meanings of gestures

We have described a possible pathway for the development of some forms of pointing. This hand configuration may first become part of an infant's own orientation toward objects and events of interest. Because this action manifests her interest, others around her may respond by also paying attention, and she can learn that this action functions to direct others' focus and achieve enjoyable moments of shared engagement. The action has now become an intentionally communicative gesture for the social act of pointing out objects and events of interest—that is, a declarative. Pointing, as we have discussed, can be used for many different social acts beyond pointing out objects and events, such as making requests, informing, and asking or answering a question. So a question that arises is, how does a child learn to use and understand this gesture in so many different ways?

From our perspective, the meanings of gestures are based on the social routines that children learn to participate in.[36] As well as discovering the enjoyment of sharing attention children are also learning about other social acts such as making requests, as described earlier in this chapter. This involves a combination of the various interactive patterns used in other social routines. Pointing can also be used for asking and answering questions. This process of applying successful activity patterns learned in one situation to a new situation was described by Jean Piaget in his books on the development of intelligence in infancy.[37] This process can also be seen in a video recording of Jeremy's niece when she is intentionally being slow in responding to her 10-month-old son, Matejka, when he is wanting to get a doll lying on the floor. Matejka first points toward the out-of-reach doll on the floor, then when that doesn't immediately work to get the doll he pushes her hand toward the doll repeatedly. He pauses when it seems that this is working, and then finally reaches himself when his mother is still being slow, at which point she picks up the doll and gives it to him, and Matejka happily accepts it. She describes him as cycling through every action that has worked in the past. Here we can see that different gestures and actions can be used in attempts to achieve a goal.

The use of gestures for multiple functions can also be observed with other gestures. For example, Jeremy's son, Max, learned how to use a waving gesture when others were leaving. Waving meant goodbye, but he also extended this to mean goodnight, or going somewhere. Max could use it to mean that he had finished his book or his food, or once when he had lost a clear plastic toy in the bath he waved to indicate that it was lost. Max at 16 months could combine two gestures and point to the door and wave to Jeremy to indicate that he wanted to go out. A colleague's daughter, Mabel, learned how to use waving when participating in a goodbye social routine, but then she also tried to use it to initiate this routine by waving when she wanted her babysitter to leave.

Some of the gestures we have discussed, such as asking to be picked up by raising both arms or pointing, may be fairly common across families, at least in Western cultures, but other gestures may be specific to particular families or particular relationships. For example, Max at the age of 16 months developed a beautiful flowing arm movement that the rest of the family knew meant swimming. His older sister had not used such a gesture. Many babies develop other sorts of idiosyncratic acts of simple communication. Although the process through which gestures develop may be in common across dyads, the particular outcomes might vary somewhat in particular families or even specific relationships. For this reason it is important to study development within particular dyads.[38]

Action and behavior

Before we conclude this chapter we need to address a possible misunderstanding on the part of our critical colleagues. They might assume that all of our talk of basing communication in activity is just reviving the old theory of behaviorism from John Watson and B. F. Skinner and others. In other words, that it is operant conditioning that explains what is happening. That is, infants are, for example, simply passively forming associations between reaching in the presence of a caregiver and receiving the object they reach for. Or critics might be thinking that it fits with the more recent incarnation of these ideas now known as statistical learning, according to which some words are learned simply by the frequency with which they are paired with the object. This has been shown in research on early vocabulary and the same processes could be applied to gestures.[39]

Although we emphasize activity in the development of human minds, we do not endorse behaviorism and there are crucial differences we want to point out. Describing the child's learning in terms of behaviorism avoids the main question of how the world becomes meaningful for the child. The association is only there because something that the child wants happens or fails to happen. That is, the outcome has significance for the child in terms of receiving a desired object, or reaching the comfort of her caregiver's arms, or achieving enjoyable shared engagement. It is the active relationship between the child and the world that is full of significance, not just a passive association, as in behaviorism. Meaningful relationships create associations for the infant not the reverse. So talk of associations is an abstraction that is inadequate to capture the formation of meaningful relationships between the active child and others interacting in the world.

Conclusion

In order to study the development of human forms of communication we have started with cases that are as simple as possible. We have discussed views of how babies develop the ability to use gestures like pointing. We have argued that for babies to become aware of the meanings their actions have for others the infant must learn how others respond to them. This has been described as taking the attitude of others toward themselves. That is, as well as being themselves, they also begin to reflect on themselves as if from outside, from others' perspectives. The child must become capable of being both a subject as in having her own experience as well as an object, in the sense of coming to view the self from others' viewpoints. We have focused on the first year to year and half of life, but even at the relatively mature age of two, toddlers are not yet experts in understanding or using gestures like pointing. We see in their actions the influences upon their learning. For example, they will treat an adult's point as a communicative gesture, but will not do so if the action is performed by a peer.[40]

We are arguing that a central reason that infants develop thinking and minds is that they are treated as persons by their parents and others with whom they have regular contact—as we have just seen in sibling relationships. We are drawn into treating babies as persons—they are so cute and fun. And in this process babies are drawn into human interaction and develop forms of thinking and minds. If so, Kenneth Kaye suggests that scholars should keep this a trade secret:

> a baby is more organism than person, has neither a mind nor a self until late in the first year, but … adults are tricked into treating babies as communicating partners. If that is true, then psychology should keep it as a trade secret. There is good reason for letting parents deceive themselves in this regard, and nothing to be gained by taking the debate into the public arena. The trend over the past 10 to 20 years to regard newborns and young infants as intelligent, gesturing persons has been entirely benign, from the point of view of the popular lore. Its only deficiency has been in terms of a rigorous theory; it is only as scholars, not as parents, that we need to know the truth.[41]

So why are we letting the cat out of the bag? We are convinced that adults cannot help but to treat babies' actions as meaningful. Even if we are aware at an intellectual level of this view of development we still interact with babies as persons—we can't usually stop ourselves. And this is necessary for them to develop minds.

Suggested further reading

Canfield, J. V. (2007). *Becoming human: The development of language, self, and self-consciousness*. New York: Palgrave Macmillan.
Carpendale, J. I. M. (2018). Communication as the coordination of activity: The implications of philosophical preconceptions for theories of the development of communication. In A. S. Dick & U. Müller (Eds.), *Advancing developmental science: Philosophy, theory, and method* (pp. 145–156). Abingdon: Routledge.
Mead, G. H. (1934). *Mind, self and society*. Chicago, IL: University of Chicago Press.

Notes

1 Geertz (1973, p. 6).
2 For example, Carpendale and Lewis (2015).
3 In many respects this chapter is a response to Michael Tomasello's (2014) book *A Natural History of Human Thinking*. We have criticized this view elsewhere (Carpendale & Lewis, 2015), as we do implicitly here.
4 Bates (1979).
5 Bates (1979, p. 33).
6 Footnote about autism.

7   Tomasello (1995).

8   Liszkowski and Tomasello (2011, p. 16).

9   We feel that the evidence is fairly clear that babies at this young age do not yet have a mature grasp of the effects of their gestures on others (they do not appear to be acts of deliberate communication) or an appreciation of others' gestures as communicative. These skills develop as a crucial component of the process by which we develop communication. However, we need to point out that some of the positions that we criticize in this book hold that such skills are written into our genetic make-up. These are often called "rich" accounts as they assume that minimal exposure to interactions is sufficient to trigger such understanding.

10   See Wittgenstein (1980, p. 31).

11   Lock (1978).

12   Mead (1934, pp. 80, 81).

13   Mead (1977, pp. 164, 191, 192, 193). The bottle example is relevant because it requires a different sucking actions to which the baby becomes attuned, even infants who have a mixed regime.

14   Seyfarth and Cheney (2003, p. 168).

15   Mead (1934, p. 78).

16   Mead (1922, pp. 163–164).

17   Frisch (1966, 1967).

18   "Awareness or consciousness is not necessary for meaning in the process of social experience" (Mead, 1934, p. 77). "The mechanism of meaning is thus present in the social act before the emergence of consciousness or awareness of meaning occurs" (Mead, 1934, p. 77).

19   The examples of conversations of gestures described above are not self-conscious, or "significant" in Mead's terminology. The first animal is not aware of the meaning of its gesture for the second animal. That is, it is not reciprocal—the meaning of the gesture is not shared by both animals. So meaning is not something mysterious hidden in the head that is transmitted to others with words. We seem to experience something like this as adults, but this is a developmental achievement. In human interaction meaning gradually becomes conscious allowing one or both individuals to take both sides of the conversation. But it is originally a social process that can be anticipated by an individual, not the other way around. We are bodies interacting in social space.

20   This is an example of what has been referred to as a "protodeclarative" because it is thought to be an early form of declarative (i.e. the infant is "pointing something out"). In fact, we could drop the "proto." When adults use the same pointing gesture to direct others' attention or to make a request we don't call it a protodeclarative or a protoimperative just because mere gestures are used rather than words.

21   Cooperrider and Núñez (2012); Wilkins (2003).

22   Bates (1976).

23   Liszkowski, Carpenter, Striano, and Tomasello (2006).

24   Liszkowski, Carpenter, and Tomasello (2007).

25   Fogel and Hannan (1985).

26   Murphy and Messer (1977).

27   Franco and Butterworth (1996).

28   Michael Tomasello now teaches at Duke University.

29 Darwin (1877).
30 Adolph et al. (2008).
31 Carpendale and Carpendale (2010).
32 Fogel and Hannan (1985).
33 Shinn (1900).
34 Bates (1976).
35 Kettner and Carpendale (2018).
36 Canfield (2007); Winch (1958).
37 For example, Piaget (1952).
38 There are many different social situations involving coordinated attention between infant and adult. Infants gradually develop skills within these situations. These sorts of patterns of interaction include forms of following others' gaze in situations of increasing complexity, pointing of different types for making requests or to direct attention, and giving and taking, games in which infant and adult take reciprocal roles. From our perspective, infants develop skills in all of these common social routines (Bibok, Carpendale, & Lewis, 2008). Their ability to engage in these different forms of interaction is not based on one underlying insight about others as intentional agents. Rather, as infants develop and coordinate these various social skills their activity begins to appear to be based on an underlying insight. That is, for us as observers it might appear that various forms of interaction with others are based on an underlying insight or cognitive ability but these may have originally developed as separate social skills (see e.g., Carpendale et al., 2018; Carpendale & Lewis, 2015).
39 Word learning has been discussed increasingly since the 1990s. It has been shown that infants can discriminate sounds they hear within continuous repetitions of novel syllables (Saffran et al., 1996). However, this does not negate the argument that we have constructed in this chapter. An article by Catherine Tamis LeMonda and her colleagues provides an example of just how this can be done in that they show how the child can pick up on regularities in what is said or done to them but that this takes place within a communication in which both parties construct an understanding (Tamis-LeMonda et al., 2014).
40 Kachel, Moore, and Tomasello (2018).
41 Kaye (1982, p. 248).

Chapter 5

Thinking about the social world
How do children understand others?

In which we describe how children come to understand their social worlds beyond the insights achieved in infancy.

One afternoon when Jeremy's son, Max, was about 4 years old he asked Jeremy to leave the kitchen. Jeremy knew that Max wanted a cookie and thought that he wanted to be alone because he didn't want anyone to see him take a cookie. This deviousness shows an important step in the development of Max's understanding of other people; that is, if he could just get Jeremy out of the kitchen Jeremy wouldn't know that he had taken a cookie! Although this was a great insight, what Max didn't think about at the time was that Jeremy might start wondering *why* Max asked him to leave the kitchen—that is, Jeremy might be *suspicious*.[1] The understanding of suspicion is a further step in thinking about what others might think. But the first step of understanding how others form beliefs based on what they have seen or heard has been a topic of great interest in developmental psychology.

Although babies are already quickly becoming skilled in interacting with other people, as we have discussed in the first chapters, they still have a lot to learn about their social world during childhood. The gestural skills of toddlers outpace those of chimps, but the achievements of preschoolers take another quantum leap.[2] Consider the following statement made by Max at 2 years, 4 months: "Anne went away from her house. Hannah really sad." Barely able to combine words, this comment shows the beginnings of an understanding of the social and emotional world, and the fact that a friend going away might make his sister feel unhappy.[3] This skill becomes far more complex in the following few years. In this chapter, we apply our general position on thinking to the topic of children's understanding of other people beyond what they have grasped in infancy.

Our understanding of our everyday world, interacting with other people, is generally straightforward and so well mastered that we are rarely aware of it because we have grown up to be embedded within social relations. We take this for granted even in the language that we use in familiar settings and other factors like politeness. There are occasions when we don't understand someone's action, and these lead us to speculate about why they may have done something. But for the vast majority of our everyday experiences such as buying a cup of coffee, queuing for a bus, or saying good morning to a friend or co-worker, we have no difficulty in such easy interaction. That is until we experience problems in this area. For example, if we meet an individual with autism who has a profound difficulty in interacting with others, even an exchange of greetings may easily go off the rails. Autism is characterized by problems in communication and understanding other people. Within an interaction, both participants need to be familiar with how to interact and to comply with norms and practices.

Knowing what others know

Let's return to the particular skill, illustrated above, of Max trying to ensure that Jeremy didn't know he had taken a cookie. Over the past 40 years, researchers have focused on this skill, known as understanding that people can have *false* beliefs. *False belief understanding* doesn't mean falsely believing in Santa Claus or the Easter Bunny, but rather understanding that someone would have a mistaken belief if they were not in the room when something happened. Max's suggestion that Jeremy should leave implies that he knows that if his father was not in the kitchen when Max took a cookie, Jeremy wouldn't know about it. This sophisticated grasp of beliefs seems to indicate an important step in social understanding. It shows an appreciation of how the mind works and how people acquire beliefs. This insight has been assessed by presenting children with scenarios in which a story character ends up with a false belief. For example, the classic test conducted by Heinz Wimmer and Josef Perner[4] involves a character from German folk tales, Maxi (not Max Carpendale's namesake). Maxi had been out shopping with his mother and he puts his chocolate away in the blue cupboard and then goes out to play. While he is outside his mother uses some of the chocolate to make a cake and puts it back in a different location, the green cupboard. Children are told that Maxi is hungry and is coming back to get his chocolate and they are asked where he will look for it. Of course, it seems obvious that Maxi would look for his chocolate where he left it in the blue cupboard and 5-year-olds tend to say this. But, surprisingly, 3-year-olds usually get this question wrong by saying that Maxi would look in the green cupboard where his mother moved the chocolate, even though Maxi was outside at the time so he couldn't have known that the chocolate was moved.[5]

This apparent lack of awareness that people can hold false beliefs seems to be why 3-year-olds have an odd understanding of games such as hide-and-seek. They may always hide in the same place, or they may call out, "I'm hiding. Come and find me!" Although they enjoy the game, for them it is something like peak-a-boo. They don't yet understand that the whole point is that it's best if the seeker does not know where the others are hiding! At the age of 3, children also have difficulty understanding that they themselves can have false beliefs. This can be demonstrated in a test in which children are shown a well-known container such as a box of Smarties (a candy common in Canada and the UK). They are asked what is in it, and kids, being experts on candy, say, "Smarties" or "candies." But then the experimenter opens the box and shows the child that it really contains something quite different, and boring, such as pencils. They are then asked (when they stop crying), "what did you think was in the box at first?" Three-year-old children, surprisingly, tend to respond by saying, "pencils," not considering that they initially had a false belief. If they are asked what their friend would think is in the box "all closed up," they usually claim that she would also know that the box contains pencils. This counter-intuitive finding has resulted in a great deal of research.

Beyond these simple situations, understanding beliefs can get much more complicated. For example, when Max, was about 8 he was invited to his friend Jacob's birthday party, and Jacob told Max what he wanted for his birthday—a fingerboard (a scaled-down toy skateboard manipulated with fingers). Later, when Jeremy was out with Max and Hannah on the present buying shopping expedition, they started talking about it and it came out that Jacob had actually told *everyone* that he wanted a fingerboard. Max and Hannah both realized that maybe everyone would buy him the same present! But, on the other hand, if all the kids invited started thinking like Max and Hannah then he might end up with no fingerboards! In fact, this is exactly what happened.

This sort of thinking involving beliefs about others' beliefs can get complex. There are further levels of understanding regarding how we come to believe things. For example, if two people watch a film together, but one goes out to buy popcorn at a critical moment, she may have different, and mistaken, beliefs about the film due to missing key information. This situation is like the false belief test that 5-year-olds have mastered, but 3-year-olds still struggle with. But adults and even older children understand something more than this. They can appreciate that even if two people do watch an entire film together they may still interpret it differently because the same ambiguous information can be interpreted in various ways. This is a further understanding of knowledge according to which people may interpret the same, but ambiguous, information in different ways. Such an understanding of interpretation begins to develop around the ages of 7 or 8 in very simple situations such as a word or a sentence that has two meanings, but this is a complex issue that continues to develop through adolescence and young adulthood.[6]

A grasp of interpretation is involved in understanding some forms of humor, such as puns. These are premised on the fact that words having different meanings (see Chapter 3). Children start understanding this type of humor beginning about age 6. This is when Jeremy's daughter wanted to be told jokes and asked for joke books for her birthday. Her friends of the same age were also interested, but her younger friends just seemed perplexed by the jokes. When Max was 5 he made up a joke: "What does a sea otter say when he says goodbye?" … "Sea you." He could make up the joke because he understood the sea/see distinction and that both words sound the same. Understanding different interpretations is also involved in sarcasm and irony, as discussed in Chapter 3.[7]

Emotions are another dimension of the social world that children must learn about. Even before their second birthday some children learn to talk about emotions such as happy, sad, scared and so on. By about the age of 4 children have mastered many of the so-called basic emotions to the extent that they can identify the situations in which they are usually experienced. But there is still much to learn about these complex mental states. An understanding of emotions can be assessed in a number of ways. For example, in a test known as the *Chandler bystander task* children are presented with a story depicted in a series of drawings in which a young girl is saddened by seeing her father take off in an airplane.[8] Later, at home, a parcel is delivered to the young girl by a mail carrier. The prospect of receiving a present cheers the girl up momentarily, but after opening the present and seeing that it is a toy airplane she once again feels sad, this time because she is reminded of her father leaving. At various points in the story children are asked questions about how the girl would be feeling and why, and as a final question they are asked what the mail carrier would be thinking about why the girl was sad. Of course, as a late-arriving bystander, the mail carrier knows nothing about the girl's father leaving on an airplane, and would not understand why the girl was crying after getting such a present.[9] Although this convoluted story involves the apparently simple emotions of happy and sad, the increasingly complex situation makes the emotions the girl would feel more and more difficult to understand. Other emotions may be difficult to grasp for various reasons. For example, embarrassment, shame and guilt involve an interpersonal dimension because they require understanding other people's perspectives on the self.

Why do some children become advanced in social understanding?

We have given the average ages at which children go through the transitions in understanding beliefs and emotions that we have described. But not all children develop these forms of social understanding at the same age. So why do some children learn about beliefs and false beliefs earlier than others? What is it about some children's experience that may give them a leg up compared to their age mates? It turns out that number of social factors are linked to children's social development. Judy Dunn conducted some of the early pioneering research on this topic with a longitudinal study of 50 families, charting the influence of family interaction on how children learn about others in psychological terms. She and other researchers found links between children's social experience and their social understanding. The more mothers referred to mental states in talking to their 2-year-old the more advanced the child was a year later.[10] Conversely, children who grow up in poor quality institutions such as Romanian orphanages lag behind their age mates in false belief understanding.[11] One of the early findings was that children with more siblings were advanced in their understanding of false beliefs; they were up to a year earlier in passing a false belief task.[12] This same pattern was found when the first study in the UK was replicated in Canada, Australia, Japan, Greece, and the US, although some other studies did not always replicate this finding of a "sibling effect."[13] This suggests that the social interaction that children experience plays an important role in the development of false belief understanding. But it is not just having a lot of other people in the house. Instead it seems to have something to do with the quality of social interaction children experience. It could be related to interaction with brothers and sisters, but having siblings also changes the way that parents talk to their children, and so it could be due to the sort of language they hear.[14]

Another source of evidence that language may be important is that deaf children are often delayed in their development of an understanding of beliefs, but, interestingly, they are not delayed if their parents are also deaf.[15] If their parents are deaf this means they would be fluent in sign language and so these children would be exposed to complex interaction and sign language from early on in development. But hearing parents who have a deaf child are unlikely to be proficient in sign language and so their communication would not be as fluent. All this suggests that it is exposure to complex conversation (verbal or sign) that may be important for children in learning about beliefs. There is now consistent evidence that family talk using psychological words such as *think, know, remember* and *want*, is linked to children being advanced on tests assessing their understanding of false beliefs.[16]

Explaining how children develop social understanding

Now that we have a description of the transitions in children's development of social understanding and some idea of the social factors that may be linked to such development, a next step is to explain *how* children develop this understanding. How do children learn about their social world and understand what they or others feel and believe?

Our view is that children's ability to think about their social world and reflect on others' thoughts and beliefs is linked to their ability to talk about human activity in psychological terms. How does this ability develop? In earlier chapters we have discussed how infants become immersed in social interaction just as they learn how to act in their physical environment. They gradually come to use gestures such as pointing in order to perform various social functions such as to make requests, to inform others, to ask or answer questions or to point something out. Once a baby has learned a gesture for making requests it becomes possible for her to learn to use a word such as "want," which is obviously psychological. A word might first be used along with the gesture, and later can replace it.[17] Based on these well-understood routines children can then begin to use words. When making a request they may also say, "juice" or "milk," or simply say "more" to mean "want."

Children learn about emotion terms like happy, sad, and scared, as well as intentions and beliefs. We suggest that grasping these sorts of words is based on children's natural reactions in everyday encounters. For example, it is easy for adults and older children to discern a young child's happy or frightened expression on seeing an animal bounding towards them in a park. Parents may then talk about this and the child learns these routine patterns of activity in which it is appropriate to use such words. Children do not learn the word by introspection and mapping it onto an inner entity.

It might seem that learning words like happy and scared would be more difficult than objects labels like "ball." But when a child is happy or is afraid of a large dog this is obviously manifest in their activity, and words for such ways of responding and experiencing events are learned through this outer manifestation. These terms are used to talk about happiness and fear, but this is not something inner and mental that is separate from, and causing, an outer behavior like jumping for joy. For example, a baby in our study of infant communication, Isla, used a baby sign for "scared" for the first time when she was just 13 months old! Her mother showed fear because she had just found Isla standing on a bedside table. Isla used the sign later when she was 16 months and she was frightened by the house alarm going off.

These patterns of interaction are described by Ludwig Wittgenstein as forms of life.[18] They are daily events that typically emerge in exchanges between individuals. We expect that some ways of coordinating actions and attention with others will naturally emerge; they are an expectable aspect of human interaction, just as a whirlpool is an expectable pattern or structure that will emerge in fluids flowing under certain conditions. Language is based on these typical forms of life. The very regularity of human interaction is rooted in our biology. This doesn't just mean that actions are encoded in our genes but rather they are the outcome of engaging within a system of interacting factors: the child's developmental system.[19]

The processes that we have just discussed regarding social factors range from daily encounters with brothers and sisters to the language children hear. These each play a role in social cognitive development. They can be understood as indications of a good cooperative caregiver-child relationship, in which parents and others try to understand their child's point of view and discuss events that are likely important in the child understanding what is going on around them.[20] Such communication is essential in learning how to talk about human activity in psychological terms. Once children have mastered the ability to use words to refer to what other people do, then they may use this skill to think about this aspect of their world.

What is the link between how infants develop an early understanding of others as they learn gestures such as pointing, that we discussed in Chapters 2–4, children's later use of language and their ability to talk about beliefs and thinking? We don't think that there is a hard line between each of these developmental achievements. To see this gradual blending from one aspect of communication to the other we need to observe young children in their first attempts to use words that extend their skills with gestures and are tied up with others' attention. For example, shortly before his second birthday, Grey started to say, "look" when pointing to direct others' attention. He began using the word "see" shortly before this, in order to coordinate this joint experience. Words like look and see are not usually considered mental state words that refer to some mental process, but learning how to use them correctly does depend on some understanding of others' attention and therefore some social understanding.[21]

Similarly, Isla used the word "look" for the first time at 20 months. She was sitting in the back seat making some scribbles on a drawing board while her father was driving and her mother was sitting in the passenger seat. She said this while holding out her drawing for her mother to see. Her mother turned around and said something like "Oh wow, did you draw that? I love it!" For the next 5 or 10 minutes, Isla kept saying, "Look," and waiting for her mother to turn around and respond. Sometimes, her mother couldn't see the board properly, so she would say, "Let's see," and Isla would move the board so that her mother could see it. Words like "look" and "see" can be used in many different forms of interaction, many of them involving a psychological dimension because they involve others' attention and whether others have seen something and so know about it. How children use words builds on earlier forms of interaction involving a shared focus between themselves and others.

Other more complex psychological words could be learned in similar ways. For example, a 3-year-old girl, Christy, said, "you forgot" when her mother brought her some toast but it didn't have any jam on it. "Forgot" is psychological term that might seem to depend on understanding memory and how the mind works, including its fallibility. It could be learned in circumstances such as this breakfast scenario where something expected is not done by someone else. That is, its meaning emerges within everyday human activity.

In keeping with our analysis in Chapter 4, we are aware that when talking about action and behavior the usual response is to assume that this is behaviorism. As one commentator put it, "the term behavior tends to set alarm bells ringing in cognitive science."[22] There is almost an instinctive tendency to associate action with behaviorism; if the current way of thinking about mental states is questioned, it is assumed that there is just behavior which is passively shaped by external reinforcement. Again this reflects a position that does not recognize that there is another possible option that is neither mentalistic nor behavioristic. Both of these options, ironically, share the same starting point; they involve splitting mental life from physical movement in that we are either trapped in detached minds or are only understandable at a behavioral level. It is from the very start that the problematic assumptions are made and they follow us all the way to the end. From the relational perspective that we endorse, we begin with the active infant and examine the origins of human understanding within his or her activity with others and the world. Our intelligence is an emergent property of this interaction.

The "problem of other minds"

We have described how children learn about other people from the perspective we take in this book, but there are also proposed theories that we have argued against.[23] We will now look at a perspective that is held by several of our colleagues. Tamsin German and Alan Leslie set up the "fundamental problem of theory of mind" as follows: "given that beliefs, desires and pretends can be neither seen, heard nor felt, how does the young brain succeed in learning about them?"[24]

First, it is the young child who learns about other people not just her brain. From the perspective of their definition, German and Leslie set up a common way of describing the problem faced by young children in coming to understand others. Many others share this starting point, even if they disagree about their proposed solution. We contend that their view of the mind then results in what is known as "the problem of other minds" that philosophers have mused on for centuries. The assumed conundrum is that somehow young children must come to understand the mind and invisible mental entities when all they have to go on are the outer physical movements caused by the other person's invisible inner mental states. It is assumed that children must make the leap from observations of someone's actions to an inference about their mind.

This view of the mind as a detached inference making entity was clearly articulated in the 1630s by René Descartes, and hence is generally referred to as Cartesian. Most modern theorists would be scandalized to be associated with Descartes because he split the mental and the physical. However, the default view of mind in a good deal of work on social cognition shares much with Descartes. This is the view that our minds are private and accessible only to us. We believe we can introspect on our own mind, and that our minds are inaccessible to others. They are hidden and private.

This view of the mind has long history. The essential idea can be found in the even earlier thinking of Saint Augustine in his *Confessions*, in which he writes about his early life. Augustine imagines himself as an infant attempting to communicate with others. He therefore assumes that babies have a mind to begin with and must figure out other minds. We have already mentioned Mead's analogy that beginning from the perspective of the individual, it is as if we start off like prisoners in isolated cells who must somehow learn to communicate with each other. Each prisoner has a mind and can think and must learn to communicate his or her thoughts to others. This assumes individual minds as the starting point and thus results in the problem of how we come to know about other minds.

The way the problem is set up in what has come to be known as the "theory of mind" tradition is typically accepted without question. It goes unnoticed and without realizing that there is nothing empirical about such starting assumptions. This common way of setting up the problem that children must solve is simply assumed. As the philosopher David Jopling points out, we have to examine the questions we start with.[25] Psychology prides itself on being a science so we might think that the basis for this starting point is somehow empirical, but in fact it is a philosophical assumption about the nature of the mind. It is not examined, but simply taken for granted. This view takes the mind as the starting point, which then results in the problem of figuring out that other people have minds. This first step follows us to the end. In Ludwig Wittgenstein's words "The decisive movement in the conjuring trick has been made, and it was the very one that we thought quite innocent."[26] This way of setting up the problem actually brings with it several possible solutions. The three that are usually cited and pitted against one another are the theory theory, the innate module view, and the simulation theory. From each perspective, children encounter "the problem of other minds." Given their predominance in the contemporary psychology we will discuss each theory briefly here.

The most commonly voiced suggestion is that children are like little scientists and they form a theory about the mind that applies to themselves and to others. This theory that children form theories is called the "theory theory," because it is a theory that children hold a theory. The catchy phrase "theory of mind" has caught on and has taken on a life of its own. The term has also made its way into the public media, even if it seems highly implausible that 4-year-old children form a theory about the mind or anything else. In fact, children can understand that objects usually fall without us needing to call them theoreticians of gravity or physicists. But many researchers continue to use the phrase, ignoring its link to the theory theory.[27]

A second theory, also assuming that the same problem must be solved, is that because social understanding is so important in our human way of life nature would not simply leave this cognitive ability to chance, and therefore it is claimed that a theory about the mind is likely to be primarily in our genes. From this perspective, this understanding is thought of as an innate neuro cognitive mechanism, or module, that does the "computation" necessary for children to understand others.[28] In Chapter 8 we discuss problems with such claims that knowledge can be innate and whether such claims are consistent with current knowledge in biology. In Chapter 9 we review criticism of the idea that the mind is like a computer. In terms of the current discussion, we note that this perspective is the most obviously Cartesian because the dilemma children are assumed to face is explicitly described as the problem of other minds and these researchers further claim that the answer is written into our genetic make-up.

The third popular contemporary account is that understanding others does not have to depend upon us forming theories about mental states because we all have our own minds and we can just imagine or "simulate" how others would think and reason by analogy.[29] This simulation theory has a long history. The philosopher Thomas Hobbes[30] wrote in the seventeenth century that given the similarities between people we can look into ourselves in order to understand others. Certainly, as adults, we can do this, although we may rarely do so. Yet, we have already developed social understanding. Can babies do this? We don't think so. In fact, this simulation approach already presupposes some social understanding in order for the process to work.[31]

There has been an extensive literature criticizing, modifying and even blending all these general theories.[32] We, and many others, have contributed to this debate, but here we will take a different approach. Instead of criticizing the individual theories we look at the underlying assumptions that all three theories have in common. In spite of their disagreements all of these theories actually share the same starting assumption concerning the problem that children are thought to face in coming to understand their social world.

As adults we can have the experience of introspecting and examining our thoughts, and we feel that these thoughts are private and inaccessible to others. However, sometimes we easily understand the thoughts and feelings of others. And, as Gilbert Ryle reflected, hiding one's thoughts may be a conscious intentional act.[33] A "poker face" would not be so difficult an accomplishment if minds were completely opaque. Good card players master this ability to conceal their reactions to the hand they are dealt but this is a gradual achievement, and some may even rely on wearing dark glasses or learn the complexities of double bluffing. We can see the beginnings earlier on. For example, Max at age 5½ years and Hannah, not yet 8, were playing a board game, Clue, in which the goal is to collect clues and figure out who is the murderer. Players compete, so it is important keep the clues that you collect secret. At one point Max said, "Hannah's starting to laugh and have silly grins. I think she's found something out." Hannah had not yet learned how to conceal her thoughts, and even her 5-year-old brother could figure out that she knew something important about who the murderer was.

As adults, we can act in even more sophisticated ways to introspect and imagine how we might feel in various situations. This often leads us into the trap of taking the mind as given and then some may even assume that babies must also have the same experience. This feeling then feeds back into the theories that psychologists come up with to explain children's social development. Adults and older children may be able make inferences about others in the sense of reflecting on how we feel, but Wittgenstein's point was to explain that we cannot introspect in order to learn the meaning of words to do with beliefs, intentions and desires. We apply this argument to the development of social understanding. There is a tendency to impose our adult understanding onto babies—to "adultomorphize" them—and then psychologists build their theories on this assumption as the foundation. However, many scholars have pointed out irresolvable flaws in this foundation that can't just be patched up. Our adult experience of having a mind and being able to introspect is the end point of a long and gradual developmental process. This is not where we start from. To think that the ability to introspect could be a part of how children come to understand the mind is to put the cart before the horse.

How do the various theorists interpret the findings that we reviewed above, showing that social interaction is so important in social cognitive development? There is evidence that, in general, having siblings, being securely emotionally attached, and hearing psychological talk are all linked with social cognitive development, in that these children develop false belief understanding earlier. From a theory theory perspective, this is assumed to just provide more evidence for the young scientist to figure out a theory, or it may be claimed to trigger innate responses. According to this view, when children hear more mental state terms such as *know* and *think* they simply learn the meaning of the word by mapping it onto their own inner experience.[34]

This idea that children could learn about the mind by introspecting on their own thoughts is based on the assumption that they can look "inside themselves" and somehow observe the mental entities underlying their actions. This implies, further, that the way children learn the meaning of some words is by linking them to their own mental states in order to learn words such as think, wonder, remember and so on. It is this Cartesian model of the adult mind and language that Wittgenstein argued against in his private language arguments. Although there is considerable controversy about this argument (or arguments), what Wittgenstein meant by a "private language" was not simply a language that only one person speaks, perhaps because he or she had just invented it or the individual was its last living speaker. Rather, he was referring to a language that was necessarily private because the way the words get their meaning is through a private connection between the word and some private inner sensation. It was this idea of being able to introspect in a way that is not accessible to others and apply a label to the sensation that Wittgenstein thought was the crucial mistake. As we have already discussed in earlier chapters, meaning can't work that way. Instead it depends on shared experience with others, and not some private matching between words and sensations.

The "problem of other minds" is one that philosophers encounter, not children. Babies just interact with animate and inanimate objects. Various aspects of their worlds respond in different ways. Other people are more lively than things. Babies begin with no clear distinction between the physical world and the people who surround them—at first they live in a sea of experience. But babies' experience with objects is very different from that of interacting with people. In James Mark Baldwin's words, things have a "stay-putness" whereas "persons are actually intrusive; they go off like guns on the stage of his panorama of experience; they rise and smite him when he least expects it; and his reactions to them are about equally divided between surprised gratifications and equally surprised disappointments."[35] Through these sorts of experiences infants differentiate people from things—babies learn different ways of interacting with people compared to things.

We encounter others directly as persons, not indirectly as scientists theorizing that others are persons. It has been fashionable in psychology to assume that children observe other bodies and have to hypothesize that they may have minds,[36] but infants just interact with people directly and their contribution is initially stage-managed to facilitate more complex forms of interaction. So, these are not just flaws in the theories we have considered but with the underlying error they all begin with—"the problem of other minds."

A further spin off consequence of the Cartesian view of private, hidden minds arises in research with other closely related animals such as chimpanzees. For Descartes, only humans have minds and souls. Current researchers, of course, would distance themselves from this but there is still the search for a dividing line.[37] Instead, Darwin's and Mead's theories lead to an expectation that there will be continuity between species and, in both, a naturalization of the mind. This means that we need to base an explanation of the mind in a natural world in which, as well as biology, we also take social interactions to be part of children's natural environment within which they develop ways of thinking. This is because babies' biological characteristics partially create the social setting in which they develop.

One problem with defining mental state terms is knowing where to draw the line between these and words that do not refer to mental states.

Consider words like trick, hide, look, and see. As we discussed with reference to the early utterances of Isla and Grey in the previous section of the chapter, these verbs would not normally be considered psychological words, but to use *hide* appropriately requires an understanding of beliefs and false beliefs: the whole point in hiding something is that others don't know where it is. Furthermore, if we think of intentions as mental states that are linked to action, then this should include words like try, attempt, and so on. Even if we say that a child reached toward the chocolate bar, this implies that she intends to grasp it, that she believed it is really a chocolate bar and not a fake or an empty wrapper, and that she wants the bar for some reason, most likely to eat it. Thus, this use of the word "reach" appears to be tied up with mental states, which are themselves intricately tied up with talking about human forms of life, ways of interacting in the world. But if we include such a word as a mental state term then where would we stop? We might have to consider many other words like walk and run, and so on. There is no easy way to draw a clear line around this category of words. And this very problem suggests that maybe those who use the term "theory of mind" are approaching our understanding of mental states from the wrong angle.

Conclusion

In this chapter, we have explored ideas about how children develop an understanding of their social worlds, of themselves and others in psychological terms. We have argued that the three theories that have dominated debate in the research literature and popular analyses of the mind in TV documentaries are based on problematic assumptions. In particular, we have looked at the question of how children learn the meaning of psychological words. Our view is that psychological talk is about human activity, which is necessarily enmeshed in purpose, emotions, interests and so on. For example, a 3-year-old girl watching a group of musicians talk about what song to play next turned to her father and said, "are they deciding?" She was, of course, right. Her question illustrates our view that talking about thinking does not refer to inner mental entities that cause behavior, but is about human activity. Once a child has learned to talk about their own and others' actions in psychological terms they can then think about what they and others know, believe, wonder and so on. They can then experience a psychological level of introspection. This is a developmental outcome of the processes we have discussed throughout this book. It is not what a baby starts from.

The same applies to more complex forms of action. Children's ability to understand others and themselves must be intimately involved in the complexity of their interactions, from their sensitivity to criticism to understanding bullying and aggression. It is also involved in the way they engage in arguments, their understanding of humor, sarcasm, irony, politeness, and similar aspects of communication. As soon as we broaden our view of understanding other people to include these intricate forms of action, we then see that understanding is linked to how we treat others and how they react to us. For example, consider the anecdote of Jeremy's son, Max, at age 8, speculating about how cave men might have made up words for things. He thought that he had solved the problem for object labels by pointing to and labeling a pterodactyl, but then he added, "but what about *thank you*? That would be hard!" This expression does not refer to an object so we can't point to it, although pointing doesn't solve all the problems, as we have discussed previously. "Thank you" is an essential part of language but it also seems to be related to our understanding of others, our social understanding and politeness, as well as perhaps even to morality, and how we treat other people. The same issue arises with saying sorry. It is hard to know if these are simply parts of language and social understanding, or more broadly, whether they necessarily involve aspects of how we treat others, within a moral framework. The fact that we want to say both suggests that the distinction collapses at this point. It reflects the conclusion what we call language is a part of our social activity more broadly conceived; that is, of our way of life, our means of being in the social world, in which morality is centrally involved. This is what we must explain in the next chapter.

Suggested further reading

Carpendale, J. I. M., & Lewis, C. (2006). *How children develop social understanding*. Oxford: Blackwell Publishers.
Carpendale, J. I. M., & Lewis, C. (2015). The development of social understanding. In L. Liben & U. Müller (Eds.), *Handbook of child psychology and developmental science, vol. 2: Cognitive processes*, 7th edition. Oxford: Wiley Blackwell.
Hobson, P. (2002). *The cradle of thought: Exploring the origins of thinking*. London: Macmillan.

Notes

1 There is an interesting case of a chimp in the paper that launched discussion about "theory of mind" by Premack and Woodruff (1978) in which a subordinate animal discovered a reward (a banana) in one location, went away to

"guard" another location until the more dominant chimps checked the new location and lost interest. When they were no longer obviously attending, the subordinate one rushed to the location of the food to eat it. However, a more dominant one spotted this and retrieved the banana. The big question here is how much did each chimp appreciate the perspective of the others?

2 We appreciate that a quantum leap is tiny (it's at the microscopic level) but that the metaphor wrongly means a massive shift of view!

3 The child cannot simply be copying her parent here as adults would not usually construct such a sentence.

4 Wimmer and Perner (1983).

5 We have reviewed this literature extensively (e.g. Carpendale & Lewis, 2006, 2015).

6 For example, Carpendale and Lewis (2006; Carpendale and Chandler (1996).

7 Carpendale and Lewis (2006).

8 Chandler (1973).

9 Chandler (1973).

10 Dunn (1996); Dunn et al. (1991).

11 Indeed these early effects persist into adulthood even after enrichment programs (see Mackes et al., 2020).

12 Perner, Ruffman, and Leekam (1994).

13 See Carpendale and Lewis (2015) for a summary.

14 The research on social factors has been extended in a number of ways. Secure attachment has been found to be related to earlier development of false belief understanding, as is forms of parenting, and social and economic circumstances. All of these social factors are linked to the development of children's social understanding. Social deprivation is linked to delays in social understanding. Blind children tend to be delayed in false belief understanding (see Carpendale & Lewis, 2015).

15 Woolfe, Want, and Siegal (2002).

16 Astington and Baird (2005); Carpendale and Lewis (2015); Devine and Hughes (2017, 2018).

17 Greetings are an example of a form of communication that could begin with a natural reaction. Infants are naturally happy to see their caregivers and so they naturally respond in such situations. This natural reaction could then gradually develop into a greeting as it becomes a routine form of interaction, and words could be added to this routine pattern of interactivity.

18 "The origin and the primitive form of the language game is a reaction: only from this can more complicated forms develop. Language—I want to say—is a refinement, 'im Anfang war die Tat' [in the beginning was the deed] ... I want to say: it is characteristic of our language that the foundation on which it grows consists in steady ways of living, regular ways of acting. Its function is determined *above all* by action, which it accompanies" (Wittgenstein, 1976, p. 420).

19 "Forms of life consist of basic human activities that are rooted in man's biological and social nature. Forms of life cut across cultural boundaries, because they are basic forms that human life takes in all cultures" (Saari, 2004, p. 141).

20 There has been a debate over the past four decades about whether the child's early speech develops because parents and others are responsive to their actions labelling objects and actions in a contingent manner. However, case

studies in cultures (Ochs & Schieffelin, 1982) and subcultures (Heath, 1983) suggest that toddlers can pick up speech just by observing others interact.

21 Campbell and Bickhard (1993); Russell (1992).

22 Hendriks-Jansen (1996, p. 113).

23 Carpendale and Lewis (2006, 2015).

24 German and Leslie (20040, p. 230). In German and Leslie's (2004) words, it is the "theory of mind" mechanism that "allows the young brain to attend to … mental states despite the fact that such states cannot be seen, heard, felt of otherwise sensed" (p. 107).

25 Jopling (1993).

26 Wittgenstein (1968, §308).

27 This is a current view of the mind in which "intentions underlie and cause bodily movements" (Meltzoff et al., 1999, p. 24). This is an approach that the philosopher Gilbert Ryle described as a "ghost in the machine" (Ryle, 1949). James Russell described it as a "picture of a purely mental willing entity trapped, as it were, inside the body, able, if it pulls the right levers, to cause the body to move as it intends it to move" (Russell, 1996, p. 173).

28 There are various versions of this position that have been proposed over the last few years. According to some, what is innate is a mechanism that allows children to pay attention to mental states (e.g., German & Leslie, 2004), but since these mental states are claimed to be invisible it is not clear at all how this could work nor how it could be innate (see also Chapter 8). See Carruthers (2006) for a detailed analysis from this perspective.

29 In psychology this was put forward by Paul Harris (1991), while in philosophy it was proposed by Robert Gordon (1986).

30 Hobbes (1988, p. 82).

31 Over the past 40 years in Developmental Psychology researchers have argued over an intriguing piece of data. Even in the delivery room if you stick your tongue out at the newborn she or he may appear to return this gesture (Meltzoff & Moore, 1977). Debate hinges on whether newborns can imitate, with simulation theorists attributing the very young infant with an ability to make "like me" comparisons, and basing the development of social under-standing on this skill that is claimed to be innate (Meltzoff, 2011). Meltzoff (2011) claims that because infants are born with the recognition that others are like them they can ascribe their own experience of internal feelings linked to behaviors to others. However, evidence of neonatal imitation is con-troversial. Very young infants do stick out their tongues, although this may be the only behavior that they consistently match (Anisfeld, 1996; Anisfeld, Turkewitz, & Rose, 2001; Ray & Heyes, 2011). But they also do so in response to many interesting or arousing situations including watching an object moving toward and away from them, having their palms touched, and even listening to music such as *The Barber of Seville* (Jones, 2006). Because of this research, Jones (1996, 2009) has argued that the observation that infants match others' tongue protrusion could be more simply explained as a response to something interesting. Furthermore, infants stop making these matching responses after about 2–3 months, and imitation is a hard won skill of later infancy about the age of 1 year (Jones, 2007). Therefore, we sub-scribe to the idea that they are simple behavioral reactions that do not require any imitation on the part of the newborn (Carpendale & Lewis, 2015; Carpendale, Lewis, & Müller, 2018).

32 For example, Carpendale and Lewis (2006, 2010, 2015).
33 Ryle (1949).
34 Slaughter et al. (2009, p. 1054); Meins et al. (2002, p. 1724). There is a problem with the uses of words referred to as "mental state words." Consider the different uses of words such as "think." We might say, "It's raining, I think," if we are not quite sure in order to express degree of certainty. (Descartes wrote, I think therefore I am. But when the bartender asked Descartes if he wanted another round, and Descartes, replied, "I think not," he didn't cease to exist. He was using the word in a different sense.) Researchers in this area recognize the problem that words are used in different ways and they develop coding systems to deal with it, so that they can isolate the uses of these words that actually do refer to mental states.
35 Baldwin (1906, p. 60).
36 See for example, Gopnik and Wellman (1992); Carruthers and Smith (1996).
37 Coulter (2010).

Chapter 6

Becoming a moral being

Early development, emotions, and neuroscience

In which we explore research and theory on prosocial and moral development.

Understanding others as persons is one crucial ingredient to being human. In this and the next chapter we explore the development of this ability in how we come to understand the norms and principles of human conduct. We start with how researchers have looked for early roots of morality in the young children and even infants. In searching for the source of this ability a number of possibilities have been explored, including a central role for our emotions. Both this and the next chapter consider a range of theories recently proposed to explain moral development. We point out what we think is problematic about them as well as what we can learn from the diversity of approaches. We first discuss claims that babies already know something about morality, specifically about helping versus hindering others. We then review research with infants a few months older who seem to enjoy helping others. A related area of development is the ability to give objects and share with their siblings and caregivers. Emotions are yet another topic of great importance in discussions of morality. We consider various different ideas about the role that emotions play in morality. Finally, to preview discussion in Chapters 8 and 9, we consider the possible roles of biology in understanding moral development.

Do babies have moral lives?

Do babies know anything about morality? Surprisingly, in a 2010 article in the *New York Times*, the psychologist Paul Bloom argued that they do. He wrote expansively about "the moral life of babies," claiming that they are born with some innate knowledge of good and evil. In his words, babies have "a rudimentary moral sense from the very start of life," and that, "some sense of good and evil seems to be bred in the bone."[1] This fascination with what babies might know about morality has been picked up in the popular press in magazines and TV shows. Bloom was somewhat more cautious, however, writing an article in the prestigious journal, *Nature*, along with his colleagues, entitled "social evaluation by preverbal infants." Without defining exactly what "social evaluation" involves their article describes infants' skills in judging others in a more neutral manner. But the temptation is to think of infants' evaluations of good and bad actions as moral. We should examine these strong claims.

To support the argument that babies are born with innate knowledge, Kiley Hamlin, Karen Wynn, and Paul Bloom draw our attention to research that they interpret as indicating that young children already "know" about objects and simple arithmetic. They do not, however, mention the criticism of this research and this interpretation. They then go into more detail about studies regarding babies' apparent knowledge of morality. In these experiments, babies watch a sequence of scenarios meant to portray the social events of helping or hindering involving geometric shapes with eyes (Figure 6.1). For example, they watch a red ball with eyes apparently attempting to go up a hill. That is, it moves up, then slides back down, and then up again, as if it is desperately, but unsuccessfully, trying to reach the top of the hill. Then a yellow triangle, the good guy, comes to the rescue by pushing the ball up to the top of the hill. In another scenario a blue square, the bad guy, blocks the goal by pushing the red ball down to the bottom of the hill. The shapes and colors were alternated so that half the time the helper is the yellow triangle and blue square is the bad guy and for the other half of the babies the roles are reversed, in order to ensure that any effect found is not due to babies preferences for particular shapes or colors.

Hamlin and her colleagues wanted to see how the babies would evaluate the actions of the helper and the hinderer in these scenarios. In order to do so they presented the babies with the two objects

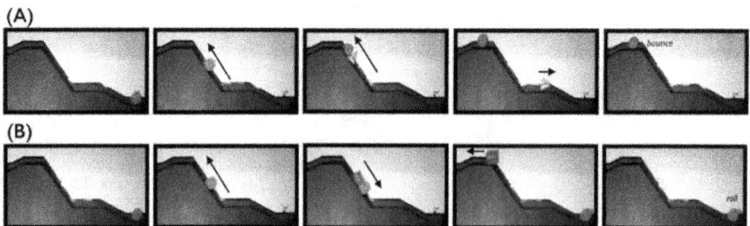

Figure 6.1 Helping (line A) and hindering (line B) events watched by babies
Source: Hamlin (2015).

corresponding to the shapes that had just performed the helping and the hindering. The experimenters were interested in which object the babies reached toward first. Most of the 6- and 10-month-old babies reached for the helper and not the hinderer—the good guy not the bad guy. This was interpreted as approving of helping rather than hindering. These researchers also wanted to see if the babies had formed expectations about how the ball character would react to the helper and the hinderer, so they showed the babies movies in which the ball either approached the helper or the hinder. The 6-month-old babies did not differ in looking at either scene, but 10-month-old babies looked longer when the ball approached the shape that had pushed it down the hill, compared to when they watched the ball approaching the helper. Hamlin and colleagues interpret this as indicating surprise when the ball approached the hinderer.[2]

In other research, babies watched various simple morality plays with scenarios such as one character helping a protagonist who is attempting to open a box, whereas a second character jumps on the box instead, slamming it closed. In another event, the protagonist puppet rolls a ball to another puppet who cooperatively rolls it back, whereas a third puppet, the bad guy, consistently runs off with the ball instead of returning it. In these studies 5-month-olds preferred the good guy, as indicated by which shape they reached toward.

This research was interpreted by Hamlin and her colleagues as showing that "the capacity to evaluate individuals on the basis of their social interactions is universal and unlearned."[3] Bloom, of course, acknowledges that babies are not born as moral philosophers and still have a lot to learn about the cultural dimensions of morality as they grow up. But he states that, "Babies possess certain moral foundations—the capacity and willingness to judge the actions of others, some sense of justice, gut responses to altruism and nastiness."[4] These are strong claims that raise a number of questions.

In spite of the attention this research has attracted, it has also been criticized on both empirical and conceptual grounds. Although Hamlin and her colleagues have published a number of studies and report strong effects, other labs have not always been able to replicate her results. One study that did find the same effect was with older infants from 12 to 36 months of age.[5]

Furthermore, the babies in this research were not newborn. They were 6, 10 or 12 months old, although one study was done with 3-month-olds.[6] So it is problematic to claim that babies are "born" with knowledge when this is assessed many months later. This would be equivalent to the logic of claiming that a student already understands mathematics in

September based on testing her knowledge the following June and after she has completed a course on calculus. Babies learn an incredible amount during their first year. At 6 to 10 months of age babies are doing a lot of things that we don't want to claim are innate. For example, Bloom expands on some of the things that the babies did in the experiments. He states that they tended to "smile and clap during good events and frown, shake their heads and look sad during the naughty events." One toddler even smacked the bad puppet. Smiling is an action that is not simply "bred in the bone." Although it has biological roots, it develops over the early months in babies' first year, and its development depends on experiencing social relations (discussed in Chapter 2). Clapping is a conventional gesture that must be learned. We can't say that it is innate—babies are not born knowing how to clap, let alone understanding the convention that this means joy or appreciation.[7] Shaking one's head is also a conventional gesture that takes some time to learn.[8] If infants can learn this conventional gesture by the time they are in these studies then they can also learn about the patterns of human activity related to morality such as facilitating or blocking an agent from reaching a goal.[9]

The meaning of the simple morality plays, like the study with shapes and hills that babies watch in this research, is obvious to adults. In doing science we must guard against the tendency to assume that babies understand the scenario in the same way. Over a hundred years ago William James and James Mark Baldwin called this tendency the "psychologist's fallacy."[10] We should carefully spell out everything that is assumed here. What is required in order that babies could prefer helping to hindering? They should understand the patterns of human activity we know of as helping and hindering. They need also grasp that the circle with eyes is a character with intentions and goals, and it is attempting, unsuccessfully, to reach the top of the hill. That is, they must understand the goal as well as the fact that the circle is unable to reach its goal. And, furthermore, they need to be aware that assisting a character in fulfilling her aims is preferable to blocking the attempt to reach the goal. Of course, this not always the case because there can be situations in which reaching goals can be harmful, but this doesn't apply in the simple case of climbing a hill.

We are not suggesting that infants must "know" all of this in a reflective sense like adults, but rather in a practical sense of having learned about typical patterns of human activity. Could babies, as Hamlin, Wynn and Bloom claim, be born with the knowledge we have outlined on which understanding helping and hinder is based? Our answer, throughout this book, has been No. As we have outlined in the book's introduction and will discuss further in the Chapter 8, there is no simple way of explaining how it is possible to get from genes, which play a role in forming proteins, to neural interconnectivity and knowledge. Helping and hindering are aspects of human activity that children learn about. For example, between 6 and 10 months babies learn about the goal of grasping as being the end point of the action of reaching. They show this understanding in their ability to anticipate the object to which a hand is reaching, as seen in the way they look toward the correct object, and the shape the hand is held in depends on the size of the object about to be grasped. Being able to anticipate if a hand is reaching toward a large or small object from its shape (an open grip for a larger object or almost closed for the smaller one) depends on the baby's own ability to perform that reaching action.[11] Another example of babies learning about human activity patterns comes from research on infants' anticipation of being picked up by their parents. This can already be seen beginning at 2 months of age when babies have learned enough about their parents' actions of picking them up that they can stiffen their bodies in order to coordinate with their parents' actions. This coordination becomes smoother shortly after, at 3 to 4 months of age.[12] These are examples of babies learning about patterns of human activity.

This sort of research raises two questions. How do these abilities develop, and what do they lead to? We can't abdicate by shifting the problem to biologists—there is no direct route from genes to moral understanding. Instead this is a difficult and fascinating developmental problem. We now turn to further prosocial development.

Helpful toddlers: The roots of altruism?

In continuing the search for morality in young children, we carry on with the theme of helping and now move from babies to toddlers. The fact that young children want to help their parents has long been noted by observers of children in early diaries.[13] In a seminal study published in 1982, Harriet Rheingold studied toddlers' helping more systematically.[14] This is something that has been right before our eyes—many young children spontaneously try to help with what their parents are doing. Rheingold pointed out that toddlers become interested in getting involved in the activities of others. We could call this the "Tom Sawyer effect," after Mark Twain's hero who purposefully took advantage of his friends whom he knew would insist on helping him whitewash his fence.

This line of research has been more recently extended in a series of interesting studies conducted by Felix Warneken and Michael Tomasello, and other researchers. Warneken and Tomasello found that 14- to 18-month-old toddlers spontaneously help a clumsy experimenter who, for example, has dropped a clothes peg while trying to pin laundry on a clothes line.[15] In another scenario, when toddlers see an experimenter carrying a large stack of books, attempting to place them in a closed cabinet, they will helpfully go and open the cabinet door. These young children will help even if there are obstacles in their way, and they don't need praise, rewards, or even to be asked for help. Toddlers at 20 months of age will even stop playing with interesting toys in order to help an inept adult who keeps dropping things.[16] These studies are very cute and have also attracted attention in the popular press.

The question now is what does this interesting evidence mean for explaining the evolution and development of morality? Warneken and Tomasello claim that this is "some of the earliest manifestations of altruism in human ontogeny: Children acting on behalf of others without a benefit for themselves."[17] Some evidence of helping has also been found in chimpanzees, and Warneken and his colleagues suggest that this means that the "roots of human altruism may go deeper than previously thought, reaching as far back as the last common ancestor of humans and chimpanzees."[18]

As scientists, we have to be careful in how we describe the phenomena we are studying. It is important to ask if what toddlers are doing is really helping, in the adult sense, or is it an interest in participating in the activity of adults? What toddlers do is very interesting and may be involved in the development of morality, but we cannot be sure that this is equivalent to altruism in the adult human sense. In fact, such acts by toddlers are not always, or even usually, actually very helpful. Parents describe their children as helping, but they also say that they tend to do chores when their child is having a nap or is busy with something else because it is just easier to get things done. When they do become involved, toddlers seem to be more interested in participating in the activity than in getting the job completed. They may want to help with laundry, but for them that could be unfolding as well as folding the clothes.

If our daughters and sons at 18 months want to get involved with washing the dishes we call it helping, but if they want to help flip tiddlywinks we call it playing. But do they really notice any difference? Perhaps this evidence is more carefully and simply explained as toddlers wanting to play with the big kids. To count an action as "helping" the child should understand the goal of the activity. One mother told us that a toddler wanted to use the big adult sized broom but not a small broom especially purchased for him, even though he had difficulty handling the heavier broom. William did just the same at around 15 months, so perhaps this activity is more about copying what your parent does or the joyous reaction of family members. Another young boy was observed contently picking up toys and putting them away in a box, only to empty the box out again so that he could do it all over again. Here the enjoyment seemed to be in the activity and he did not appear to understand the overall aim of tidying the house.[19] Here is another observation suggesting that young children enjoy doing what adults are doing: a 4-year-old girl, Taya, who wanted to help her grandmother with washing the dishes said, "You're not letting me play" and then corrected herself to say, "You're not letting me help."

In her original article, Rheingold had stated that a "fundamental characteristic of human infants that underlies helping, and many other prosocial behaviors, is their interest in people and their activities."[20] This is a very important, yet still overlooked insight. If this is what underlies the apparent helping, then it is this characteristic of human babies that needs to be explained. Instead of assuming that a human action manifests some form of genetic predisposition to altruism, we may need first to explain the development of interest and enjoyment in participating in others' action or simply their attention. Perhaps this activity is one of the roots of morality, an early form of interaction which hints at what we later call morality.[21] Interest in others and caring about them are essential for the development of morality. Babies need to be concerned about others; this is the ground on which morality can develop, but it is not moral conduct itself.

Showing and giving

> If I help myself to part of your sandwich, it is not the same as your sharing it with me.
>
> —Kenneth Kaye[22]

This difference between taking and giving is so obvious that it prompted Kaye's quip. Yet it is a distinction that children have to learn about. But what, exactly, is it? One difference involves the recognition of the other as a person—that is, as someone with goals and wishes, not just something that can be treated as an object. Taking without asking seems to neglect the owner's rights, or perhaps assumes that he or she has already given permission, so it involves ideas about possession.[23] This social understanding is crucial for our everyday interaction with others, yet it is an awareness that children must gradually develop.

More broadly, giving is an essential activity woven into the social fabric of our daily lives. Sharing food must be a crucial aspect of survival in hunter–gatherer societies serving the vital function of exchange. The role and importance of exchanging resources may vary across societies but it is difficult to imagine a human way of life without such social acts. Writing almost a hundred years ago, Marcel Mauss discussed giving across many societies, highlighting the economic, moral, legal and even religious significance of these acts.[24] Cultural practices also involve obligations to receive gifts that are offered with expressions of gratitude—even if you do not like the socks that grandma has knitted you. Such gestures are based on assumptions about possession.[25] They both vary across cultures and develop in children. Given the incredible complexity of such social acts of exchange, we now turn to examine how an early understanding of giving develops in infancy.

If we are interested in the development of concern for others, and if toddlers' helping at 14 to 18 months is considered early evidence of altruism, then their actions of showing and giving objects to others at around 12 months might be viewed as even earlier evidence of altruism. There has been a long history of interest in these actions that emerge around infants' first birthdays.[26] But, again, it is important to avoid assuming that this action is the same as giving in older children and adults. When we focus on how infants' interest in people and their activities develops and how it comes to underlie helping and many other human social activities, then earlier roots of this interest in others may be found in infants' activities of showing and giving.[27] Rather than an earlier example of altruism, giving may be better understood as a form of coordinating action with others in enjoyable routine patterns, games in which infants learn their parts and anticipate what happens next.

A problem with interpreting human infants' showing and giving as evidence of altruism is that ravens also show and offer objects to their mates. Simone Pika and Thomas Bugnyar argue that these activities are declarative gestures, and they "may function as 'testing-signals' to evaluate the interest of a potential partner or to strengthen an already existing bond."[28] Instead of assuming that ravens are innately altruistic, there may be other ways to explain the emergence of this interesting behavior. Ravens' tendency to explore different objects likely helps in finding new sources of food, and they may pick up interesting, shiny objects. Their mate might also be attracted to the object in their beak and the raven could learn the effect their action has on their mate. Children may also learn that showing objects to adults works to attract their attention. Furthermore, with human infants the pattern could arise through a different developmental pathway. It could be a game initially driven mostly by adults. The concept of giving is important across cultures,[29] but, although we describe what infants are doing as "giving," it is important to be aware of the differences and the complex developmental pathway from this early activity to adult abilities.

Emotions and morality: And now with feeling

The role that emotions play in morality has been a topic of debate for centuries. The philosopher David Hume was perhaps the best-known scholar who emphasized their importance. Immanuel Kant, in contrast, is known for arguing for the importance of reasoning in morality. More recently the debate has re-emerged, and some of the prominent analyses have been provided by Jonathan Haidt, Joshua Greene, and Marc Hauser. Haidt argued that morality is primarily reducible to evolved emotional gut reactions, and that moral reasoning is merely justification after a choice has been made. From this perspective, people are not really like moral judges using reasoning to decide the right thing to do, but instead are more like lawyers trying to argue their case, to persuade others, as well as justify their actions to themselves.[30]

An example of Haidt's research focuses on moral judgments about incest. He tells participants about a hypothetical scenario in which a brother and sister have consensual sex. Most people state that it is wrong, even if the reasons they come up with, such as risk of pregnancy, are shown not to apply in this situation. Haidt argues that this suggests that the judgments are based on intuitions because the reasons supplied are inadequate. Thus, Haidt claims that an aversion to incest has evolved in humans and when he presents people with scenarios involving incest they feel that it is wrong, and even when all of their reasons are shown to be irrelevant they still feel that it is wrong.[31]

Many researchers study morality, exploring different aspects of this multifaceted domain. In making sense of these variations it is important to think about what question is being addressed by each investigator. Not only does the definition of morality vary across studies, the question grappled with also varies so that some disagreements may be due to researchers talking about different things. Haidt focuses on the social psychology of how people talk about morality to persuade others and to justify their own actions. He and Greene reduce it to evolved emotional responses that are justified after the fact. Although Haidt does include moral reasoning in his model he does not focus on explaining this aspect and he believes it is rarely used. Rather than being used for figuring out what to do, he argues that its primary purpose is for justifying what one feels like doing, based on evolved intuitions. Haidt thus attempts to explain much of our everyday interaction, such as selling a used car and justifying one's actions, using post hoc rationalization. Here he may have some valid points. If the question is why is there so much injustice in the world, and how is that people can be nastier than you can believe, then Haidt's approach may provide some useful insights. If we are interested in how an individual justifies cheating someone when selling a used car, then the sort of approach taken by Haidt may be appropriate.

Haidt and Greene claim that this covers the vast majority of the moral domain.[32] We suggest that this overstates the case. Even if moral reasoning is a small part of our social world that does not mean that it is unimportant. The occasional but crucial moral issues we encounter and grapple with may be of central importance in our lives and identities.

Haidt focuses on the question David Hume asks at the beginning of his book *Enquiry Concerning the Principles of Morals*,[33] published in the mid-1700s, in which he asks if morals are derived from reason or sentiment. Haidt takes Hume's writing as support for the claim that decisions are based on emotional intuitions and that any reasoning comes later. However, Hume goes beyond that claim to develop a much more complex position, that such thinking is not a simple matter of gut reaction; instead reasoning is also important in educating our intuitions. So, in fact, over 250 years ago the *Enquiry* argued explicitly against the possibility suggested by Haidt that intuitions are innate. For Hume intuitions are the result of experience and thinking.

There are dimensions that are overlooked. Is morality about right or wrong, or is it just about conforming to local customs? There is something beyond conformity. It might seem that the main problem is to explain how things go wrong, how and when people act immorally. But perhaps the bigger problem is actually to explain justice, and the fact that we develop the ability to recognized and protest against injustice. These opposing forces are simply assumed by Haidt but he does not grapple with trying to explain how it develops. But that is what others such as Piaget and Kohlberg took as their central problem which we explore in Chapter 7. Before we do this, we need to consider research from a neuroscience perspective.

Can morality be explained by neuroscience?

It might be thought that recent research in neuroscience can help us explain morality and find the basis for a sense of fairness in the brain.[34] In one sense it is obvious that there must be a neuroscience side to explaining morality because we are biological beings, and therefore, thinking about moral matters, just as thinking about anything else, must involve brain activity. Therefore, there has to be some neurological level of analysis. Clearly we need neurons in order to think. But we should be cautious about jumping from this simple truism to expecting a complete understanding of morality at the level of neurons. Here we need to be cautious. Although neurons are required for consciousness and for morality, they are not conscious nor are they moral. It is the person not her neurons who does or does not adhere to a moral code of conduct and thinks about right and wrong. Morality emerges at the level of interpersonal relations, not neural activity. We can study changes in how children understand helping or lying, and no doubt there would be changes in their brains as neural pathways are set up and they develop more complex understandings of their social world, but we could not appreciate the changes in their understanding of these actions by only studying the changes in their neural interconnectivity. In other words, if we did not understand the nature of human obligations, promises, and indiscretions, we could not learn about this dimension of human experience merely by studying how brain tissue functions.

Furthermore, if we are trying to reduce morality to biology why stop at neurons? If we consistently apply the logic of looking for something biological to explain morality then we should continue to a more basic level, like the movement of ions across the cell membranes when a neuron fires. The problem really starts with splitting biological from other factors rather than thinking of a developmental system made up many levels of interacting factors. If a person is described in terms of protons and electrons something is missing. Although neurons are necessary, we can't find meaning at that level.

When we review research on morality and neuroscience it is important to be clear on how the researchers define the concept and what it is that they are actually studying. Although researchers use the same term, they may mean different things. So, it is important from the outset to look at how morality is defined in neuroscience research. Jorge Moll and colleagues, for example, state that, "Morality is considered as the set of customs and values that are embraced by a cultural group to guide social conduct, a view that does not assume the existence of absolute moral values."[35] Their definition overlooks the limitations of this view of morality discussed above and seems to reduce morality to a conformity to ways of doing things in particular cultures with no way to explain change in moral norms. Is this really a complete definition or instead a change of topic? Many researchers working in this area seem to define the notion out of existence. What they study and refer to as "morality" is quite different from how developmental psychologists conceive of this aspect of human conduct. We see the word in the title of research papers, but when we read the method section where they actually explain what they did we might wonder if they are actually studying conformity and not morality. When we set off to investigate something we should begin with a good idea of what we are looking for.

One typical neuroscience approach to morality involves an attempt to localize the brain structures involved in morality. There are two general methodologies. One approach to study people with damage to particular parts of their brain. A famous example is Phineas Gage's often mentioned unfortunate accident with explosives in 1848 in which a tamping iron was fired through part of his brain. Although he amazingly recovered from this horrible accident, he was no longer an upstanding citizen. This is interpreted as evidence that something about the areas damaged in his brain where involved in his moral nature.[36] Many other cases also involve damage to particular parts of the individual's brain and this can then be compared to any deficits the individual might have.

A second general approach is based on neuroimaging studies of individuals' brains while they are asked to make moral judgements and decisions. This is an attempt to examine what parts of the brain appear to be active when participants are thinking about moral topics. Due to practical constraints, a typical study involves putting volunteers into an fMRI machine and presenting them with scenarios that have moral implications and encouraging them to think about various moral topics. Sometimes the manipulation of participants' thinking just involves presenting them with different words that vary in their moral associations. The fMRI signal is based on blood flow. This produces images representing increased blood flow in different parts of the brain; but much of the "signal" shows after the data are "cleaned." This is a signal-to-noise calculation, taking into account the fact that blood flow in the brain is continual and is influenced by several factors like movement of the head, changes in heart rate and/or breathing patterns, blood pressure and environmental influences like the amount of carbon dioxide inhaled. The additional blood flow associated with brain activity has to take these factors into account.[37] Once the image is produced it could be asked what does it really tell us? Evidence of increased blood flow has to be interpreted by drawing on what is known about the functions that those areas are typically involved in. Brain regions, however, tend to be involved in multiple functions. For example, in one study Joshua Greene and his colleagues[38] reported that when participants were presented with personal moral dilemmas parts of the brain associated with emotions were active, whereas when considering impersonal moral dilemmas other brain regions were found to be active that are linked to abstract reasoning and problem solving. However, the case is not so clear-cut because some of the areas associated with emotions are also connected to memory and language.[39]

The goal of neuroscience research on this topic is to determine what parts of the brain are involved in morality. Although a number of studies have been conducted isolating various brain regions, we won't review this field because the general conclusion after all of this research seems to be that, "many brain areas make important contributions to moral judgment."[40] It would be surprising or improbable if this were not the case because morality is such a complex, multifaceted issue. This leads us to the question of what morality is, and how we define and isolate the moral domain. It will be a central concern of Chapter 7. It is not neuroscience as a whole that we are evaluating here but rather particular approaches within it.[41]

Morality cannot be simply reduced to neural activity. Instead, we believe that biological adaptations set up the infant for the kinds of social interaction in which human development occurs. This is the approach we have taken throughout this book. Examples of such adaptations could include emotional engagement and interest in others, as well as other factors such as being born early, which necessitates social interaction and further development within such interaction. Communication, meaning and thinking develop in interaction.

Moral modules: From genes to justice?

In Chapters 8 and 9 we review and critique the position endorsed by Steven Pinker and others that the mind consists of a series of innate neuro-cognitive mechanisms, or modules, that evolved to solve particular problems encountered by early humans. This same approach has also been applied more specifically to morality. John Mikhail argues that humans have evolved innate modules that are the source of moral decisions. Mikhail's evidence, which even he admits is weak, is that children by the age of 3 know something about morality and that all human languages seem to have words to deal with moral issues.[42] But by the age of 3 children have learned lots of things including, if they are North American or British, about Barbie dolls, and we don't want to assume that there is a module for this understanding. The fact that, as far as we know, all human languages have ways of talking about moral issues is very interesting and important, but it does not mean that this knowledge is innate. Rather it means that moral issues form a vital dimension of human existence and language has to be adapted to allow us to reflect on and communicate about such issues. We expect that all languages would also have words for hello, goodbye, sorry and thank-you, and so on, because these are important aspects of human forms of life that we would expect to find in all cultures, but an innate module is not needed to explain them. Mikhail's third source of evidence is that "prohibitions of murder, rape and other types of aggression appear to be universal or nearly so."[43] This may be true but it is what has to be explained.

Proposing a module, as so many psychologists are keen on today, does not simplify or finish our task. This sort of claim is just a promissory note—it is an IOU. We still need an explanation for how such a module could have evolved and how it develops. That is, how do we get to modules from the factors that influence our biological inheritance?[44]

Summary and conclusion: Evolution and the moral developmental niche

We want to reiterate the point that in questioning claims that morality can be explained as simply innate, we are certainly not rejecting a Darwinian view that morality is rooted in human biology, and in that sense has an evolutionary story. Instead we are questioning the nature of that development. There are two contrasting ways to think about evolution. One is focused on genes and the other on the whole developmental system in which babies develop as persons. Humans don't simply inherit morality. Rather, biological characteristics play a role in setting up the human social and emotional developmental system in which morality develops. This may sound like splitting hairs, but we think that there is an important difference between these two possibilities. These are based on quite different views of the nature and origin of human thinking.[45]

From our perspective, we should be looking for quite different biological capacities. We would not be looking for genes that would somehow result in neural circuits that influence reactions in moral situations. Rather, the process is a great deal more complex and we need to explore the developmental story; we would look for the ways in which human babies are well suited to create and engage in social relationships in which communication and then thinking gradually emerge. This is what we have been discussing throughout this book.

Morality develops within conditions that must be at least potentially found across cultures. So the question then becomes what are these conditions of human forms of life and how do they make it possible for morality to develop? The general theme of this book is that thinking is necessarily social; minds and thinking arise through social processes. Thus we would look for the ways in which human babies are born being well suited to enter into as well as play a role in creating the social environments in which they develop human forms of thinking, including thinking about moral matters. In the next chapter we examine the complexities of this form of thinking that take us well beyond genetic influences.

Suggested further reading

Carpendale, J. I. M., Hammond, S. I., & Atwood, S. (2013). A relational developmental systems approach to moral development. *Advances in Child Development and Behavior*, 45, 125–153.

Notes

1 Bloom (2010).
2 Hamlin, Wynn, and Bloom (2010).
3 Hamlin, Wynn, and Bloom (2010, p. 559).
4 Bloom (2010).
5 Margoni and Surian (2018) did a meta-analysis of 26 studies. See also, Tafreshi, Thompson, and Racine (2014); Cowell and Decety (2015); Salvadori et al. (2011); Scarf et al. (2012); Scola et al. (2016); Decety et al. (2016); Carpendale & Hammond, 2016.
6 There is some evidence at 3½ months of age but it is with looking time methodology (Hamlin & Wynn, 2011) and so more difficult to interpret.
7 As we write (November 2018) the University of Manchester Students union has banned clapping at its meetings in case such activity upsets members of the student body who are on the Autism Spectrum. So, clapping is not universally appreciated. For discussion about hyper-sensitivity to specific types of room design in autism spectrum disorder see Kanakri et al. (2017). For the literature on what makes an individual with autism sensitive, see Lucker (2013). See Carpendale and Ten Eycke (in press) for an example of an infant using clapping to make a request.
8 Kettner and Carpendale (2013).
9 Carpendale, Hammond, and Atwood (2013). As we have discussed throughout this book, we could also ask if it even biologically plausible to claim that babies are born with moral knowledge? Although Bloom doesn't spell it out, the usual assumption is that such knowledge is rooted in genes that can evolve and be selected for. We devote space in Chapter 8 to reflect on recent research in genetics that makes it clear that there can be no simple direct route from genes to knowledge. Claims that abilities are innate shut down attempts to unfold the complex developmental process through which these abilities develop. This smoke screen must be rejected in favor of studying the process of development.
10 James (1890); Baldwin (1906).
11 Ambrosini et al. (2013).
12 Reddy, Markova, and Wallot (2013).
13 Hay (2009).
14 Rheingold (1982).
15 Warneken and Tomasello (2006, 2009).
16 Warneken and Tomasello (2013, 2014).
17 Warneken and Tomasello 2009, p. 459).
18 Warneken et al. (2007, p. 1418).
19 Carpendale, Kettner, and Audet (2015).
20 Rheingold (1982, p. 115).
21 Carpendale, Kettner, and Audet (2015).

22 Kaye (1982, p. 147).
23 Rochat (2014).
24 Mauss (1967).
25 Rochat (2014).
26 Rheingold, Hay, and West (1976).
27 Hay and Murray (1982).
28 Pika and Bugnyar (2011, p. 1).
29 For example, Mauss (1967).
30 Haidt (2001).
31 Haidt (2001); Haidt and Bjorklund (2008); Greene and Haidt (2002).
32 Haidt (2001); Greene and Haidt (2002).
33 Hume (1751).
34 For example, Greene (2003); Greene and Haidt (2002); Moll et al. (2008).
35 Moll et al. (2005, p. 799).
36 In fact, there is controversy about this case. For more discussion see
    Macmillan (2008).
37 Miller (2008). For a description of how signals are "cleaned" or "denoised"
    in fMRI analyses see Caballero-Gaudes and Reynolds (2017).
38 Greene et al. (2001).
39 Miller (2008).
40 Greene and Haidt (2002, p. 517).
41 It is important to consider the implicit assumptions that underlie this
    approach. It assumes that the mind processes information like a computer;
    that some neural systems may be specialized for morality. It is simply
    assumed that these neurological circuits/mechanisms have evolved and that
    such modules are genetically determined, or "hard-wired." In Chapter 8 we
    critique the underlying assumption in this approach that meaning must be
    fixed—it would have to be were such modules to be able to work. It is not
    clear that Greene and others really want to accept the full implications of this
    (because they do talk about some cultural influence but they downplay this
    so much that it is hard to tell what if any role this plays in their approach),
    so they leave the difficult questions unanswered. Others like Cosmides and
    Tooby (2013) are not shy about placing their money on a form of genetic
    determinism that implies fixed limited knowledge. The alternative to this
    view that is the focus of our attention, is that the brain is shaped by social
    interaction and that meaning is social. We therefore contend that we cannot
    have evolved neural mechanisms that compute meaning. Instead, humans have
    evolved adaptations that set up the forms of interaction in which humans
    forms of thinking emerge, but the emergence is the interesting part of what
    makes us human.
42 Mikhail (2007).
43 Mikhail (2007, p. 143).
44 Marc Hauser, in his book *Moral Minds* (Hauser, 2006a), also argues that
    morality is like language in the sense that there is a universal and innate
    grammar for human morality. The arguments we have reviewed earlier in
    this book about Chomsky's view of language as an innate module apply just
    as well to Hauser's attempt to explain morality in the same way. In fact, he
    does not even acknowledge let alone respond to the many devastating (in our
    view) critiques of Chomsky's view of language. Our goal in this chapter was
    to present our view of moral development that follows from the general

approach we have presented in this book, and to set it in the context of other approaches to morality. But there is much more work on the evolution of morality that we have not addressed. To do so would require a whole book. For example, we have not covered the work by Dennis Krebs (2011) on the evolution of morality. The extent to which our approach converges with his depends on what he means by the evolution of moral mechanisms. Our view is that the human forms of thinking we are concerned with in this book emerge within social interaction. The evolutionary and biological sides of the story are involved in providing an account of how these social conditions evolved and develop.

45   In the broadest sense we could say that the ability to play soccer is inherited but developing this skill is quite different from growing the legs needed for the game. Skills for the game include running, controlling the ball, learning the rules and coordinating one's actions with others on your team in order to achieve actions like passing the ball and attempting to make goals and win the game. This is winning but within the constraints of conforming to the agreed upon rules. This is a social and culturally specific activity. Despite the interest shown in the World Cup, soccer is not played in all cultures. Situations we describe as involving morality, however, must, we assume, arise in all cultures. The idea of soccer being biologically based seems ludicrous, which is why no one looks for a specific gene for performing the activity. But if such research were to be done, undoubtedly there would be genes linked to successful performance. Are these genes for soccer? No. They would be genes associated with traits that are useful in soccer such as quick reaction time, cardiovascular stamina, fast twitch muscles for sprinting, balance, coordination, as well as intellectual abilities needed for anticipating patterns within games and personality suited for various positions on the team. To be clear, these are not genes for these traits that somehow determine the traits but rather are part of a developmental system that can lead to these traits.

Chapter 7

Knowing right from wrong
Or, how does morality develop?

In which we explore the nature of morality and attempt to explain its development.

> Two things fill the mind with ever new and increasing admiration and awe, the more often and steadily we reflect upon them: the starry heavens above me and the moral law within me.
>
> —Immanuel Kant[1]

This quotation from the influential German philosopher Immanuel Kant was chosen by his friends to be inscribed on his tombstone. What is this "moral law," and where does it come from? In this chapter we consider several possible answers to this fundamental question. As we suggested at the start of Chapter 1, Kant also argued that comprehending "the moral law within" us is fully as difficult and fascinating a problem as understanding "the starry heavens above" us!

The importance of children developing an understanding of morality is non-controversial. One answer to the question of how they develop such principles might be that parents tell their children what is right and wrong. Indeed, the person in the street might argue that this is obvious. We hear repeatedly on the News of good citizens who act as "role models." The idea that others might simply copy them is a legacy of the Social Learning, or socialization, account of moral development from behaviorism in the 1960s. Such learning must be part of the story, but assuming that this is a complete explanation simply reduces morality to conformity, to just doing what our parents tell or show us. If this were the only factor there would never be any social change. Yet there are many famous examples of changes in views of morality. Why did William Wilberforce, for example, carry the day 200 years ago in taking a step toward ending slavery? Why was the Berlin Wall torn down? How did South Africa make a peaceful transition into democracy? To explain these and other examples we need something more than thinking of morality as conformity.

We concluded from the last chapter that there must a biological and evolutionary side to the story, but what is also required is an awareness of the role of social relations in the developmental system in which children develop. We explain the development of morality as emerging from social relations.

What is morality?

On one hand, everyone knows what morality is, but, on the other hand, any attempt to clearly define it becomes a great deal more murky. To begin with, it involves such a broad range of issues concerning conflicts among people ranging from lying and honesty to murder and genocide. We teach our children about the Nazi Holocaust and the Killing Fields of Cambodia, as well as more recent events like the "ethnic cleansing" in the former Yugoslavia and Myanmar, the genocide in Rwanda and Assad's bombing of the suburbs of his own capital Damascus in February 2018, followed by individual regions across the rest of Syria, notably Idlib in 2020. These examples are not, unfortunately, just isolated incidents and they are very complex. As developmental psychologists, we focus at the very small-scale level on how we interact with and treat other people in everyday social activity. In this sense, morality can be thought of as a dimension of our interpersonal interaction, a concern for others. It arises when we must coordinate our interaction with others and, thus, it has to do with the way we treat others as persons. This is a broad definition that even includes politeness and treating others with respect. This is the ground on which interaction is based. We are a moral species because our human lives are embedded in interactions with others which necessarily contain a moral dimension.

An additional issue, however, must now be considered when we think about morality. In the past, discussions about ethics have only had to deal with coordinating conflicting interests in the present, not with the implications of time. However, humans now have the increased technological power to alter conditions on our planet in ways that affect the quality or even the possibility of life for so-called *Homo sapiens* ("wise man"). We should be concerned about the effect of what we are doing on future generations. This also applies to other species. The rate of the extinction of species in recent years due to humans is now approaching that during the five great periods of extinctions. Our power to affect other forms of life on this planet raises the question of whether we now have some responsibility along with that power for the rest of the biosphere.[2]

Even simple acts like buying a cup of coffee have moral implications. Is the drink you so desire fairly traded, organic and was the plant shade grown? Is it in a disposable cup? What are the implications of supporting that type of coffee for the farmer and the environment, and what are the effects on future generations? The same concerns can arise with our other purchases from shoes to shirts because we can think about whether they were made in sweatshops by workers who were not given a living wage. Our choices about the way we live our lives from taking the bus or riding a bicycle to turning off lights all affect our carbon footprint and, therefore, influence the lives of our children and our children's children through climate change.[3] And who we vote for, if we can vote, may have a larger effect in either positive or negative directions concerning taking action to reduce greenhouse gases.

From this brief discussion it is clear that there are multifaceted ways in which we affect the lives of others. We have barely scratched the surface of the complex issues here, without attempting to pin down a hard and fast definition of how morality is conceptualized, let alone how it develops. It ranges from the way we treat others in everyday interaction to wider political issues, including how our lifestyle affects how others live or die. With this backdrop, we now turn to discussion of views of morality, and how this essential aspect of what makes us human develops.

Why moral thinking is not simply passed from parent to child

Let's reflect further on the common view that we simply absorb our parents' statements about what is right and wrong. First let's examine the position that children are simply passive in this process. We will spell out the implications of this position and suggest that it is far from satisfactory. From first principles, we could ask, how did their parents learn about morality? Well, it must have come from their grandparents, and so on. But where does that process come to an end? If we learned moral principles from our parents and they learned them from their parents, it's turtles all the way down.[4]

Who came up with these moral principles to begin with? Of course, they can be attributed to some ultimate authority figure like God or gods, but many people are no longer satisfied with that explanation. We could also wonder about different moral principles derived from different gods. So, who is right? All the protagonists of wars may claim that God is on their side. The amount of blood that has been shed throughout history in God's name is simply unimaginable. In the crusades, for example, women and children were slaughtered in God's name. As just one example, in the 1209 siege of Béziers in southern France one of the leaders of the Crusader army, in response to a crusader asking how they should tell the Cathars from the Catholics, was reported to have said "kill them all and let God sort them out." Whether or not he actually said this, everyone in the city of 20,000 was killed in God's name regardless of sex, age or, indeed, religious faith. Furthermore, this appeal to a higher authority does not account for a number of other problems.

Religious texts must still be interpreted, and such interpretations change over generations. The view that moral thinking is simply passed on by parents does not explain how the principles held in a culture change over time. Changes in moral norms may not be just arbitrary, and in many cases may be an improvement. There have been widespread views, once commonly held, that we now consider immoral such as slavery and men owning their wives and children. For example, the usual story is that democracy originated in ancient Greece, but as Terry Deary pointed out in his Horrible Histories series for kids, "they didn't get it quite right at first."[5] That is, it was only male landowners who could vote. If we consider it an improvement to give more citizens the right to vote then we could track when women could vote in different countries. It was only in 1893 that the first country gave women the vote[6] and it took the First World War for this to be granted in the UK and several European states. In Canada, First Nations citizens were allowed onto the electoral roll only in 1960. In some contemporary countries, voting for all citizens is suspended and in all nations the dividing line between freedom to work and slavery is a complex one. It was not until 2015 that women voted in Saudi Arabia and this was only in local elections. The right to vote is only one aspect of democracy. Citizens still need to participate and use that right, sometimes in spite of voter suppression, and some countries (such as the US, the UK, and Canada) still have voting systems that often do not result in a government that reflects the actual voting patterns. Not all citizens in such countries are necessarily free. For example, 21 cockle-pickers drowned in Morecambe Bay in 2004, five miles from Charlie's house. They were working as slaves within full view of the public, the police and other government agencies.

A further problem with the idea that moral norms are simply passed on, as parents and children will testify, is that it just doesn't work. As parents ourselves, we know that children don't always do as they are asked to do. If children reject what their parents tell them this does not necessarily mean that they are rejecting good advice to be upstanding citizens, while turning to the dark side and into trouble. The alternative is also possible. That is, progressive social change, improvement in our ways of treating others, may arise because young people question existing practices. Instead of just adopting values, children may question the ethics of their parents' conduct. Many contemporary young people educate their parents about moral and sustainable practices—for example, that wasting water, burning fossil fuels, or dumping used engine oil or plastics may not leave the planet in a sustainable condition for their children and their children's children. Children's questioning of their parents' ways does more than show that we do not simply conform to tradition. This reveals the assumptions behind practices that are taken for granted and exposes key moral questions.

For example, consider white children growing up in South Africa during apartheid. Many of their parents would likely have endorsed the idea of segregation, yet their adolescent children started to question it and later voted against it. Or consider youth in Nazi Germany. In one famous example in Munich, portrayed in the 2005 film *Sophie Scholl: The Final Days*,[7] a brother and sister joined the Hitler Youth, but then they thought about what they were being told and rejected the dogma being imposed on them. They left the group and started what they called the "White Rose" to oppose the Nazis. This was a very brave but also extremely dangerous undertaking showing how they had thought deeply about these moral issues, and it demonstrates the strength of their commitment. Tragically, they were caught, quickly "tried," and beheaded. Consider a more recent example of children changing their parents' views. In a 2-year longitudinal study on the coast of North Carolina 10- to 14-year-old school children enrolled in a school program about the impact of climate change on their local environment. At the end of the study it was found that the children had also influenced their parents' views. In fact, this effect was particularly strong in girls greatly increasing conservative fathers' concerns about climate change.[8]

These examples of young people thinking for themselves, however, are, unfortunately, not always the way it is, as we know from the unfortunate history of Nazi Germany. Many children did take on and believe the propaganda of the Hitler Youth, often with their parents' blessing, but sometimes in opposition to their parents' views. Some children even turned their own parents in to the authorities. There are many complex social, historical as well as developmental factors involved that go beyond what we will address. The complexity of such issues is sometimes well presented in the form of novels such as *Stones from the River*,[9] which follows the stories of people in a small town in Germany leading up to and through the Second World War. These and scores of other examples show that pressure from others is not the only way in which children adopt moral norms. If we simply followed others' behavior then our actions would not be "moral" in the sense of needing to distinguish right from wrong. The excuse of just following orders was rejected at the Nuremberg trials. Although they may not always do so, young people can and do think for themselves, and this must be explained by any account of moral development. The fact that the socialization assumption has difficulty with this suggests, again, that it is incomplete.

A further problem concerns the issue of relativism. If morality simply involves adopting the norms and values of a culture (what our parents tell us), then it is not possible to say anything about other moral systems, because there are no means of evaluating them. Consider Warren Jeffs's defense against being charged with forcing a 14-year-old girl to marry and have sex with her older cousin (over and above his marrying of over 60 wives). Jeffs claimed that charging him was religious persecution because this was the way things were done in his community, his culture, even though he was also a citizen of the US. There are several cultures where marrying at that age may be less contentious, but this raises questions about whether (or when) there is an age at which a bride or groom cannot give full consent. If morality is just the way things are done in a particular society then how can we question the way things are done in other cultures? How can we say that stoning a woman to death if she has been accused of adultery, or has been sexually assaulted, is not right? We also need to explain how after generations of women were exploited in Hollywood and elsewhere without the indignation that is currently so evident that the #MeToo movement finally emerged.

There is a difference between the fact of moral relativism—that cultures do vary in moral norms—and the issue of whether this means they *should* vary. If we address the question of whether moral perspectives are of equal value or whether some are better in some sense than others, this raises deep questions. Clearly views about morality do vary across cultures. We also know that even young children appear to take a complex approach to this question. For example, one study comparing 5- to 7-year-old Brahmin children in India with American children, revealed that the Brahmin children thought that it was wrong to eat beef, to address their father by his first name, to cut their hair or eat chicken after their father's death. But, at the same time, these two groups of children agreed that it was wrong to ignore a beggar, break a promise, kick a harmless animal or steal flowers.[10] Such agreement still leaves open the question of whether there might reasonable grounds for deliberating about moral principles or if selecting a moral system just like choosing your favorite flavor of ice cream.

We run into this paradox because it is completely understandable that we are hesitant regarding imposing a way of thinking about moral issues on other cultures. We are gun-shy from many horrendous historical examples of doing just this, such as residential schools in Canada, where First Nations, Inuit and Metis children were sent in an attempt to "kill the Indian in the child" through denying them the opportunity to speak their languages and practice their culture. A far less extreme example is that we shouldn't impose a cultural convention like wearing green on Saint Patrick's Day. When Jeremy's son, Max, was six he refused to wear green on Saint Patrick's Day because he had heard that Saint Patrick had driven all the snakes, lizards, and weasels out of Ireland and into the sea. Max liked lizards and weasels because weasels use things that are thrown away, and he said that they break cars, and cars cause pollution and, besides, it's bad for biodiversity.

The socialization view seems to reduce to moral relativism because there is no way to evaluate those differing moral systems that are imposed on children across different cultures. Yet there may be cases in which we do want to evaluate different moral beliefs. What about the ethics of gangsters such as killing someone who "rats" to the cops? Or consider so-called "honour killing" in which in some traditional societies parents may kill their own son or daughter if he or she embarrasses the family or clan, by, for example, holding hands with their girlfriend or boyfriend in public. These murders are referred to as "honor killings" because they are premeditated and their goal is to cleanse collective dishonor from the family and clan, and in doing so the murderer becomes a hero for restoring honor to his group.[11] These situations may arise when families move to different cultures and experience conflict between cultural values, but the solution is extreme.[12]

A further aspect to the paradoxes around moral relativism concerns the size of cultures. How big does a group have to be to be considered a culture? Does a group of gangsters count as one. What about sub-cultures? Would a family be considered a small one? If so, then we couldn't say anything if in our neighbor's house the husband beats his wife, or the wife beats her husband,[13] because that is just the way things are done in that family culture. Perhaps their parents taught them that this was right. Ironically, if morality is just what parents teach then it seems to reduce to this privacy. But morality cannot simply be a private way of doing things.

Our final concern about the socialization approach is that from this perspective becoming moral is like learning a set of virtues such as the boy scout principles of being honest, brave, loyal, and clean, and so on. Lawrence Kohlberg, whose theory we discuss below, called this the "bag of virtues" approach, according to which once children acquire such a list of virtues they have become moral. This system doesn't work as it has difficulty in dealing with situations in which such virtues are in conflict. For example, imagine you are in Europe during the Second World War and you are hiding someone in your attic. In middle of the night the SS pound on your door and ask if you are hiding anyone. Should you tell the truth? Should you follow the boy scout virtue of always being honest? Or, instead, should you follow the virtue of trying to save someone's life? These rules are in conflict; they don't provide a simple solution. It is not possible to just look up the answer in the rule book. Instead this dilemma requires some thinking. Or consider another case in which you have a friend who is very hungry and you have no way of feeding your friend except by stealing food. Here is a setting in which a virtue of saving someone's life is in conflict with the virtue of not stealing. These are examples where simply following the rules doesn't work and some thinking is required to decide on what is the right thing to do.

Although the socialization assumption may help us understand part of what we think of as moral, it cannot fully account for our moral worlds. And thus we have to turn to other ideas. Jean Piaget believed that the view that we pick up on or simply accept a code from previous generations was not sufficient to explain how it is that children become moral beings. Over and above the question of whether this really is morality or just conformity, many of the examples we have used in this section show that children often construct a moral code that is different from, and sometimes in opposition to, the values of their parents. The psychologist R. Q. Bell became a staunch critic of the behaviorism that he was the product of. He pointed out that, even at a behavioral level, children influence their parents as much as being influenced by them—so morality is something that we can catch from our kids within a subtle negotiation process.[14] Granted, we do learn from our parents, but we need to understand how rules are made and modified.

Reasoning and morality: Thinking about moral matters

One of the best-known psychologists working in the area of moral development was Lawrence Kohlberg. A source of his motivation to study this topic was to understand the Holocaust. His PhD dissertation in 1958 was a ground-breaking attempt to examine the development of reasoning about moral issues. Kohlberg focused on events in which moral principles are in conflict, and he asked people to attempt to resolve these difficult quandaries. Perhaps the best known of Kohlberg's dilemmas involves a man faced with the decision of whether to break the law by stealing a drug he could not afford in order to save his dying wife. Although this might seem an abstract question from a fairy tale far removed from most of our everyday lives, this same issue is evident in the case of the AIDS epidemic in Africa where the price of drugs charged by pharmaceutical companies prohibits many lives from being saved. In the words of Canada's former ambassador to the UN on AIDS, Stephen Lewis:

> It's like all the wars of the twentieth century wrapped into one. Thirty million people have died; 34 million live with the virus. There are two and half million new infections last year, of which 330,000 are children. More than 50% of those infected in Africa are women.[15]

Another dilemma used by Kohlberg involves euthanasia—a woman, dying in pain, pleads with her doctor to give her an overdose of morphine. Here following the law is in conflict with an individual's right to make a choice. Since Kohlberg constructed this dilemma, the law in many countries has been rewritten in attempts to deal with this challenge and provide options for end of life issues.

Reasoning was essential for Kohlberg because mere behavior cannot be moral. Consider an act in isolation of the reasons for the action. For example, if we know that someone is not paying their taxes should we simply judge this act is immoral? If someone doesn't pay their taxes because they refuse to support a war that their government is waging then the act could be considered highly principled, even valiant. Or consider witnessing a scene in which young man pushes over an elderly person. If the camera pans back so that we can see the larger context and we realize that the young man has in fact acted heroically to push the elderly person out of the way of an on-rushing truck then we see that the act was deeply moral. These examples explain Kohlberg's emphasis on the reasoning underlying an act.

Kohlberg's focus on the process of reasoning contains a developmental dimension that he was most interested in. He described a series of stages, or forms, of reasoning through which individuals develop. Each increases in complexity and is able to deal with more complicated situations. To understand why people do or don't act morally we must first understand how they think about the issues involved. Kohlberg drew on Plato's view that knowing the good would lead to doing the good. He thought that if people were able to figure out the right thing to do, this would be important in understanding their subsequent moral action. Of course, he realized that there was no direct link between knowing the right action and doing it, but he thought that reasoning was an essential step toward acting morally.

Jean Piaget on lived morality

We started with Kohlberg in order to introduce important ideas about morality. In fact, he drew on ideas from Jean Piaget.[16] They are both generally thought to have focused on the role of reasoning in moral development. Kohlberg was inspired by Piaget, but his approach was, in fact, quite different. Piaget started with children's activity, with the way they played together and their gradual development of a practical, lived morality—a way of getting along with each other. So, kids usually get this figured out and they also form strong emotional bonds with their peers. It is the practical level of understanding how to interact with others that Piaget began with. He was concerned with "the morality of the queue rather than the morality of the pulpit."[17]

One of the methods Piaget used in studying morality might be considered somewhat unusual. He played marbles with lads, and asked them questions about the rules. The younger boys told him that the rules could not be changed and that you can't make up a new rule; it was as if they viewed the rules as external to them and set in stone. They thought that the rules came from some authority like their father or ultimately from God. The 12- to 13-year-old boys, in contrast, said that, sure, you could change the rules or make up new ones—as long as everyone agreed. They understood the rules as based on mutual agreement so that they could get on and play without always arguing. So the question is how they had developed this fine grasp of democracy over this time period. Piaget's answer was that the boys stopped playing marbles at around the age of 14, so that the 12- to 13-year-olds he interviewed had no older boys imposing their views on the younger ones. Instead the older boys could work it out among themselves, among equals. For him, it was this relationship of cooperation based on equality and mutual respect that allowed for this development in understanding of rules as based on mutual agreement. Although other topics raise much stronger moral dilemmas, Piaget studied games as one of his approaches to morality because it is an example of how rules are passed on and accepted from one generation to another.

It is clear that Piaget's idea that moral norms are constructed by children within social relations contrasts with the view of morality as imposed from external sources—the socialization perspective. He argued that forms of morality develop in different types of relationships. Within interactions with parents children may have moral norms imposed on them. These are relationships of constraint in that children are expected to follow instructions and in simply doing so they do not need to understand the moral norms being imposed upon them. If the child is supposed to respect the adult, a parent may simply impose a view and does not expect to be questioned. This sort of situation is not well-suited to reaching understanding.

In contrast, for Piaget the best means of coming to understand others and develop moral norms is within cooperative relationships among equals. This form of relationship is based on mutual respect and so everyone feels obliged to explain themselves as well as to listen to others. In doing so, individuals are likely to reach mutual understanding and can work out a resolution that everyone agrees with. This type of relationship is best suited for reaching mutual understanding and developing moral norms. This process is usually possible among peers because they tend to be equal and thus can work out ways of interacting that everyone agrees on. It's fun to play with friends, but if you don't treat your friends right, you soon won't have any left. Of course, any relationship may involve a mixture of constraint and cooperation, and bullying can occur among peers. Conversely, parent-child relationships vary in how cooperative they are; children's relationships with their parents may involve cooperation to some extent.[18]

A next step is that children gradually become conscious of this practical morality through a process of becoming aware of and being able to talk about those principles that have guided the way the child interacts with his or her peers, what Piaget referred to as conscious realization. This is not a verbal report of introspection on inner psychological processes. Instead it is becoming able to reflect on those ways of responding to their friends that they have not really thought about before, just done. For Piaget, this is the way children construct moral norms, beginning in actual interaction with others. Children gradually become aware of their way of engaging with others that embodies the principles that underlie their way of interacting with their friends.

Piaget studied a number of aspects of morality including the more typical topics concerning justice. For example, he examined how it is that children come to understand lying. A first form of understanding emerges within relationships of constraint with their parents. At this point young children said that lying is bad simply because they get punished. Their explanations showed no understanding of the interpersonal consequences of lying. Piaget argued that children have a natural tendency to make things up, to fantasize.[19] Then they are told by their parents that this is bad, but they don't really understand why. It is only when they live as members of society within a web of trust and expectations that they begin to understand the interpersonal consequences of lying. Once they realize the consequences of misleading their friends, the betrayal of trust involved, then children understand lying. This is much more likely to occur within cooperative relationships among equals. When Piaget talked with children about lying, the younger ones told him that you shouldn't lie to an adult, but it was alright to lie to kids because you wouldn't get punished. The older children said exactly the opposite. They said that sometimes they had to lie to adults because of their silly rules, but it was really bad to lie to a friend! So this is something that cannot simply be told to children. They don't understand it until they experience it, and to do so they must experience cooperative relationships.

For Piaget, notions such as the idea of justice are not something children are born with and it is also not simply imposed by society on them. In fact, it can't just be imposed by parents because their children would not understand it. Instead Piaget proposed a third solution which is in keeping with the thesis of this book, that is the idea of justice may emerge within relationships of a particular type—cooperative relationships. There is the potential for the idea of justice to naturally emerge within certain conditions, just as the structure of a whirlpool consistently arises in fluids given certain situations. The whirlpool does not pre-exist in any sense, but it will naturally emerge given the right conditions. Similarly, justice is an idea that will naturally emerge within cooperative relationships because everyone is considered equal; so all positions in a moral conflict are listened to and coordinated in reaching a solution that is acceptable to everyone.

We might have given the impression that moral development is simple and straightforward, but in fact it can be nothing like that and kids have their own goals and so they will often make mistakes. When a 3- to 4-year-old first says, "that's not fair!" it may be that at least partly she just wants her turn. But children usually like playing with each other so if a child's initial clumsy attempts to get his own way fail and he ends up playing by himself next time he may try for a better balance with others' wishes in the hope of having more fun by playing with his friends. Thus, there is the potential to move toward a better balance between goals. We need to explore further how they and we do this.

Morality through interpersonal agreement: "The method of morality"

> It is as social beings that we are moral beings.
>
> —George Herbert Mead[20]

Morality concerns right and wrong, correct and incorrect. We feel obligations to do the right thing. Thus, it involves adhering to standards of correctness.[21] But where do such moral norms come from? If we are moved to act, either through social pressure or our biology, then this does not seem to count as a morally based action. The big question is how could ethical standards emerge from a world of causes? Some contemporary scholars believe that moral rules are innate, evolved, and thus contingent. That is, they just happen to be that way due to chance and they could have been different. Another position is that these moral rules are just culturally specific practices—the current way of doing things in a particular social group. Both of these approaches have a series of problems that we have already discussed. Our goal in this book is to explain human intelligence as emerging in our everyday interactions, so we must account for how moral rules form within this world of causes.[22] In looking for naturalistic explanations we do not restrict ourselves to physical causes. Instead we also include higher levels of social interaction, which might be termed the social process. In this way we can explain the emergence of normativity through interpersonal agreement.

If morality is neither innate nor merely based on social conventions, then the third option is that it is based on agreement among all rational persons involved—moral norms are what no reasonable person can reject. The universality of such a judgement is arrived at through taking the perspectives of all rational agents involved and coordinating these perspectives to reach agreement. This fits with the main argument of the book, that our thinking emerges within social interaction, but this link with moral understanding still requires some unpacking. How is agreement reached? How do persons develop to this point?

Using another metaphor, Kohlberg proposed the idea of "moral musical chairs." In their imagination individuals rotate through the various positions in a moral conflict so that they can appreciate all perspectives involved. A decision made with such experience of the different perspectives should be moral. Kohlberg's ideas are based on George Herbert Mead's earlier approach to this problem. For Mead the sense of universality of moral judgements, which the philosopher Immanuel Kant stressed, arises because we are part of a community; it is through our relationships with others that we can "take the attitude of the entire community, or all rational beings...; that is, everyone who can rationally appreciate the situation agrees. The very form of our judgment is therefore social, so that the end, both content and form, is necessarily a social end."[23] According to Mead, this is a method for reaching a moral decision. Importantly, for Mead this is a conversation with the community, it is not simply conforming to the views of the community.

Jürgen Habermas[24] is a contemporary philosopher who proposed a universal morality based on the idea that moral norms are those that can be agreed upon by all involved in a conflict in a practical discourse. This discussion requires the social conditions of an "ideal speech situation" in which there is no coercion. Everyone can talk freely and present their position on a conflict. Of course, not all conversations are actually like this ideal form, but less happy examples are distortions of the potential. Thus, discourse ethics attempts to derive a universal morality from the presuppositions of the form of communication, which is concerned with reaching mutual understanding. This requires respecting others and explaining one's own view and listening to theirs. Habermas argues that morality is already present and presupposed in everyday communication. The moral ideas of equality and respect already underlie the actual communicative practices of everyday life. In everyday conversation we listen to others and respond to their position, and in this way respecting others as persons with their own views underlies the practice of conversation. It is assumed in what we do. This is similar to Piaget's view that morality is already there in our ways of interacting with others rather than being something imposed from the outside. Habermas is concerned with the practical, lived aspect at the level of the ways of interacting on which conversation is based. Piaget's interest was the emergence of morality at the level of lived interaction, whereas Kohlberg focused on verbal reasoning.

What all these scholars propose, in common, is a process for making moral decisions, what Mead called a "moral method," not just a set of rules to be followed. Some moral conflicts may be routine and the best action may be clear. Other conflicts, however, may be set in more complex circumstances in which previous rules cannot simply be applied. Here we need a process of coordinating the conflicting viewpoints to arrive at a moral outcome, a balanced solution that is acceptable to all persons involved.

Emotions have to play a role in getting this whole process off the ground. That is, other people have to matter for the developing children. They need to be valued in themselves, to be *someone* not *something*.[25] It is not that persons could develop and then get together and realize that it is to their advantage to all agree on a social contract. This would be backwards in developmental thinking. Concern for and interest in others must develop early on and then be the basis for the development of morality.

It seems that we have assumed something here in our account—the idea of persons who communicate and give reasons to each other. But how do we explain the development of children up to this point, because very young children cannot give reasons? We have to take a step back to explain why and how we come to live in a space of justifications. This is what the whole book has been about. That is, we have presented a view of the development of thinking, of giving reasons to others, which depends on a social life of mutual engagement.

The reason for reasons

> Man is a rational being because he is a social being.
> — George Herbert Mead[26]

If at least an aspect of the development of morality is linked to reasoning, to figuring out the right thing to do, then it is important to explain the human ability to use reasoning. Reasons emerge from our social relations, from interpersonal obligations and the need to maintain our emotional relationships with others. If we ignore a friend and don't respond to a greeting we are expected to explain, to give reasons for this omission, because this action, or lack of it, has significant interpersonal consequences. We are bound by moral norms and feel obliged to explain and justify our actions to others. We care about others and their views of us.[27] Furthermore, we feel that others should account for their actions as well; they should explain themselves. There are many other social species from bees to baboons who do not coordinate their interaction by explaining their actions. Giving reasons is first a social process to maintaining relationships and it is later co-opted as an individual form of thinking. The concepts of responsibility, excuses, and blame arise from social relations. Because it is social it is also an emotional process through being based on our relationships of care and concern for others.

Infants and toddlers must be prevented from touching a hot stove because they cannot understand the significance of such an action. Later, when they have mastered enough language, they are given a plethora of explanations for acting or not doing so in order that they can understand the prohibition. These involve a grasp of the physical world, or the physical consequences of their action. Other reasons concern the social world, centered on the interpersonal consequences of actions. This human form of communication then changes emotional relationships—reasons are now exchanged. We explain why we do, or refuse to do, something. By means of a reason an action that might seem to involve rejecting the child, such as leaving the room, can be transformed into another act such as going to get something for him or her and returning. This is the attachment theorist John Bowlby's idea of *goal corrected partnerships* when language begins to provide a new way to maintain relationships for the preschooler.[28] Grasping a reason involves understanding another's perspective and the other's views of the self.

Reasons are also for other people because they are required in order to influence others' views of ourselves. Thus, we would expect that they develop when children become sufficiently aware of others' view of them. This depends on being self-conscious, of being able to think about others' view of ourselves. The analysis of coyness in Chapter 2 is part of this process but does not yet involve such perspective taking. This approach results in a route in which morality emerges out of everyday human interactions, building upon communicative practices in which justifications and explanations are expected.

Summing up the social conditions for the development of morality: A natural history

The development of morality is interwoven with human forms of life. It cannot be reduced to what we are instructed to do or to simple conformity. It is this problem of explaining how children construct and accept moral norms that we address here. The approach taken by Piaget in the 1930s contains neglected insights that are still highly relevant today. He was interested in the practical morality that children work out in their interaction. They don't understand moral rules that are simply imposed on them by adults until they have worked them out themselves and understood the reasons for them. Indeed, children reconstruct moral principles in their practical interaction in cooperative relationships, and then they gradually become aware of them. Cooperative relationships develop among equals, so children are obliged to explain themselves and listen to the others—a situation best suited for reaching mutual understanding. They listen to their friends if they want to keep them and continue playing. In their negotiations children work out what is fair for everyone involved. This is similar to Mead's view of considering all perspectives, or Habermas's ideal speech situation. This is a balanced form of interaction because if one child is getting a bad deal in the resolution of some coordination of interests she can say, "that's not fair," until some resolution is reached that they are all happy with. In this sense the best resolution of the conflict of interests is a moral one that cannot be rejected because it is based on good reasons that are accepted by all.[29] So it is the logic of interaction that is important in the sense of coordinating interests to reach a balanced resolution. This cannot be overturned by particular interests because all the children have agreed.[30]

The position we have outlined might seem overly optimistic given the amount of injustice and oppression we see around us in the world every day. The world of human experience is moral but this doesn't mean that people are always nice to each other—far from it! As Kurt Vonnegut has noted, people can be nastier than we can believe as well as nicer than we can believe.[31] Clearly, moral decisions and actions do not always, or even often, occur. Cooperative interaction is not always, or perhaps is only rarely, fully achieved in actual relationships. Many other factors are involved that may reduce cooperation. But what requires an explanation is how it is that we can *recognize* injustice. It is this potential that gives us a source of moral norms and a way in which it is possible to evaluate moral decisions and actions, a way to decide if one decision is better than others. A resolution that includes more perspectives on a particular conflict is more complete, and therefore, preferable to others. This is a method or a moral process from which moral norms can emerge. Thus, we root thinking and morality in the natural world, which for humans is embedded in our social relations.

Suggested further reading

Carpendale, J. I. M. (2009). Piaget's theory of moral development. In U. Müller, J. I. M. Carpendale, & L. Smith (Eds.), *The Cambridge companion to Piaget* (pp. 270–286). Cambridge: Cambridge University Press.

Notes

1 Kant (2015, p. 1).
2 Jonas (1984). This was not a worry in the past when humans lacked the ability to change our environment to such an extent that it has a negative effect on future generations. More accurately, it is our awareness of how we transform our environments that has changed, due to the speed at which it now occurs. For thousands of years, humans have altered the landscape, but more recently the ability to do so has increased exponentially. This applies to water, air and our food supply, as well as driving other species to extinction. Perhaps a salient example is cutting down forests. Although reference to logging first appears in the historical record around 3000 BC, the process was slow. The UK for example, was once covered in forests. Denuding the land was at first highly labour intensive, a very slow process that took centuries, and there always seemed to be another country or another continent to log. This was before our planet was thought of as finite, a concept that, although perhaps intellectually grasped, still seems to elude our practical appreciation. By the late 1600s there were hundreds of sawmills operating in Eastern Canada and New England. Now a 200-ton tree, growing on the west coast of North America for over a thousand years, can potentially be felled and sent to a sawmill in under an hour. And smaller trees can be harvested in mere minutes. What can now be done by three people with modern machines would have taken a least a dozen fellers a day to accomplish in the 1930s. In 1890 it would have taken weeks, and a

hundred years earlier in 1790 would have taken months if it was even possible to fell such a large tree (Vaillant, 2005). By the 1920s most of New Zealand's vast Kauri forests had been cut down. Some of these trees were already growing when Jesus Christ was born. Of the few Kauri trees left, the largest named *Tane Mahuta* (Lord of the Forest), estimated to be between 1,250 and 2,500 years old, is visited by bus loads of tourists very day. In Joni Mitchell's words, "they took all the trees and put 'em in a tree museum." In fact, there is a fascinating museum in New Zealand devoted to Kauri trees. This is an example of just one way in which our ability to change our environment has accelerated (Vaillant, 2005).

3 This dimension of morality is becoming much clearer with current evidence regarding climate change. For example, Gwynne Dyer's (2008) book *Climate Wars* explains the effect of an increase in the average world temperature of two degrees. The estimated decrease in food production for India would be 25%! This means that a quarter of India's population—about 300 million—may go hungry. These are figures calculated for the World Bank, one of the most conservative institutions on the planet. The implications for China are even more shocking. These few figures, that are now out of date, emphasize just how the choices we make affect other people's lives and therefore are moral issues.

4 This expression is used to explain the problem of infinite regress. In a variant on a traditional Hindu myth that sixteenth- and seventeenth-century Western philosophers mused upon, if the earth is held in place on the back of a turtle, the answer to the question "What holds that turtle in place?" is a slightly larger turtle. The same answer is given to the question repeated an infinite number of times.

5 Deary (2014).

6 This was in New Zealand. Partial voting rights were granted in several countries before, including the Isle of Man in the UK in 1881.

7 Taika Waititi's *Jojo Rabbit* (2019) contains a similar set of moral dilemmas for a much younger child, treated in a much more ironic way.

8 Lawson et al. (2019).

9 Hegi (1994).

10 Shweder, Mahapatra, and Miller (1987).

11 Discussion of this point and the example of the Sweden can be found in Wikan (2008).

12 For example, Unni Wikan (2008) describes the case in Sweden in which a 26-year-old woman was killed by her father because she had chosen her own boyfriend and had walked with him in public. Her younger brother had tried to kill her earlier and had been jailed for threatening her. In fact, in some cases the whole family may be involved in the killing, and the brother may actually kill his sister because he may get a lighter jail sentence due to his younger age. However, we can see a response to this in a case in 2006 in Denmark in which nine people were found guilty in the murder of an 18-year-old girl. She had eloped with her boyfriend and her brother killed her two days later. The father had ordered the killing and was actually given the harshest sentence. This case contrasts with cases at about the same time in Germany and Sweden. In the case in Germany a young woman was killed by her three brothers because she had divorced her violent husband from an arranged marriage. In Sweden a young man was murdered by his girlfriend's

brother while the girl's parents watched or may have participated in this particularly brutal murder. In each of these cases one person was convicted and because of their youth they were given reduced sentences. In Canada a man and his wife are both on trial for killing their three daughters and the man's first wife. Their son is also charged in the murders. In a rare case in India, 8 community elders have been sentenced to death for their role in the torture and murder of a young couple and their friend 20 years previously. The girl was of high caste and the boy was from the untouchable caste. Various sources report that several hundred young couples are killed each year, when they break caste laws.

13 The evidence on aggression within couples does not exactly fit the stereotype: while men inflict more damage on their female partners, acts of aggression between the sexes are more common in females against males. See Archer (2000).

14 Bell (1968).

15 Stephen Lewis Foundation (2012).

16 Piaget's position from the 1930s, however, tends to be overlooked even though it is still highly relevant for current debates. This may be because it is thought that Kohlberg built on and extended Piaget's ideas, so they are assumed to be incorporated into Kohlberg's theory (Carpendale, 2009). Kohlberg's theory and research on moral reasoning has been very influential for decades, but it has also been heavily criticized for a number of reasons. In particular, it has been claimed that in focusing on reasoning Kohlberg neglected the role of emotions in morality.

17 Tesson and Youniss (1995, p. 106). That is, morality in everyday life rather than imposed in the abstract.

18 Piaget (1965).

19 This is a perennial problem discussed in psychology. For example, Maggie Bruck and Steven Ceci (1997) have been arguing for 20 years that we cannot trust children's accounts of events—for example, their testimony in court—because they are susceptible to misleading cues in the questions asked of them. The evidence shows that adults are equally as influenced by suggestive questions (Loftus et al., 1978) and that if asked questions that are not misleading children give very accurate accounts of events (Brown et al., 2013).

20 Mead (1934, p. 385).

21 These take different forms (Smith, 2006; von Wright, 1963), such as logical, social conventional and moral norms, each of which develop in different contexts. Logical norms involve necessary outcomes of coordinating our action on the world. Social conventions and rules of games are sets of agreements about coordination of action with others, such as agreeing what side of the road to drive on, and how to play chess. Moral norms involve situations of conflicting interests that could involve consequences for others.

22 Smith and Vonèche (2006).

23 Mead (1934, p. 379). Further: "On the one side stands the society which makes the self possible, and on the other side stands the self that makes a highly organized society possible. The two answer to each other in moral conduct" (Mead, 1934, pp. 385–386). "The method for taking into account all of those interests which make up society on the one hand and the individual on the other is the method of morality" (Mead, 1934, p. 389).

24 Habermas (1990).

25 Spaemann (2006).
26 Mead (1934, p. 379). In Mead's time it was not just acceptable to write using sexist terms, but it was prescribed.
27 In the causal world of natural science how do we find room for reasons? How is it that persons do things for reasons rather than causes? We are bound by norms and are obliged to explain and justify our actions. We live in a "space of reasons" (Forst, 2005, p. 67), yet this human space emerges from a causal world, if we attempt to root our explanation of human intelligence in the natural world. We are not machines; our actions are not caused in this way, we do things for reasons. How do we account for the emergence of the fact that humans live in a world of reasons, that is, we give and expect reasons from each other, we inhabit a "space of justifications." How is it that we come to live in a space of reasons, of justifications? We feel accountable to others, yet how did the potential for this second nature evolve and how does it develop? Our actions are meaningful. In fact, within interaction we are condemned to be meaningful (Heritage, 1984, p. 110; Merleau-Ponty, 1962). That is, whatever we do some meaning will be read into it.
28 Bowlby (1969).
29 Mead (1934).
30 It is a balanced resolution. Of course, this is a partial equilibrium, as all equilibria are partial. So logic has to do with the working of arguments but arguments and language are based on simpler forms of human life, and so we can look for the emergence of logic earlier on in interaction. For example, there is logic to how two people coordinate getting through a door or how they carry a table together, and so on.
31 Vonnegut (1997, p. 12).

Chapter 8

From molecules to minds
Can genes determine thinking?

In which we consider the role of genetics in human development, and analyze the role of the brain in human forms of thinking.

On October 12, 2008, Richard Garriott, a video game developer, is reputed to have paid 30 million US dollars to travel in a Soyuz spacecraft to the International Space Station, carrying with him a small memory device, which he dubbed "the immortality drive." On this micro-chip he had stored his own digitized DNA sequence as well as the sequences of a select group of people including video game players, musicians, the physicist Stephen Hawking, the comedian Stephen Colbert, the professional wrestler Matt Morgan (known as "The Beast"), and the cyclist Lance Armstrong, winner of the Tour de France a record seven consecutive times. This was before Armstrong was stripped of all seven titles for using performance-enhancing drugs. The only woman mentioned was the Playboy Playmate for that year, Jo Garcia, who is also a "gamer." Garriott's goal for this very expensive trip was to preserve human DNA sequences from what he viewed as an elite group of humans so that if some catastrophe should occur on the Earth this time capsule could be used to clone these individuals, and presumably gaming skills would also be preserved.

There are many difficulties with the assumptions behind Garriott's action, even before we consider subsequent revelations about exactly how Lance Armstrong won all those races. Garriott's choice of these individuals reveals what he values about their social contributions. His plan for the whole project reveals one theory of human development. Unfortunately for Garriott, his immorality, and that of the others, is not ensured simply by preserving their DNA sequences because the biology of getting from DNA to persons is actually far more complicated. In fact, his assumptions are based on a misunderstanding of how genes work. It is easy to see how this project might have been conceived, given the view of genes available in the public media. Even during the excitement of mapping the human genome many biologists were voicing the concern that discovering the sequence of amino acids across every gene on all the chromosomes is not sufficient to explain human development. The notion that genes contain information or a genetic program that determines development is still widespread today, especially in the popular press. However, these are views from the 1960s and 1970s,[1] and developmental biologists, geneticists and philosophers of biology are now claiming that we are in a "post genomic era" in which it is essential to recognize the importance of development in evolution. These and much older analyses suggest that genes are one part of a complex interactive developmental system. We need to take a closer look at the biology involved in order to understand the role of genes in development. To do so we start on an incredibly intricate voyage that begins with genes and culminates in persons. Of course, no one can provide a complete account of human development without a role for biology, but the story is much more complex than usually assumed. In fact, in the end we will see that it is not so easy to draw a sharp line between biology and social factors.

Instinct and innateness revisited

If our task in this book is to explain the development of thinking and minds, then couldn't we solve this problem by saying that human forms of thinking are just programmed into our genes? It is increasingly common for theorists to do this by claiming that traits and forms of thinking are innate, or "hard wired," or that humans are "endowed" with various forms of thinking,[2] "specified by our genetic program."[3] When the term "innate" is used in current debates the underlying assumption seems to be that there is some genetic mechanism that explains the human ability being referred to. Often the terms innate and genetic are treated as synonyms. This reference to the innateness of our skills resonates with the excitement about neuroscience and the mapping of the human genome. At the same time, however, some researchers are advising more caution, saying that even a rudimentary understanding of how genes actually work tells us that genes are one part of a complex system, which we can only understand by looking at the bigger picture.[4] To anticipate the conclusion from this part of the story, we believe that there is no simple short cut from genes to being human, and that instead the many strands of influence include our interactions with other people. To see this we need to examine the concepts of instinct and innateness.

The notion of instinct is ancient. It was described in Greek literature some 2,500 years ago and it is probably far older than that.[5] The origin of this idea in antiquity appears to be related to defining clear differences between humans and other species. The actions of humans were assumed to be based on reasoning, whereas animal behavior was instead thought to derive from simpler biological mechanisms.[6] The concepts of instinct and innateness seem to be a part of our everyday thinking, our folk wisdom.[7] The general notion is that some behavioral patterns are the result of the organism's intrinsic nature, whereas other characteristics are due instead to influences from the environment.[8] Older phrases expressing this notion of instinct, such as "bred in the bone" or "in the blood," have now been replaced in public discussions with "in the genes" or "in the DNA." For example, a hardware ("do it yourself") store advertisement in New Zealand reads, "DIY is in our DNA."

As well as having its roots in antiquity, the idea of innateness is also an everyday concept. The experience of having siblings who are different, or parents' experience if they have more than one child, provides everyday encounters with differences in the same family. Discussions often revolve around how a child acquired some ability with math, music or athletics. Did it come from her mother or her father? Or perhaps instead it was due to some important experience, such as an influential teacher.

The now-familiar terms, *nature* and *nurture*, were apparently introduced by Richard Mulcaster in 1582. Mulcaster, a British teacher, viewed nature and nurture as working together collaboratively in influencing the development of children.[9] This view of thinking about nature and nurture, unfortunately, has been eclipsed by the tendency to think of nature *versus* nurture separately as competing explanations. Sir Francis Galton in 1874 played a role in setting the two terms in opposition, starting a tradition that has continued ever since.[10] The Canadian biological psychologist and geneticist Michael Meaney argues, however, that the goal of understanding development is hindered by the "rather arcane notion that we can partition the cause of individual differences into distinct genetic *or* environmental spheres of influence."[11] Instead of separating nature versus nurture, we need to think about interactions because "the genome cannot possibly operate independent of its environmental context."[12]

The classic dichotomy between nature and nurture is remarkably persistent. It has been declared stone dead many times but, unfortunately, it continues to be resuscitated. Developmental resources, however, cannot be easily classified into nature or nurture.[13] And explanations of complex traits such as forms of thinking based on separating the influences of genes and environment are, in Meaney's words, "inconsistent with even the most rudimentary understanding of gene function."[14] Therefore, we need to gain at least a "rudimentary understanding" of how genes function in order to be able properly to assess current claims that various human traits are "innate."

Although psychologists often use the word "innate," it is not clear if there is, in fact, an agreed upon definition. The philosopher Matteo Mameli and biologist Patrick Bateson identified 26 different ways in which the term is used and found problems with all of them.[15] When psychologists use the word they generally mean biologically given and not influenced by the environment during development. The notion of innateness is generally considered antiquated and confused by biologists, but it is still used in psychology in explaining forms of thinking.[16] The phrase "hardwired" also seems to be used interchangeably with "innate." Sometimes used in quotation marks, to indicate that it is only used metaphorically, the "hardwired" reference derives from a computer's functions that are built into the hardware. Each machine comes from the factory that way and cannot be changed without replacement parts. This metaphor implies that here is no role for interaction with the environment in the constitution of thinking.

Steven Pinker's central claim about innateness, outlined in Chapter 1, is exemplified by statements such as: "We do not learn to have a pancreas, and we do not learn to have a visual system, language acquisition, common sense, or feelings of love, friendship, and fairness."[17] He equates human psychological processes with the functions of our vital organs. Even a sense of fairness develops in the same way as a heart or liver! But then on the next page he states, "But if the mind has a complex innate structure that does not mean that learning is unimportant."[18] In *How the Mind Works*, Pinker states that his "book is about the brain, but I will not say much about neurons, hormones, and neurotransmitters. That is because the mind is not the brain but what the brain does, and not even everything it does, such as metabolizing fat and giving off heat."[19]

We suggest that if Pinker had said more about the brain it would have ended up being a very different sort of book. His claims would not stand up to views from neuroscience about how the brain develops. We need to be better informed about neuroscience: "A basic knowledge of what genes can and cannot do is necessary to constrain and inform hypotheses about how genetic variability may relate to cognitive variability."[20] Pinker does note, in passing, that these modules or mental organs do have to be "assembled." Of course, he does have to acknowledge this rather obvious point that development must occur, yet in doing so he leaves open the questions of how this happens and the importance of the process. This is an obvious point, but overlooking it obscures its central importance. In fact, no traits are present in the fertilized egg—the zygote—they all have to develop. But Pinker never returns to spelling out how that actually happens. We suggest that pulling this hanging thread would unravel his whole position and change it into quite a different approach. If Pinker is serious in his claim that human children do not have to learn about fairness, and that such psychological abilities simply grow like an arm or a leg, he has a complex task ahead of him to explain how this actually happens. But it is not something he even bothers to hint at, it is simply assumed that it is in fact possible. The implications of this point are what we spell out in this book. We have used these researchers as examples, but their general approach is also endorsed by many others.

The approaches taken by Pinker and others like Leda Cosmides and John Tooby put development in a black box.[21] The logic of their argument is that the leap from genes to thinking is unproblematic. Placing the mysterious processes of development into such a box allows them to avoid an explanation.[22] We, as developmental psychologists, want to look inside their black box to unpack the complexity involved. There is a further reason for doing so, beyond the fact that development is our area of expertise. We need to bring these processes out into the light of day to examine them in order to determine if they are actually biologically plausible.

It might seem that claims about innate forms of thinking are rooted in biology and so they therefore gain some cachet. In fact, however, the more we know about neuroscience the less likely it seems that supposed innate modules can simply be determined by genes. The emerging field of evolutionary developmental biology takes development seriously and assumes that it is necessary to explain the developmental processes that contribute to the construction of a trait during development. Indeed, this is not a new line of thinking. The Canadian psychologist Donald Hebb argued, over 50 years ago, that theorists who propose explanations requiring innate modules for thinking should have some obligation to determine if, in fact, this claim is biologically possible.[23]

It is unlikely, of course, that any scientists are completely hard-core genetic determinists; everyone must acknowledge that the environment (or more specifically that the organism's interaction with factors in their environment) also plays a role. However, this may be acknowledged as an aside, and the importance of that role may be underestimated and overlooked. What is more consistent with biology in this "post genomic" era is that the idea of genes as stable inner entities and the environment as a pre-existing outer force breaks down when we see how particular aspects of the environment play a role in turning genes on and off, and how the organism influences the environment being experienced.

Recent analyses of the interactions between genes and the environment have suggested that these are complex. For example, Marian Bakermans-Kranenburg and Marinus Van IJzendoorn have conducted a series of meta-analyses of studies which examined children with identifiable genetic mutations influencing the important neurotransmitters serotonin and dopamine, which are vital for several brain functions including attention, motivation memory and reward. Their work suggests that children with these mutations are susceptible to behavioral problems if their parents are inconsistent or controlling. But, if their parents are nurturant then they are less susceptible to these behavioral problems and can do very well.[24] These differences have been discussed with the metaphor of children characterized as dandelions who do reasonably well in a range of circumstances, in contrast to orchid children who do very poorly in stressful environments, but flourish in enriched supportive conditions. This metaphor has been taken up in the popular press, and although it is helpful in understanding the results it implies that a child is either a dandelion or an orchid, whereas in contrast to this categorical view it is actually continuous and children vary in how much they are dandelion or orchid-like.[25] Given that Bakermans-Kranenburg and Van IJzendoorn published analyses which pool the data from thousands of children we can be fairly confident that the patterns they demonstrate reveal interesting and unexpected interactions between genes and environmental influences.

Our goal is to overcome the unhelpful dichotomy between genes and environment, or nature and nurture. We want to bring in more recent work in biology emphasizing the many levels of interacting factors involved in development—there is much more than simply "genes and environment." We have to consider a whole developmental system within which children develop—and a critical part of this system involves interacting with other people. We feel that we would understand the patterns identified by Bakermans-Kranenburg and Van IJzendoorn were we to add this constructivist perspective to their interesting data.

Studying twins

Twins, especially those who are identical or "monozygotic," who share the same genotype, have been studied closely to separate the effects of genes and the environment.[26] The topic has been of great interest in the popular press, where research is portrayed to provide convincing evidence that genes determine outcomes such as personality. There are famous examples of identical twins reared apart who nevertheless seem to be very similar.[27] One of the best-known examples is the so-called

"Jim Twins" widely reported in the media in 2014.[28] These twins, Jim Lewis and Jim Springer, appear to have an unusual set of similarities, including their career choice, the names of their wives and children, and even both the brand of beer they drink and the cigarettes they smoke. Another well-publicized case of twins is the brothers Oskar Stöhr and Jack Yufe, which may help us to understand these case studies a little better.[29] They were born in 1933, but their parents separated and Oskar was raised by his mother in Germany as a Catholic and Nazi. Jack lived his father in Trinidad as a Jew, also spending time in Israel on a kibbutz. Despite their different lives, however, an amazing set of similarities was evident when they arranged to see each other. At an airport they were both wearing wire-rimmed glasses and similar shirts. They found out that they both liked spicy food, were absent-minded and kept rubber bands on their wrists. The fact that this sounds like a Hollywood movie may not be a coincidence. What is not mentioned is that the brothers had met before. Indeed, they had been in contact for 25 years. Furthermore, they sold their life stories to a Hollywood producer, suggesting that they may have had a financial interest in emphasizing their "coincidental" sameness. Similarities can be found between any pair of people if one spends enough time at it, especially if they were born at the same time, as twins obviously are. We should take a more careful look at evidence than is given by newspapers whose interest is more in selling papers than reporting science.

The idea behind twin studies is that if those who are separated at birth and grow up apart end up being similar, this indicates that their personality must be mostly genetic. It has long been thought that identical twins with very similar genes who are raised in different environments, provide us with an ideal research design for separating the effects of genes and environment—"a natural experiment." But such situations are rare. Most twins grow up together for several years, or they are raised either by members of the same family or by adoptive parents in similar social and economic circumstances. In addition, such twins were often aware of each other's existence and have frequent contact. In one review of 121 cases of separated twins, only 3 cases were separated in the first year of their life and did not know that they had a twin.[30] One flaw in this sort of research is that it is often because of the similarity between the twins and the fact that they have known about each other that researchers become aware of them. Many twins are found through appeals in the media, which requires that they know about each other. In fact, in one early study in 1937 pairs of twins who were not similar in personality were not included in the study due to the expense of transporting the twins to Chicago.[31] The attraction of an all-expenses-paid trip to Chicago during the depression might have been a motivation for twins to exaggerate their similarity. The researchers were aware of this problem and after the initial study they attempted to recruit more twins. For example, they corresponded with one twin who was interested in being in the study but his brother was described as a "hoodlum" and he refused to cooperate. This illustrates the point that twins who are different are not so likely to agree to become involved in this type of research. In these studies, researchers may have thus unknowingly selected for similar twins in their study.

These potential flaws in the way many twin studies are conducted make it difficult to draw firm conclusions. There are differences between the results of the studies and what reaches the newspapers. The cases in which the twins are quite different in personality are not so well reported, perhaps they are considered less newsworthy. Twins also share far more than the same genes. They have many biological factors in common including the environment within the womb.[32] These concerns should not cloud the influence of genes. When large studies of monozyotic and dizygotic (identical vs fraternal) twins are compared, the identical twins show a greater consistency than fraternal ones. This amounts to about 40% for personality attributes and 60% for more specific higher order skills like self-control.[33] Even this higher figure leaves 40% to be explained only by the factors that we discus here and the influence of the child may not be direct—genes may express themselves in behavioral characteristics that elicit particular responses from and interactions with care-givers.

What do genes do?

We now turn to examine the claim that forms of thinking are the output of innate modules, and that the "modules' basic logic is specified by our genetic program."[34] What is the connection between genetics and the "modules", which nativist theorists argue are essential mechanisms responsible for thinking? We need to take a close look at what genes actually do. The popularity of The Human Genome Project and the widespread use of the metaphor in the popular press reveals the common view of genes as containing "instructions" or information in a "program." Now that we have mapped a human genome do we know how to build a person? No. It's worth unpacking this metaphor to develop a more complex understanding of the role of genes in development. If we have a master chef's shopping list this does not enable us to produce the meal she could prepare. Similarly, having a list of building materials or being surrounded by stacks of lumber does not give us a vision of a building an architect might have designed, nor does having sheet music alone necessarily help without a concert pianist to interpret it. And yet even these are misleadingly simple analogies because they cannot touch the complexity of getting from genes and molecules to minds and thinking. Genes are obviously crucially important, but they are one part in a complex system. Suppose, for a moment, we take the blueprint metaphor seriously. Blueprints still have to be interpreted by an experienced builder; they would be relatively meaningless to someone lacking experience with the processes and materials involved in construction. It is not just a straightforward process to go from the architect's ideas, sometimes imperfectly portrayed in the plans, to the final house. Modifications may occur on the way due to many facts such as availability of materials and so on. So how does the need for an interpreter fit into the blueprint metaphor for genes? The metaphor is misconceived, and any theory requiring such an interpreter is a non-starter.

In fact, genes are far less than blueprints. They do not specify how the various parts actually go together. Genes are involved in forming proteins so it could be said that they are more like a shopping list of the materials needed to construct the structure, like a list of bricks, mortar and lumber. Even here, however, we are overplaying their role because genes are turned on and off by various factors from the level of the cell to forms of social experience. So, if we continue with the building metaphor, then genes are more like a catalogue for the local hardware store or building supply. DNA is involved in the production of RNA molecules, which result in sequences of amino acids produced in the cell. But this is still not everything that is required to produce particular proteins. The folding of the polypeptides into three-dimensional proteins necessary for proper functioning is not specified by the DNA. The correct folding depends on the typical conditions within the cell,[35] and misfolding may result in diseases. We are not suggesting the hardware store catalog as a replacement for the ideas of a blueprint. Instead we are exploring the weaknesses of these metaphors. We are not reducing the leading role usually given to genes to a mere bit part. Indeed our crude metaphor must not obscure the key role played by genes; they are an essential part in an exceedingly complex system. But our goal is to bring out the equally important parts played by many other aspects of this intricate system.

It seems that in psychology an implication of claiming that something is inherited is that it is "genetic," or simply encoded in the genome. But, as Michael Meaney points out, this is so,

> only if one assumes that there are no other biological mechanisms for inheritance. This is simply untrue. There are multiple potential

mechanisms of inheritance, involving, for example, the passage of epigenetic marks through the germline, the passage of maternal RNA molecules into the embryo, the potential passage of prion proteins from parent to offspring, the biochemical state of the gametes at the time of conception, and the transmission of nutrients, bacteria, or antibodies from maternal circulation to that of the offspring, and so on.[36]

Even though all the cells in our body are genetically identical, they develop very differently in different parts of our body. We are sitting on cells that we could be thinking, or seeing, with if they had developed in other parts of our body. Despite being made up of genetically identical building blocks, different organs such as the liver and the brain produce only cells of the appropriate type.[37] The same point applies to behavior. The queen bee and worker bees in the same hive may have the same genome, but they develop and behave in extremely different ways depending on the amount and quality of food they are given. These aspects of the environment influence the expression of a series of genes.[38] The Jekyll and Hyde transformation of certain species of grasshoppers into locusts provides another example.

As a further example of the interaction between genes and environment, consider a strain of mice that was selected to be aggressive. After the process of artificially selecting aggressive individual mice and breeding them for successive generations these mice were more aggressive than other mice. It might be assumed that they have "aggressive genes." However, even after 39 generations when these mice were raised with other mice, rather than in isolation, they were not aggressive.[39] This emphasizes the important role that the rearing environment plays in a trait such as aggression.

How can we expand our psychological imagination to avoid the simple explanations that genes are blueprints? Here we merely want to point out the many levels of interaction that rule out explanations assuming that thinking can be simply "innate" or "hardwired." Such is the complexity of these links between genes and behavior, that we cannot say that genes *determine* traits. Instead they are one of many crucially important factors in a developmental system. In the words of the neuroscientist Simon Fisher:

> Genes do not specify behaviours or cognitive processes; they make regulatory factors, signalling molecules, receptors, enzymes, and so on, that interact in highly complex networks, modulated by environmental influences, in order to build and maintain the brain. I

propose that it is necessary for us to fully embrace the complexity of biological systems, if we are ever to untangle the webs that link genes to cognition.[40]

There is a strong tendency to overlook these tangled webs because there are deep roots to the intuition that some characteristics deriving from an animal's biology are independent of the environment and so must be genetic.[41] But these roots are not scientific. This fundamental assumption has survived a half-century of critique and evidence.[42] To dispel the tendency to think in this way, consider some examples of the influence of environmental factors. For instance, sex might be considered to be innate and determined by genes. But in turtles, sex is determined by the temperature at which the eggs are incubated. For some species eggs that are incubated at about 30°C develop into females, whereas those incubated below this temperature develop into males.[43] Although this system has worked well through evolutionary millennia, it may become problematic with climate change and warming temperatures. As we have mentioned, in bees, whether the larvae develop into workers or queens, vastly different in size and behavior, depends on their rearing history. These aspects of the environment influence the expression of a series of genes.

The interplay between genes and the environment can be very complex. For example, in rats maternal licking of their pups influences the regulation of genes which are involved in the newborn's brain development. The amount of that licking is influenced by the level of stress experienced by the mother. We might also consider that the ability of male rats to use their penis to copulate is "innate," but this does not mean that it is determined only by genes. Instead it is caused by a typical aspect of the environment in which rat pups develop—their mother's licking. Differences in the amount that mothers lick the genital area of male and female pups influences the gene expression of the rat pups' developing spinal cord. This differential licking is influenced by the male pups excreting more of a chemical that elicits maternal licking. These examples show the complex interaction of many levels of factors in development in addition to genes, including several aspects of the environment. It is also clear that the influences between these levels are bidirectional.[44]

These examples undermine an oft-held assumption that evolution makes development reliable by being insensitive to the environment. In fact, developmental biologists argue that reliable development can be due to consistency in the environment.[45] But this is an interactional process—as we see in the example of maternal licking in rats, aspects of the organism may influence aspects of the environment.

The blueprint metaphor of genes is an attempt to understand the regular outcomes of development, but perhaps there are alternative analogies. Consider an example from environmental biology. The outcome of mature forests tends to be consistent given similar contexts of development. But we can't say that there are genes for forests! So how do we explain their regular development? Let's consider a temperate example. After a forest fire in some regions of the northwest coast of North America, one of the first species to re-colonize the land is fireweed. These plants are followed by low shrubs, and then deciduous trees, such as maples. But because of the shade produced by these trees, only certain species of trees, tolerant of shade, can thrive. These are Douglas fir and, especially, western red cedar and western hemlock. Along the pacific coast, a series of mature forests end up consisting of primarily cedar and hemlock. This is a fairly consistent pattern in the development of a mature forest in some bio-geo-climatic zones in this part of the world, yet nothing about this predictable outcome is specified in the genes of any of the species involved. Rather the common pattern is a natural outcome of the changing conditions produced by each interacting specie's characteristics. There is a relatively stable outcome given the regularity of the environment and the way factors within it interact. The example of ecological succession provides an alternative analogy[46] that may facilitate seeing that there can be stability in the outcome of development even if this is not pre-existing in genes. Instead, it emerges through interaction among species with a stable typical environment.

From molecules to minds

The phrase, "A gene for ..." has become common in the popular press. We hear about a gene for language, a gene for intelligence, a gene for obesity, a gene for impulsivity, and so on. This phrase, although widely used, is also highly misleading. Reflecting on the example of behavioral problems, Michael Meaney remarks that these statements "drive many scientists slightly mad, since the data are merely correlational and do not imply a cause-effect relation between the genomic variant and conduct disorder."[47] That is, particular genes may be more commonly found with certain disorders but this does not imply that they are simply a direct cause of the disorder. The story may be considerably more complex. The story of the FOXP2 gene and its role in language illustrates this problem. There is strong evidence that this gene is linked to language. But this still does not mean that it is a "gene for language" because it is also involved in the development of lungs and other processes. Furthermore, other species such as mice also have a gene that is very similar, yet mice do not develop anything like a propensity for symbolic communication—except in Disney cartoons. The bottom line is that genes perform a role in making molecules, and we have to get from those molecules to minds.[48]

To gain an appreciation of the role of DNA in the biology of cells, Meaney suggests that we begin with an example of just one gene to show its incredible complexity.[49] He focuses on the gene that codes for the glucocorticoid receptor, which is present in every cell. This gene can have dramatically different effects in different types of cells. Glucocorticoids are hormones secreted by the adrenal cortex. They bind to the glucocorticoid receptors in the cell. When they are not bound to glucocorticoids the glucocorticoid receptor is found in the cytoplasm of the cell associated with a chaperone protein. A glucocorticoid binding to the glucocorticoid receptor becomes dissociated with the "chaperone protein" (which it has bonded with) and instead becomes associated with a different protein. This pair then moves into the nucleus of the cell where the glucocorticoid can now bind to certain sites on the DNA. Where this new binding occurs will influence different processes in the cell such as those involved in cardiovascular activity, appetite, metabolism, immune responses, and electrolyte balance. The activated glucocorticoid receptor can also become associated with other factors, called cofactors, which change the effect it can have on the DNA. The cofactor may just influence the size of the effect on the DNA, but it can also change the genes that the activated glucocorticoid receptor acts on, so it may function very differently depending on what cofactor it is associated with. In fact, depending on the type of cell in which this binding takes place, the activated glucocorticoid receptor can have different influences, even opposite effects! For example, Meaney explains that, "activation of the glucocorticoid receptor promotes cell survival in liver cells but activates apoptosis (cell death) in thymocytes."[50]

The glucocorticoid receptor can also influence the DNA and how the cell functions in other ways. For example, it can be involved in decreasing inflammation because it binds to a protein, stopping that protein from accessing DNA targets that are involved in the activation of inflammatory responses. But this only works when there is an increase in those proteins which activate inflammation. The glucocorticoid receptor gene may be active in almost every cell in the body but with very different functions. In fetal mammals it is important in the transition to breathing air, but in the brain of more mature individuals the activation of glucocorticoid receptors is linked to a decrease in the generation of neurons and the ability for the connections between neurons to change in strength. In addition, the same gene can produce different versions of the glucocorticoid receptor, which in some contexts can have different effects.

So, the gene for this protein has many functions depending on the type of cell in which it is active. In fact, we have only scratched the surface of the complexity of just this one gene by focusing on the level of protein interactions in the cell. Many other effects emerge as we move up the levels of complexity.[51] The gene can only be understood as it functions within a particular cellular environment. This provides just a taste of the incredible complexity and the interaction of multiple factors in developmental outcomes.

The bottom line here seems to be that the role of genes in development is amazingly complicated! According to Douglas Adams, the author of the *Hitchhiker's Guide to the Galaxy*, there is a theory that as soon as we completely understand the universe it will instantly be replaced by one that is infinitely more complex. And there is another theory that this has already happened![52] An important lesson for our task of accounting for the development of human thinking is to be aware of the multiple levels of interacting factors in the developmental system, and in the case of human thinking to consider the essential role of social interaction.

The effect of interactions between genes and the environment is vividly illustrated in classic research with rhesus monkeys by Stephen Suomi and his colleagues. Their studies examined the interaction between type of rearing and serotonin, a neurotransmitter involved in the regulation of emotional behavior. The serotonin transporter gene produces a protein that regulates the amount of serotonin in the synapses, and so influences interaction between neurons. One version of this gene is linked to problems during infancy and poor control of aggression. But this negative outcome is only found when these monkeys are separated from their mothers and reared by peers. The negative outcome is not found when monkeys with the same gene are reared with their mothers and peers during infancy, again showing how genes interact with experience in development.[53] We have discussed recent research on genes and human behavior at the start of this chapter showing that humans are influenced by the same processes.

Instinct and eggs

This brief summary of recent research in genetics and neuroscience shows that there is no simple way of identifying links between the molecular operations of DNA and human behavior or thinking. Instead there are multiple levels of interacting factors. But what about the idea of instinct that we started the chapter with? Aren't some animals simply driven by a biological imperative? The idea of instinct and behavior being "innate" or "inherited" was assumed by the famous ethologists Konrad Lorenz and Niko Tinbergen. What they meant was that instinctive behavior is characteristic and typical of a species, and it is evident even if individuals are raised in isolation so that there is no opportunity for learning. This view was criticized decades ago by Daniel Lehrman and others.[54] One of Lehrman's examples was the pecking of chicks. Soon after hatching, domestic chicks peck at objects such as grains of food, and they show this behavior even if they are raised in isolation. This action consists of the coordination of the head lunging forward, the bill opening and closing, and swallowing. This seems like an excellent example of what Lorenz would consider instinctive behavior. More recently Noam Chomsky stated that this is genetically determined.[55] However, such claims are made without the benefit of any research. In fact, Lehrman turned to a careful analysis of research done by Zing-Yang Kou decades ago on the embryonic development of chicks. By painstakingly opening a window on the egg, Kou was able to observe development inside the shell. At three days of age the chick's heart begins to beat, causing its head to move forward and back. This research showed that the chick's pecking action is actually the outcome of complex development before the chick hatches. Thus, this characteristic behavior is the typical outcome of the embryo's development within the constraints of its usual environment. It is the chick's development within a rigid eggshell that is one of essential the factors for this typical behavior, and this is the result of much more than genetics. Something like an eggshell—a consistent aspect of the environment—is not usually thought to play a role in development.[56]

This example shows that a typical aspect of development need not be encoded in the genome, which in any case does not seem possible. Instead, it is the outcome of a complex process of interaction among many interacting factors including aspects of the typical environment of development inside and outside the egg. As another example consider Mallard ducklings following their mothers' calls. This is a reliable behavior that does not seem to be learned. The ducklings follow maternal vocalizations even if they have not heard these calls when they were still in the egg, so they apparently have no opportunity to learn about this. However, the ducklings themselves make sounds while they are still in the egg, and it turns out that this is essential. If they are "devocalized" while they are in the egg so that they no longer make these sounds, then they no longer follow their mother's calls.[57] This shows the important role of aspects of the duckling's experience that might be easily overlooked, and it underlines the importance of the whole developmental system including the genes.[58]

Constructing the brain

So how do we get from the fertilized egg to the incredible complexity of the human brain? Even a single cubic millimeter of cortex contains about 100,000 neurons. Then, if we consider the interconnections between these neurons—synapses—there are about 1,000,000.[59] In a whole human brain there are more than 100 billion neurons and the number of synapses may be as much as 10^{14}. That is a one followed by fourteen zeros! This number is so vast it is hard to conceptualize. To gain some appreciation for the degree of interconnectivity, think of a single synapse as represented by a grain of sand a millimeter square, it would take a box with sides of 100 yards—a cubic football field—to contain all this sand.[60]

The incredibly interconnectivity of the human brain is far too intricate to be fully specified by genetics.[61] Although there is debate about what a gene is, there are perhaps about 20,000 to 30,000 genes in the human genome,[62] and up to about 20,000 of these may be involved in the development and maintenance of the central nervous system.[63] If we think of the genome as containing information, which we have shown is not correct, there would not be enough stored "information" to specify the interconnections in an adult brain—it is far too complex. Instead, the brain is shaped during development,[64] and this shaping takes place through the infant's and child's experience, a large part of which is social.

A second difficulty emerges from the problem that brains have become more complex in various species, but the number of genes has not increased at the same rate.[65] Although human brains are much more complex than those of mice, the total amount of DNA in the cells of the two species is, paradoxically, about the same: "over evolution the number of genes has not kept pace with the increasing complexity of the brain: while the total amount of DNA per cell is roughly the same between mouse and human, the human brain is far more complex."[66]

How is this possible if it is genes that spell out the structure of the brain? It is necessary to think about how our nervous system develops. Human brains increase in size by four times from birth to maturity and this continues over more than twenty years. This involves growth of the cell bodies. There is also considerable change in the connections between neurons (synapses), both a pruning of connections and also an increase in synapses after birth.[67]

Some aspects of the growth of neurons depend on their activity, on the pattern and duration of their electrical stimulation. This fits with Donald

O. Hebb's slogan that "neurons that fire together wire together." That is, they form stronger interconnections. From this neuroconstructivist perspective, "brain and environment are essential components of the same system, coupled together in time."[68]

Given the dramatic structural changes that take place, the brain a baby is born with still has a great deal of development and shaping to occur.[69] There is a tendency to assume that language, for example, is located in a particular part of the left hemisphere of the brain. But this is only in the majority of adults. In others, especially left handed individuals, language can be located in the right hemisphere, and in yet other individuals it can distributed across both hemispheres.[70] Language is only typically located in a particular area of the left hemisphere of the brain because that area appears to be well suited for processing this sort of information, and thus, language develops in that brain region. In Elizabeth Bates's words, that area of the left hemisphere tends to "win the language contract." However, if young children experience damage to that part of the brain, or even if they lose their entire left hemisphere, they tend to develop language in other parts of their brain.[71] Whether such children's language abilities are different from other children is still debated, but they don't tend to have obvious deficiencies in communication. Even the claim that language is located in particular parts of the left hemisphere is not so straightforward. Although these areas may be essential for particular aspects of language, language is a complex facet of being human that draws on many skills, some of which will be distributed across other parts of the brain.[72]

Do neurons know? Looking for thinking in the brain

How should we think about the role of the brain in thinking? The philosopher Patricia Churchland began a recent article entitled "How do neurons know?" with the statement that, "My knowing *anything* depends on my neurons—the cells of my brain."[73] In a sense, of course, this must necessarily be true; without neurons her knowing would not be possible. The question, however, is that although neurons are necessary for knowing, are they sufficient to explain this capability? It appears to be commonly assumed that it is possible to explain thinking just by studying the brain, but we argue that her knowing would also not be possible without the rest of her body and other people to interact with as well as her brain.

The brain has now taken the place of the soul. The split between mind and body inherited from Descartes has now been transformed into brain and body. Through history other organs have played this master role. In ancient Egypt it was the heart that was assumed to rule the body. The early Chinese thought that the liver and the lungs were also important in addition to the heart.[74] Although in Western cultures the brain is considered important, in other cultures the nose is far more significant. The sense of smell is important for the Ongee of the South Pacific whose lives are centered around smell, so much so that their identity is linked to their nose and when greeting someone what they say translates as, "How is your nose?"[75]

This focus on the brain implies that other parts of the body are good to have but are not essential. Particularly with advances in surgery, we can replace them but not our brains, which do the thinking and control our bodies. In directing the body, the brain is like a manager and is the source of identity. There is some truth to this. A brain is obviously necessary, but does having one explain everything about what it means to be human? Of course, it is linked to other parts through the nervous system, but when we shift to the psychological language of the brain "telling" other parts what to do, we set up a dualism between brain and body and end up in a paradox (of how to explain the divide).

Reports of neuroscience research in the popular press that we described in Chapter 1 are presented as "hard science," but some of this research is primarily a redescription of what we already know.[76] For example, if we know that people who have experienced loss show more blood flow to the nucleus accumbens when they look at pictures of their loved one who has died[77] this may turn out to be a useful piece of information, but it doesn't tell us much more about the nature of devastating grief. Only combined with other knowledge can this contribute to our understanding of this powerful human emotion.

There seems to be greater confidence in evidence that appears to be biological. In one study, women who reported loving chocolate rated seeing and tasting it as more pleasurable then women who did not report the same craving. The sight and taste of chocolate activates the craver's brain's reward system more than it does in people who do don't report such desires.[78] Have we really learned anything new with this expensive research? Yet this is considered news worth publishing and reporting in the *Guardian*. If *no* difference had been found the two groups of women, there must be something wrong with the equipment. There is no explanation here yet, just a correlation between brain activity and desire. We don't need an expensive brain scan to know that people who crave chocolate like eating it. Knowing what parts of their brain are active doesn't explain this, it just gives another level of description. Of course, such re-descriptions when combined with other knowledge may increase our understanding of human neuroscience, but this is about the location of activity rather than the nature of thinking itself.

In an article in *Discover* magazine David Eagleman discussed what he referred to as the "10 unsolved mysteries of the brain," stating that one of the top questions yet to be answered by neuroscience is, "how does the brain think?"[79] We think that this is a misleading question. Indeed, its phrasing produces a mystery. Brains don't think, people do.[80] They (brains, that is) are part of a system. In fact, only during an autopsy do they exist in isolation from a body in interaction.[81] Some activities of a person are described as thinking. Of course, brains are necessary to do anything, including thinking, but that does not mean that we should look for thinking only there, any more than we should look for morality in the hand. After all, it is the hand that holds the sword or the pen, the murder weapon or the judge's gavel. Yet for all of this we would think that it is misguided to look for a moral muscle in the finger that pulls the trigger. And we don't put hands on trial. In some cultures thieves have their hand cut off, but this is to punish the person, not just to stop that hand from stealing again. People, but not just their brains, can be said to think and make judgements and decisions.[82]

Perhaps this way of talking about the brain thinking is just harmless shorthand, and everyone knows that brains are embedded in bodies, which are, in turn, embedded within complex social networks. Although this may be true for some researchers, philosophers have warned us that the way we ask our questions already contains the form of possible answers that are acceptable.

"Of all the objects in the universe," states David Eagleman, "the human brain is the most complex: There are as many neurons in the brain as there are stars in the Milky Way Galaxy."[83] Perhaps all scientists think that what they study is the most complex thing in the universe. It is not, however, only the sheer number of neurons that excites neuroscientists, but rather the incredible complexity of the interconnections among these neurons. The brain certainly is incredibly complex, but consider for a moment the additional complexity of interconnections when we examine the brain as embedded within the body, which is embedded in the physical, social, cultural and historical world. Now the complexity of the interconnections explodes exponentially. It is this input from the environment that shapes the processes in the brain, which in turn is the organ that supports our social relations.

Neuroscience and psychology: The role of the brain

To avoid any possible misunderstanding, we strongly emphasize that, of course, there must be an extremely important side of the story from neuroscience in accounting for the development of thinking. But the move from molecules to minds or from genes to thinking is convoluted and torturous. By stressing the role of interacting with others, the neuroscience story must involve the construction of neural pathways. This is "neuroconstructivism."[84]

Although neuroscience is centrally important in a complete account of human thinking, we need to be cautious in evaluating this work because several psychological assumptions have usually already been incorporated within the theoretical bases and conclusions of this work. These tend to be invisible. This theory is, usually, the information processing framework, which we critique in the next chapter. Our students often insist that "there must be processing!" In one sense this is, of course, necessarily true. That is, when we interact with the world, and think about our world of experience neural activity will occur, but the connection to thinking is not straightforward.

A similar problem arises from a version of the information processing framework in which the mind is depicted as a computer. Thinking is also depicted as processing in a sequence consisting of input as sensing, then processing, and then output. However, the metaphor of the brain or mind as a computer rests on the false equation of the way in which "information" is processed in each system. Throughout this book we have pointed out problems with the information processing framework and we have argued for an alternative way of conceptualizing human thinking. The brain does not passively store and processes information. The perspective we have presented in this book is that the brain and the whole nervous system links us with the world of experience. It allows children to learn about outcomes of their actions and to anticipate what is coming up next.

We perceive the world in terms of potential action plans. When we are teaching someone to drive and we are approaching a stop sign, we see it in terms of putting our foot on the brake. This doesn't work on the passenger's side of the car, but my wife (CL) can be seen quite visibly to apply the brake when I drive her, even though I've been driving for 35 years. In research from this perspective, when ballet dancers watch ballet performances the motor areas of their brains involved in those physical movements are activated.[85] Human brains enable the social activity on which human thinking is based, they allow individuals to master this social process as an individual function and they facilitate social understanding through shared experience.

Conclusion

In this chapter we have turned from presenting an account of the development of human thinking to considering competing approaches. Given their prominence in contemporary discourse, we have critically examined claims about the role of biology in human development. We began this section of the book by evaluating claims that human forms of thinking are innate in the sense of being determined by genes. We have reviewed recent work in biology suggesting that although genes are a crucial part of developmental systems they don't determine anything by themselves. Instead they play a role in a bi-directional process in which individuals interact with aspects of the environment.

In examining the actual biology of the journey from genes to minds it becomes clear that this is a very complicated route. Although our biological systems obviously play an essential part in an explanation for human thinking, they do not provide the whole story: "Genes do not (and indeed cannot) *specify* particular behavioral outputs or cognitive processes, except in the most indirect way."[86] And, therefore, "We ignore at our peril the existence of molecular and ontogenetic[87] complexity and the importance of developmental context."[88] Others who have reviewed recent biology and neuroscience agree that "the routes linking genes to cognition will inevitably be tortuous."[89] In this chapter we have shown that the complexity of the developmental context includes many levels of interacting factors. An unfortunate consequence of the claim that some characteristics are innate is that it shuts down the search for an explanation instead of encouraging such research. We need to look more broadly at other factors in the developmental system leading to human thinking.

This close look at the biology involved in the development of various human traits has brought to light the complex developmental systems involved and the role that aspects of the environment play in such development. It is not just the existence of genes directing the show but rather the regulated expression of genes. For our topic of the development of thinking it is necessary to further examine the role of the environment, in particular the effect of humans interacting with others.[90]

The developmental environment consists of all the factors from the level of cells, tissues, and hormones to ecological and social factors. A number of theoreticians using different approaches are now putting development back into evolution, such as developmental systems theory,[91] niche construction theory,[92] and evolutionary developmental biology.[93] It is now necessary to enlarge the perspective to include evolution and the context in which development occurs—the developmental environment. And this is only the start of the problem of getting from neural activity in the brain to thinking.

Suggested further reading

Fuchs, T. (2011). The brain—a mediating organ. *Journal of Consciousness Studies*, 18, 196–221.

Gottlieb, G., (2007). Probablistic epigenesis. *Developmental Science*, 10, 1–11.

Mareschal, D., Johnson, M. H., Sirois, S., Spratling, M. W., Thomas, M. S. C., & Westermann, G., (2007). *Neuroconstructivism: How the brain constructs cognition, vol. 1*. New York: Oxford University Press.

Meaney, M. J. (2010). Epigenetics and the biological definition of gene x environment interactions. *Child Development*, 81, 41–79.

Spencer, J. P., Blumberg, M. S., McMurray, B., Robinson, S. R., Samuelson, L. K., & Tomblin, J. B. (2009). Short arms and talking eggs: Why we should no longer abide the nativist-empiricist debate. *Child Development Perspectives*, 3, 79–87.

Stiles, J. (2009). On genes, brains, and behavior: Why should developmental psychologists care about brain development? *Child Development Perspectives*, 3, 196–202.

Notes

1 See Stiles (2009); Stiles, Brown, Haist, and Jernigan (2015).
2 Mikhail (2007); Hauser (2006a, 2006b).
3 Pinker (1997).
4 Cobb (2020); Meaney (2010).
5 Beach (1955).
6 Beach (1955).
7 Mameli and Bateson (2006, 2011).
8 Griffiths (2009).
9 West and King (1987).
10 West and King (1987); see also Spencer et al. (2009).
11 Meaney (2010, p. 41, emphasis in original).
12 Meaney (2010, p. 42).
13 Stotz (2008).
14 Meaney (2010, p. 69).
15 Mameli and Bateson (2006).
16 Griffiths (2009).
17 Pinker (1997, p. 31).
18 Pinker (1997, p. 32).
19 Pinker (1997, p. 24).
20 Fisher (2006, p. 291).
21 Pinker (1997); Cosmides and Tooby (2013).
22 Wereha and Racine (2012).
23 Hebb, Lambert, and Tucker (1971).
24 For some of the empirical studies see Bakermans-Kranenburg and Van IJzendoorn (2007, 2011). For a review of the complexities of this literature see Bakermans-Kranenburg and Van IJzendoorn (2015).

25 Bakermans-Kranenburg and Van IJzendoorn (2015).
26 However, even monozygotic twins may differ in their DNA (e.g., Bruder et al., 2008).
27 For examples of accounts in the popular press see Callahan (2014) and Lewis (2014).
28 Joseph (2001).
29 Joseph (2001).
30 Joseph (2001).
31 Joseph (2001).
32 Joseph (2001).
33 There have been many meta-analyses on the personality of mono- and dizygous twins. A typical one is Vukasović and Bratko (2015). This suggests that 40% of personality is heritable. One of the analyses which focuses only on self-control is Willems et al. (2019). These genetic effects are complex and interactional. Some of this genetic influence seems to come from aspects of the child's influence on how the parent perceives and acts towards the child (Avinun & Knafo, 2014).
34 Pinker (1997, p. 21).
35 Lewontin (2000).
36 Meaney (2010, p. 44), citing Chong and Whitelaw (2004).
37 Finlay (2007); Jablonka and Lamb (2005, 2007).
38 Mameli and Bateson (2006).
39 Gottlieb (2007).
40 Fisher (2006, p. 270).
41 Psychologists often use the term "hardwired" or "genetically determined" and seem to assume that genes contain information in a "genetic program." But what does this really mean? Perhaps that the organism typically turns out that way? And then the problem is just handed to evolutionary biologists without an explanation, saying here we can't solve this, it's your turn (see Hebb, Lambert, & Tucker, 1971). It is not a problem that can be solved that way. We have outlined some of the complexities involved to make it clear that biologists should just hand this problem back. Genes are involved in producing proteins; DNA codes for RNA molecules, which in turn specify sequences of amino acid. But these sequences must still be folded up to produce proteins. And there is a long distance between proteins and behavior or thinking. Paul Griffiths (2009) points out that many things happen in a cell after these amino acid sequences are formed. Genes could be said to carry information only in the sense that seeing smoke is a likely indication that there is a fire. So, a Y chromosome in humans carries information about sex, indicating that the individual in question is a male (Griffiths, 2009). But we cannot consider the genes to have determined what happens afterwards. There are many elements in the developmental system in addition to genes. For example, "basal bodies and microtubule organizing centers, DNA methylation patterns, cytoplasmic polarities, membranes and organelles are all inherited" (Griffiths & Stotz, 2000, p. 35). Furthermore, "Genes are interpreted differently in different cells and at different times, as are all other factors which make up the developmental system" (Griffiths & Stotz, 2000, p. 35). A range of factors such as the mother's diet can influence the fetus's genes. We are not saying that genes are unimportant, but rather that it is even more complicated than focusing on genes, and there are many other

levels of interacting factors that are part of a complex developmental system including the environment.

42 Griffiths and Machery (2008).

43 Mameli and Bateson (2006).

44 Griffiths and Machery (2008). Biologists studying the development of embryos have known for over two hundred years that biological structures in the organism influence the development of structures that follow in development. One of the founders of embryology, Casper Friedrich Wolff, wrote in 1764 that "each part is first of all an effect of the preceding part, and itself becomes the cause of the following part."

45 Griffiths and Stotz (2000).

46 Griffiths and Stotz (2000, p. 33).

47 Meaney (2010, p. 43).

48 Fisher (2006).

49 Meaney (2010, p. 45).

50 Meaney (2010, p. 46). Thymocytes are a type of white blood cell (lymphocytes) found in the thymus, an organ of the immune system.

51 Meaney (2010).

52 Adams (1980).

53 Meaney (2010); Suomi (2006).

54 Lehrman (1953).

55 Chomsky (2007).

56 Lehrman (1953).

57 Gottlieb (1991).

58 With "a framework of systems biology that acknowledges molecular and developmental complexity, we will greatly improve our chances of untangling the webs that link genes to cognition" (Fisher, 2006, p. 292). In other words, neuroscientists seem to be telling psychologists to learn something about biology before making strong claims that depend on getting from genes to thinking.

59 Mareschal et al. (2007, p. 41).

60 Watson and Breedlove (2016).

61 Mareschal et al. (2007).

62 Greenberg and Partridge (2010).

63 Mareschal et al. (2007).

64 Stiles (2009); Stiles et al. (2015).

65 There are about 31,000 genes in the water flea, *Daphnia pulex*, a near microscopic crustacean, which grazes on algae and is prey for fish (Colbourne et al., 2011).

66 Mareschal et al. (2007, p. 44).

67 "Experience changes the brain in specific ways and the adult structure of the cortex is the outcome of a developmental trajectory in which the cortex is progressively shaped" (Mareschal et al., 2007, p. 20). This shaping of the brain involves a complex process of neurons being "born" and then migrating to positions, sometimes moving along radial glial cells which form a system of guiding threads and then growing axonal and dendritic processes to form connections with other neurons. Axons may grow along other axons forming bundles of axons or they may be attracted towards a target cell with chemical attractants secreted by that cell, or they may be repulsed by other cells. Neurons also die. There is an overproduction of neural cells during

embryonic development and about half of these cells then die. The death of a cell can be through detecting certain chemicals, or other chemicals may repress the cell's automatic "suicide program." An important factor in reducing cell death is neural activity—use it or lose it!

68 Mareschal et al. (2007, p. 71).

69 For example, Stiles (2009); Stiles et al. (2015).

70 Knecht et al. (2000).

71 Bates (1999, 2005).

72 Theorists who take a neurocontructivist approach describe the development of brains as a gradual constructive process depending on multiple levels of interacting factors. Just as the term embodiment is meant to encourage us to think about the importance of the way in which humans' bodies influences development, Mareschal and his colleagues (Mareschal et al., 2007; Westermann et al., 2007) coined the word "encellment" to bring our attention to the fact that the way in which neurons develop depends on that cell's neighboring cells. At the next level up they introduce the concept of "embrainment" to indicate that where a cell is in the brain makes a difference in how it develops.

73 Churchland (2004, p. 42).

74 For a discussion of this and other cultural differences see Greenberg and Partridge (2010).

75 Lillard (1998, p. 19).

76 In 2006 the cognitive neuropsychologist Max Coltheart challenged users of brain imaging techniques to identify any data which changed the nature of psychological theory. In 2013 he reiterated the challenge, stating that we are still searching for brain imaging data to have changed or helped us to decide between different theoretical positions (Coltheart, 2006, 2013). These articles make provocative reading for neuroscientists.

77 Beck (2010).

78 Tallis (2011).

79 Eagleman (2007).

80 Bennett and Hacker (2003).

81 Fuchs (2011).

82 This is described as the "mereological fallacy" in neuroscience: to attribute to parts of an animal what can only apply to the whole animal (Bennett and Hacker, 2003, p. 73).

83 Eagleman (2007, p. 54).

84 The proponents of this approach to neuroscience keep the notion of development as a constructive process intact. See Mareschal et al. (2007).

85 Kinsbourne and Jordan (2009).

86 Fisher (2006, p. 279).

87 Ontogeny is a biological term used to define the development of the individual. It is often contrasted with phylogeny, the evolution of species.

88 Fisher (2006, p. 280).

89 Fisher (2006, p. 279).

90 We should keep in mind the point that there are aspects of human forms of life that may be universal across cultures but still do not require an explanation in terms of a genetic mechanism leading to them. An example that the psychologist Elizabeth Bates (1984) used is that all humans eat with their hands. This is a cross-cultural universal. Do we want to say this is innate?

Well, in a sense of the word yes, this is an expectable and stable outcome of our biological heritage. But we certainly don't need to assume any sort of a genetic mechanism to explain it. Rather, as animals we necessarily eat, and, because of the nature of our bodies, it is just easier to eat with our hands than with our feet.

91 Oyama, Griffiths, and Gray (2001); Lickliter and Honeycutt (2009).
92 Odling-Smee, Laland, and Feldman (2003).
93 Stotz (2008).

Chapter 9

The myth of the desert island baby

Is the mind a machine?

In which we critically examine the claim that the human mind is like a computer.

The term *technological singularity* refers to the idea that at some point technology will become so advanced that it will take over from humans. The notion is that as computers become more advanced they will reach a point at which they can design themselves and then they will increase in intelligence to the point at which they will outstrip humans. At that point humans will be doomed because such "superintelligence" might see no need to preserve humanity, that is, unless such intelligence had human emotions and morality. Even as early as Alan Turing's pioneering work on artificial intelligence (AI) he expected that machines would "outstrip our feeble powers" and as a result "take control."[1] Among the people currently voicing concern is Bill Gates, who, although acknowledging the potential of AI, has also warned of the dangers.[2] Elon Musk advised that this is "summoning the demon."[3] Stephen Hawking went further, stating that such a superintelligence "could spell the end of the human race."[4] It has even been claimed that at some point it will become possible to "upload" human minds onto a computer or the "cloud."[5] All these speculative hopes and doomsday fears are based on the assumption that computers make an appropriate model for human intelligence. Indeed, there are theories in psychology and cognitive science that are based on this view.

In this chapter we will examine this assumption. Throughout this book we have outlined a very different account of human intelligence based on how it develops. To hint at our conclusion, we point out that the account of human intelligence we have presented is the opposite. It is not the science fiction writers' fear that emotions have to be added after intelligence is built in a machine, but rather that emotions are part of the system in which persons develop. To be clear, the work in AI that we will examine that is relevant for theories in psychology is that part of

the field attempting to model human intelligence, sometimes called artificial general intelligence. Other work in AI, sometimes referred to as
artificial narrow intelligence, concerns building tools for solving particular problems. This can be as beneficial or harmful to people as any
tool, depending on its design and use.

One crucial issue surrounding whether the computer serves as an
adequate model for the human mind concerns how core concepts like
"information" and "knowledge" are conceptualized. Although it might
seem odd to argue that such commonly used words need to be examined,
we hope to convince you that neglecting to do so results in flaws in
conclusions reached regarding the link between computers and minds.
How we conceptualize information has been raised and examined in the
previous chapter. As we argued in Chapter 1, explanations for human
development and thinking are based on assumptions about how knowledge develops. The explanation we have presented in the first part of this
book is based on a view of knowledge that differs from some other
approaches to explaining human thinking. We endorse a constructivist
view of knowledge, arguing that babies learn about their experience of
the physical and social worlds through the process of finding out what
happens as they interact with the world and other people. In this way,
they learn about what they can do with the world they experience and
thus they begin to anticipate what will happen if they act in particular
ways. Babies acquire habits as they learn about their world. These are
patterns of action and sensing, which Jean Piaget called "schemes," such
as turning to look toward a noise, reaching to grasp an interesting
object. These action plans can be combined in various ways as babies
become more skilled in doing things. We have proposed an explanation
for how human thinking develops within the social process of interaction, and we argued that the skills developed in this interaction serve as
a foundation for thought. We traced the development of forms of communication in infancy through forms of interaction on which language,
and then later forms of thinking, are based, showing that the development
of human thinking requires this developmental context.

Not all theories in psychology are based on this view of knowledge.
Now we broaden our focus in this and the previous chapter to consider
competing theoretical accounts of human thinking, and to compare our
approach to other theories. As we acknowledged in Chapter 1, there are
many approaches to human thinking. We now turn to more directly
consider them. In the previous chapter we examined the claim that genes
determine traits and forms of thinking; and the idea that evolution has
resulted in innate neurocognitive modules. We used the example of
Steven Pinker in Chapter 1 because his popular writing is widely

accessible, and because he combines many of the points we will criticize. Here we examine the claim that thinking is like computation and that the computer makes a good model for the mind.

On computers and minds: Information versus knowing

We have pointed out that theories in psychology are based on philosophical assumptions, but we have not explicitly examined these. In describing the development of thinking we cannot ignore the question of how children learn about the world, of how knowledge is acquired. This issue can easily be overlooked because it doesn't seem like a problem. You might assume that children learn just by looking around at the world. Or their parents teach them what they need to know. Anything more than this can be safely left to philosophers to worry about. Psychologists should be down in the lab studying brain scans. Why do we need to deal with philosophy if it is psychology or cognitive science that we are concerned with? Can't we use fMRI to study the mind by forming beautiful colored images based on the flow of oxygenated blood in the brain and leave epistemology to philosophers? Unfortunately, we cannot do so because our theories and methods are based on philosophical assumptions about what knowledge is. These preconceptions operate like stowaways in a Trojan horse because they already set up the question and smuggle in possible answers.

Researchers tend to just go with the current off-the-shelf theory of knowledge—the currently popular view is the "representational theory of mind." This is the view that developing knowledge of the world is something like forming a mental image, or representation, that matches the world. But the meaning of the word representation is very slippery—it can have many different meanings. James Russell[6] called it a humpty-dumpty word for this very reason—it seems that it can mean anything the user wants.[7] As we pointed out in the first few chapters, commonly held assumptions about knowledge viewed as representations have been heavily criticized.

Does the representational theory of mind rest on a mistake?

According to this theory the mind works through manipulating internal representations of external reality. The claim is that we know about the world through representing it internally, and so thinking is based on manipulating these internal representations of the world. To understand how this works consider the operation of a computer, which is often used as a metaphor for this perspective. The philosopher John Heil[8] illustrates this theory with an example of a computer program that is used to keep track of the inventory in a grocery store. It would need symbols that represent bananas and cans of soup, and the program keeps track of how many are in stock and when they need to be ordered and so on. The operations of the computer do not depend on what the symbols represent, that is, what the symbols mean or how they are linked to the world. Therefore, the same program could be used on a different computer or the same computer at a different time to keep track of the inventory of a hardware store, where the very same symbols would be used to represent glue and nails and so on. We leave to one side whether there actually are any symbols in the pattern of magnetic deflections within the computer. It is the people who use the computer who treat these as if they are symbols. It is not controversial, however, that human thought has meaning. We reflect upon real and hypothetical experiences, so our thinking is meaningfully linked to the world. This is exactly what we need to explain. Any meaning that symbols in a computer might have is just assigned by the person using the computer by typing in bananas or glue. So, the program itself is not equivalent to how symbols in human thought are given meaning.

Although the representational theory of mind is the current default theory of knowledge, the problem of explaining representations is rarely addressed. We can represent in the sense of thinking about what is not right in front of us, or re-present to ourselves. But the question is how does this work. Ironically, the concept is one of the biggest problems faced by psychologists and cognitive scientists, yet it tends to be simply taken as a premise for theories. That is, representation is not an explanation, but rather something that still needs to be explained.[9]

Many psychologists, however, assume that knowledge is simply acquired through our senses. We just open our eyes and information floods in, and we come to know more about the world. But if information, in this sense, is the same as knowledge, then, as mentioned, why aren't our cameras very knowledgeable? Whether these are film or digital cameras the images are caused by photons, but cameras still don't know about our last vacation, even if the images are still stored on their memory card. This assumption regarding representation has resulted in a misleading view of knowledge and we need an alternative.

Jean Piaget grappled with the problem of explaining knowledge and how we can re-present the world that is not in front of us, and he rejected the idea that knowledge is simply the result of perception. He argued that if our knowledge consists of some sort of copy of what we perceive, then we must know about the world in order to make the copy. But how do we get this copy if there is no way to get at the world directly? This view already presupposes that we must have some knowledge of the world, but it does not explain how we could acquire such prior knowledge.[10]

A further problem with the theory is that if the mind works by representing reality and working on those representations, not directly on reality, how can we check our representations, except against another representation or copy of the world? Suppose we read the morning newspaper and found it hard to believe a story, would we go out to buy another copy of that newspaper to check the facts? No, this seems non-sensical.[11] According to this view of the mind there is no way to get at reality directly, only through a representation, so we can only compare one representation against another. The ability to detect errors is essential, but this is not possible when two representations are compared without being able to tell if either of them is correct. If children cannot tell when they have made a mistake then they cannot learn. Clearly there is a problem with a theory that does not account for learning.[12]

One way that Piaget illustrated his view of knowledge and tried to dispel the myth of knowledge as just perception was by quoting the neurologist, Weizsäcker's remark that "when I perceive a house, I do not see an image which enters through the eye; on the contrary, I see a solid into which I can enter!"[13] That is, our knowledge of a house is not just an image, it is not just based on perception alone, but rather consists also in our understanding of what we can do with it based on our experience of interacting with the world.

Even if we agree that, in one sense it could be said that computers process symbols—though we don't see anything like symbols in the computer—how do these become meaningfully linked to the world? How symbols in a computer have meaning could only be in the sense that marks on paper can have meaning. A person is required to make sense of—to understand—such marks as writing, just as it is only the person using the computer who knows things, not the computer. This would obviously, and absurdly, need a little person—traditionally called a *homunculus*—along with a computer in our model of the mind in order to add meaning. A homunculus is actually no explanation at all; it simply pushes the explanation further off. Imagine we are admiring the operation of a new machine and we ask how it works. If the answer we receive is that it has a device in it that tells it what to do, we really have not been given an answer at all. But that is the same idea as a homunculus.[14] This would only produce the illusion of an explanation. We would also need to imagine another little person in that little person's head, and so on and on. Just as a theory that the earth is supported on the back of a turtle runs into trouble if we ask what that turtle is standing on, we don't want a theory about thinking that is "turtles all the way down" (see Chapter 7, note 5). No one would want to acknowledge endorsing such a theory requiring a homunculus, but buying into the computational view of the mind may be necessarily linked with this implication if there isn't a way to explain how symbols acquire meaning.[15]

A fundamental problem with this model of the mind arises because the word *information* is used in multiple ways. Although it could be said that computers process information, this is only in a certain sense of the word. In fact, no matter how much information computers process they still don't know anything, just as the *Oxford English Dictionary* contains a great deal of information, but it is equally ignorant.[16] Train schedules also contain information but, again, this is different from knowledge. For example, consider an illiterate slave with a message tattooed on his head. The slave's head might contain information but he does not know it—he might not even be able to see it.[17] But knowing is just what we have to explain in understanding child development.

One meaning of the word *information* refers to the transformation of energy. For example, we can talk about photons hitting the cells in the retina of a person's eye, that energy being transformed and the "information" being transmitted to the brain via neurons. This may result in the person coming to know something about a situation—to have "information," in a very different sense of the word. That is, the person sees something and knows something. Those same photons could have hit a camera, and, as mentioned above, images could be stored in the camera and transferred to a computer. Although we could talk about information being stored, neither the camera nor the computer would know anything. How is the process different when a human looks at a scene? Humans can be said to know something, and cameras cannot. We don't want to be in a position equivalent to claiming that an automatic door opener opening in response to an approaching person is the same as a person seeing someone coming and holding the door open. Information from photons in a causal sense—that is, the photons causing certain changes in a cell in the retina of an eye—is being conflated with the process of a person acquiring knowledge, of knowing.

Our knowledge is based on our connection to the world. So how are the symbols assumed by the computational theory of mind grounded in the world? This raises the issues of meaning and reference, which are much-debated topics in philosophy discussed in the early chapters in this book. One approach to this problem is the suggestion that meaning and reference work through some sort of causal connection. That is, there is some sort of causal relation between the world and the idea or concept, and this is how symbols acquire meaning.[18] If knowledge really does consist of having a representation of the world, the assumption seems to be that it is something like having an image. Let's see how this might work. Suppose that someone looks out of the window and forms a mental representation of a tree in front of them, this then presumably consists of knowledge because there is a causal connection between the tree and the mental image of it. That is, photons hit the cells in the retina of the person's eye and nerve impulses transmit information to the person's brain. The image was "caused" by the tree, and so it has been claimed by some theorists that therefore it is meaningful. But as we pointed out in Chapter 3, and earlier in this chapter, meaning cannot be attached to images. We will set aside the problem for the moment.

To evaluate this claim, the philosopher Hilary Putnam suggested that we imagine a science fiction plot in which a picture of that tree is accidentally dropped on a planet inhabited by people just like us, except that there are no trees on the planet, nothing larger than a bush. Someone on the planet who picks up and looks at this dropped photograph could be said to have formed a mental representation of the tree, and there is also a causal link back to the actual object. But can we say that this person would know anything at all about trees, even though there is a causal chain between the tree and his or her mental image? No. Having that mental representation does not imply knowledge. It is possible to take the story one step further and break the causal chain. Suppose that the picture dropped on the planet was not actually a photograph, but was really the result of an accident with spilled paints that just happened to look exactly like a tree. Now there is no causal connection between the person's mental representation—caused by looking at the image that was formed by spilled paints—and any actual tree. You or I would see a "tree," but this person may have exactly the same mental representation, but completely different knowledge. Therefore, we cannot say that the mental representation explains knowledge.[19]

The curse of computers

Of course, computers are very useful, so why is this section heading so disparaging? It is because they are taken as a metaphor to understand human minds. This is the claim that thinking is like computation. This computational view of the mind is based on the same assumption about knowledge discussed above, and so it has all the problems we have just reviewed, as well as additional difficulties. Computers can be powerful tools, but since the "cognitive revolution" many psychologists have also considered them to be an appropriate model for the mind. However complex we make programs and however powerful the processing speed the machine does not actually do any thinking. The calculator knows nothing about numbers or what it is doing. It is the designer who is intelligent. She can program the default rules and what determines a successful outcome. The same point can be illustrated with a slide rule, a device that some readers might now see only in a museum. It is a simple tool that can be used to perform complex calculations just by sliding parts of the ruler. Again, we would not be tempted to think that this ruler is performing the calculation even though it can be used for such purposes—the designer did the thinking in the first place. So why are we tempted to compare ourselves to computers? We are seduced by their apparent complexity. They appear to be more complex than calculators and slide rules, but the passive nature of the process is the same. The human tendency to look for meaning is essential in the way we treat babies because it results in babies growing up into persons, but this tendency to attribute meaning may have something to do with our propensity to attribute meaning to computers.[20]

Commonly proposed views of what thinking is are exemplified in books such as Steven Pinker's provocatively titled *How the Mind Works* in which he states that:

> The mind is a system of organs of computation, designed by natural selection to solve the kinds of problems our ancestors faced in their foraging way of life, in particular, understanding and out-maneuvering objects, animals, plants, and other people. The summary can be unpacked into several claims. The mind is what the brain does; specifically, the brain processes information, and thinking is a kind of computation. The mind is organized into modules or mental organs, each with a specialized design that makes it an expert in one arena of interaction with the world. The modules' basic logic is specified by our genetic program. Their operation was shaped by natural selection to solve the problems of the hunting and gathering life led by our ancestors in most of our evolutionary history. The various problems for our ancestors were subtasks of one big problem for their genes, maximizing the number of copies that made it into the next generation.[21]

This is a succinct summary—a more-or-less tidy story that covers many of the currently popular claims about the nature of human thinking—but is it really satisfactory? Although evolutionary theory must be an important part of the story, Pinker's use is only one possible application of the theory to these issues. Moreover, this application only follows if we first buy into the assumptions Pinker starts with regarding the nature of the mind. These assumptions, however, appear to be fundamentally flawed. Of course, we don't question the importance of evolutionary theory and neuroscience; rather, we question the result of joining these approaches to the starting position that the mind works like a computer—the computational view of the mind. It is this aspect of the set of assumptions Pinker summarizes which we examine in this chapter, that is: "the brain processes information, and thinking is a kind of computation." We responded to other claims regarding evolution and biology in the previous chapter.

It has been suggested that the most advanced technology available during any given time period tends to be adopted as a metaphor for how the mind works. This has certainly occurred with the computer. In a great deal of work in psychology the computer has been welcomed as a model for how the mind works. It seems to make intuitive sense that people process information in thinking and so do computers. But along with their ubiquity and usefulness, metaphors are also dangerous when not considered carefully. Yet we can detect no watchfulness, no caution regarding this metaphor. It is just taken for granted and the different meanings of the word *information* are overlooked. The computer might sometimes be a useful organizing metaphor for conceptualizing thinking. It also helps us to organize its components and processes in flow charts, but it is easy to slip into assuming that it is far more than a metaphor, and that it is actually a reasonable model for the mind.

An essential aspect of the computational view is that computers do what the mind does; that is, they processes information. So computers are assumed to provide an example of something like mental phenomena that is actually instantiated in a physical device. Furthermore, cognitive scientists can produce computer programs that appear to mimic human behavior for particular problem-solving tasks, and if the programs are judged to be successful then this seems to suggest that researchers have successfully captured how humans solve such tasks. If a computer program produces what appears to be the same output as a human then it is tempting to believe that researchers have identified the processes that underlie the outward behavior; and so it is claimed that the thinking is explained. For example, in studying children's mental arithmetic researchers can write computer programs that reproduce children's performance and the pattern of errors that they make. Thus, it might appear that they have explained children's thinking in this area.

There are a number of problems, however, with this position. First, it is possible to write multiple computer programs that produce similar output. So how do we know which one is the correct program that matches the process children actually use? The far bigger problem is that even if we only had one successful program, how would we know for sure that it is in fact the way children do mental arithmetic? It is possible to describe activity in very abstract terms but this doesn't mean that this is the way it is actually done. For example, consider a dog catching a Frisbee or a child tying his or her shoelaces. These actions could be described in terms of complex differential equations, but it is very unlikely that the dog or child actually accomplishes the action by using calculus.[22] Or consider flight. It is possible to calculate lift, thrust and drag based on knowledge of airfoil shapes, weight, air density, and thrust, in order to figure out take-off and landing characteristics for airplanes, and this is done in some situations, especially involving large aircraft, or high altitude takeoffs in hot weather when it is necessary to know the length of runway needed in certain conditions. But it is also possible in other situations to draw on past experience and to fly "by the seat of one's pants." Even though birds are superb flyers it is it unlikely that they explicitly know anything about the theory of flight. For example, the exquisite dynamic soaring in which albatrosses make use of lift from wind passing over waves is unlikely to involve any computation on their part. Instead, this skill is of a practical nature. The albatross has learned how to work with its environment. Similarly, "The squirrel does not infer by induction that it is going to need stores next winter as well."[23] That is, there must be a simpler way to explain the behavior of squirrels.

Or consider the example of trying to determine if another boat is on a collision course with yours. This could be done by calculating angles and speeds of the two boats; but it can also be simply determined by noting whether the other boat is pulling ahead or falling behind a reference point on the side of your boat. The lesson from these examples is that the descriptions imposed by researchers do not necessarily correspond to the actual psychological processes involved. In other words, the computer programs written by researchers do not necessarily have anything to do with how children actually solve such problems. The idea that thinking is computation is a philosophical assumption; there is nothing empirical about this claim.

Furthermore, most theories taking this computational or information processing approach are restricted in application. The focus has primarily been on particular tasks such as how children do mental arithmetic or solve problems involving a balance beam without an overall view of the mind; so far there has been no integration into general theories. Proponents of this approach claim that this is just a matter of time, but it may in fact be part of the nature of the approach.

The computational approach also only addresses certain aspects of children's thinking. In studying children's mental arithmetic, the computational approach may be able to deal with children memorizing that 5 plus 7 is 12, but there are other aspects of children's understanding of numbers that we want to explain. For example, we want to know how it is that children come to know that 5 plus 7 *has* to be 12 and they are certain of this fact. They know that it is *necessarily* so; it just has to be that way. This understanding is very different from memorizing. If a child has merely memorized that 5 plus 7 is 12, just like she has memorized her phone number, then it would be possible for her to forget the answer or to convince her that in fact it actually equals 13 or 11. But if that child really has come to understand numbers then she will know that the answer must be 12 and she will not forget—or if she does she can soon figure out the answer, and she cannot be convinced that a different answer, such as 13, is correct, no matter how many jellybeans she is offered as a reward. It is this fact that at some point children understand that 5 plus 7 just has to be 12 that Jean Piaget was concerned with. And this fact cannot be addressed with the computational model of the mind because computers know nothing about this sort of *necessary* knowledge—knowledge of what necessarily must be the case.

Constructing knowledge

If there are so many problems with the representational theory of the mind, why is it still so widely accepted? There are probably several reasons why this view persists. First, knowledge is not usually considered a problem outside philosophy. Psychologists don't generally fret about whether or not we actually know things, or how we know them. Instead, knowledge is just assumed and they don't feel a need to wonder about it—it is just taken as given. Only philosophers sit around and worry about such issues. The issue is protected by a Douglas Adams "somebody else's problem field."[24]

A second, related, reason may be that even if common assumptions about knowledge are challenged, in the ways outlined above, it seems so obvious that we do have knowledge that these objections are simply ignored. After all, we can successfully interact with the world and other people, so doesn't this show that we know something about the world and other people? Yes, it does. But this way of thinking also suggests an alternative to the representational theory of mind. Rather than thinking that knowledge consists of representations of the world, with all the problems that come along with this view, we can think of it in terms of what we can do with the world—our unsuccessful and successful actions. This is a very different way of thinking about knowledge. It is the constructivist approach to knowledge taken by Jean Piaget, and other contemporary theorists such as Mark Bickhard.

In this book we have taken this constructivist view. Babies are not born with an innate understanding of objects or people, nor is knowledge passively imposed from the environment. In contrast to the two classic positions of nature and nurture, a third option is that children gradually come to know more about the world through their actions. They make sense of the world in terms of their past experience, but new events can be different and therefore they accommodate or change in light of this new experience. This dynamic process results in a progressive movement toward more complete knowledge, though we can never step outside of our own experience in this process.[25]

According to this action-based approach babies learn that they can suck objects, see them, grasp them, drop them, and so on. They regard the world in terms of what they can do with it—its potential for interaction. In this way they develop practical, lived knowledge. This is called sensorimotor understanding (or sensorimotor intelligence), because it is based on coordinating what infants sense with their actions. In interacting with objects and people, they develop webs of potential actions on objects. Being so tied to their own activity means that infants can make some surprising errors. Early on when they are playing with a toy and it is taken from them and hidden under a blanket, babies don't look for it. Only gradually do they find objects that are partly covered by a blanket. But in the process of learning they often make a very curious error, beginning at around 8 months of age, known as the "A not B error." If a baby has found an object several times in a particular place, call it A, and then right in front of them an experimenter places the object in a different location, call it B, they still tend to look in A, where they had found it before! This phenomenon was first noticed by Piaget when he saw a young child lose a ball under a bed but then, rather than look there, the child went to retrieve the ball in his toy box. You might ask "Is this just a problem with memory?" Memory is related to knowledge so it is just a different way of describing the same error. That is, babies cannot remember objects until they have developed this way of interacting with the world based on the assumption of a stable world of objects that continue to exist. Also, in some studies babies still make the error when the object is plainly visible behind a transparent panel, so memory cannot be the only problem.[26]

As adults, we find it difficult to understand a young baby's experience because we have developed a much more complex understanding of external objects (and understanding of our understanding) and we take this experience for granted. We know that objects won't just pop out of existence the moment we turn our back on them. Yet, if we as adults choose to write an autobiography for the first couple of years of our life then, just like Saint Augustine, we may override our lack of any memories of this period of development, and impose our adult experience to assume how babies see the world.

Breaking down the common sense assumption that knowledge is simple and unproblematic requires looking behind, or beneath our adult experience to see how it is actually put together. This is what we do as developmentalists. We follow Elizabeth Bates's advice not to be overwhelmed by the complexity of our adult experience but instead to look at how it comes to be. Looking below the surface reveals a slow process of babies learning patterns of action on parts of their world and gradually fine tuning these with different objects, as well as combining or coordinating these actions. So, for example, the coordination of seeing and grasping is slowly acquired over the early months and comes to be combined with other actions, like rolling over. This demonstrates bringing together action patterns (*schemes*) to do with any activity, like interacting with a rattle. Babies can see the rattle, grasp it, suck it, shake it, hear it, drop it, and so on. The knowledge they develop about how to interact with the object is like a web of possible actions. Not all of these combined actions serve an obvious purpose or continue in a child's repertoire. For example, William at 5 months would bring his hands together and moved his arms up and down repeatedly. This ritual lasted only for a few weeks and seemed to be performed for the sheer mastery of combining his actions. These patterns are not simply combinations of bodily movements. Actions are also part of social engagement, particularly from the second half of the first year, when infants enjoy giving or receiving an object, and sharing attention with others toward an object or event.

When we talk about constructing knowledge we want to be clear that this does not mean that babies can just make up the world. Knowledge develops as a result of our necessary interactions with objects and people, and infants across the world face similar challenges in terms of attending to, reaching towards and manipulating objects. Their solutions to problems all involve the coordination of individual skills into more complex combinations or "operations." This view of development leads to various levels of knowledge, beginning with practical or "lived" engagement with the world. In learning routines using just their bodies (like William's ritual described above), particular and repeated ways of manipulating objects (at first putting them into the mouth, but becoming more sophisticated) and countless and repeated social rituals with others are steps toward the development of communication and language. An emerging ability to reflect on their own action on the world is the result of further levels of knowledge, especially as facilitated through language.[27]

Piaget's critics

We have argued for as an alternative to the representational and computational views of the mind. In order to understand our constructivist approach to knowledge, we need to consider criticism of Piaget. The Piagetian way of thinking that we have just described has not been accepted by everyone. Along with the acclaim for his theory, and his acute observations of infants and children, Piaget was extensively criticized. He has been out of fashion in many transient schools of developmental psychology since the 1960s. Piaget remarked that he was "the most criticized author in the history of psychology, and … I came through alive."[28] As an example of such a perspective, one of the better-known recent critics of Piaget's research on infancy is Renée Baillargeon, a French Canadian, now at the University of Illinois. As a graduate student Baillargeon read about Piaget's work on infancy but she felt that it made no sense to her and she thought that the idea that babies gradually develop an understanding of objects through interaction had to be wrong. She went on to build a successful career attempting to disprove Piaget's ideas about how babies develop knowledge. She felt that babies do not need to interact with their world to learn about it, and that they are born with some innate knowledge. Baillargeon has conducted a series of ingenious experiments that she interpreted as showing that babies know a lot more about objects than expected by Piaget.[29]

Doing research with young infants is challenging for many reasons and discovering what they know about objects is particularly difficult. Babies can be fussy because they are hungry, or they may just fall asleep in the middle of an experiment. But the biggest problem is that the researcher cannot just ask them questions because, of course, they can't talk yet. To deal with this problem a number of methods have been developed. For example, if a visual pattern is shown repeatedly until the baby is thoroughly bored with it, just like an adult, she will lose interest and stop paying attention. Then if a different visual pattern is presented and the baby still pays no attention then it seems that baby cannot tell the difference. However, if the baby perks up again and looks at the second pattern, this is used as evidence to suggest that she must be able to tell the difference between the two patterns. This looking time method can also be used to assess babies' ability to distinguish sounds or other aspects of their perception. What is far more controversial, however, is extending this method from studying babies' perceptions to inferring their understanding.

Let's examine one example of how Baillargeon and others have extended the use of babies' looking time to consider their *conceptual* understanding of objects. In her early research, she set up experiments in which babies watch various events, some of which were seemingly impossible. For example, she showed babies a drawbridge apparatus apparently swinging back right through a box instead of stopping when it should have hit the solid object. Unseen by the child, the box was quickly moved out of the way by a research assistant. The goal was to assess babies' reactions to these seemingly impossible events. Baillargeon found that when compared to possible events (the drawbridge swinging and stopping at the box), some babies as young as 3½ months looked a few seconds longer at the impossible event. She argued that this longer looking time shows that these infants knew that the box was there and expected the drawbridge to stop when it hit the box, and they were surprised when it continued to move through the location of the box. Baillargeon interpreted this as showing that young babies know that objects have a solidity with cannot be penetrated. This is a perspective on knowledge about objects that is credited to the infant much earlier than Piaget expected. He believed that the infant's repeated exploration of the world is required to learn about the world of objects.[30]

Baillargeon's work has been very popular. Perhaps it fits with the current zeitgeist in which parents are asking when they can start using flash cards with their young babies to teach them multiplication because they want their kids to grow up to be another Einstein or Mozart. The headline of this "neo nativist" work could be: "Babies know much more than we suspected." We also think that babies are wonderful and there are all kinds of amazing changes occurring in infancy. But flash cards are not needed, nor does the evidence suggest that they influence development.[31] All that is needed is to be interested in your baby and to play and talk with him or her. So, has Baillargeon disproved Piaget?

Criticism of the critics

The current state of the field is that most textbooks of developmental psychology present Piaget, usually inadequately, and then describe the research conducted by Baillargeon and others such as Elizabeth Spelke and Karen Wynn. Wynn, for example, claims to have shown that babies understand numbers and can do simple arithmetic.[32] The story usually ends here with the proposition that, although Piaget was a pioneer in this research, he was shown to be wrong by Baillargeon and others. This is unfortunate, first, because most textbooks fail to present an adequate view of Piaget, and, secondly, because they stop the story at Baillargeon and her colleagues. In fact, the debate continues and gets more interesting. The response to the neo-nativist research program has involved criticism of both the methodology and the conclusions drawn from the research.

To consider the level of methodology first, a number of researchers have pointed out many potential problems. As mentioned, the method used by Baillargeon and others, based on differences in how long babies look at different events, was developed to figure out what young babies can see and hear, without being able to ask them. It shows that babies can tell the difference between various stimuli or events. But that's *all* it tells us. The rest is interpretation of any differences in looking time. This is fine for research on determining what babies can see or hear because all we want to know is if they can detect differences. But when it comes to research on babies' knowledge of objects our inability to test alternative views becomes problematic. We know that babies look longer in some situations, but we don't know *why*. The claim is that they do this because they are *surprised* about something, and from that Baillargeon and her colleagues infer that babies know about objects. However, other researchers have pointed out that babies may look longer for many other reasons.[33] For example, it is well known that infants attend more to objects or events that are familiar, if they have seen them a few times before. However, if they have seen them many times then they look longer at something new. So, time attending can be affected by just the number of times babies have witnessed a particular scene. This means that the researchers have to be very careful to ensure that these effects of familiarity and novelty are not the cause of the longer looking time. In fact, when researchers have conducted detailed tests for some of Baillargeon's experiments, controlling for such effects they have found that longer looking time can be explained by novelty and familiarity. This strongly implies that the preferential looking does not necessarily tell us anything about babies' knowledge of objects.[34]

There is still continuing debate between Baillargeon and her critics regarding the methods and interpretation of particular experiments, but even if we assume that the research shows that babies have some knowledge of objects at about 3½ months, what does this mean? Is this understanding at 3½ months the same as the knowledge of objects at 18 months that Piaget was talking about? To answer this question we have to evaluate the conclusions Baillargeon draws, which means we need to know more about what Piaget was claiming.

The unknown Piaget: Understanding Piaget from within

A second aspect of the response to the neo-nativist research concerns interpretation of the research—that is, what do the findings mean? We should first be clear that criticism is essential in science, and Piaget's theory is no exception. Science and the development of knowledge involves criticism, as Alexander Pope noted:

> Trust not yourself: but your defects to know,
> Make use of every friend—and every foe.[35]

Criticism, however, is valuable when it is well informed, that is, when it is based on a solid understanding of the position it attempts to undermine. But if it is not first based on an adequate grasp of that position then it misses its mark. Many studies have been conducted to test claims that the researchers apparently believed that Piaget asserted, but, in fact, he actually never made such claims.[36] So, criticism itself needs to be carefully evaluated. When this is done it seems that there has been a tendency for Piaget's work to be misunderstood or even misrepresented. Any theory needs assessment for further development, and, in fact, Piaget claimed to be his own best critic.[37] But once Piaget's theory is better understood the criticism will be different, and more interesting.[38]

We have mentioned Baillargeon's experience of reading Piaget and feeling that it made no sense to her. Other psychologists, especially within the North American tradition, may have had similar experiences when reading Piaget because there are a number of challenges in understanding his work. The first may be what some commentators describe as Piaget's obscure writing style, although this may be due to the different intellectual tradition that forms his background. Related to this, is the quality of the translations of his books because his original work was written in French, and some of his books still have not been translated.[39] A second issue is that Piaget wrote so much and he did not always write about the conceptual and philosophical issues that underpin and motivate his work. And this brings us to the third and most difficult challenge in reading Piaget—the ideas! Psychologists rarely question the assumptions that Piaget critiqued, and his concern with how knowledge develops was the backdrop to all his work even if it was not always spelled out explicitly in all his books.

Towards the end of his life, when Piaget was asked how he felt his work had been received he expressed mixed feelings, stating that, "I am pleased by it, of course. But it is pretty catastrophic when I see how I'm understood."[40] He also said that he felt he was understood "more from without than from within."[41] What did he mean by this? The real problem seems to be the interdisciplinary nature of Piaget's theory. That is, he was doing more than just psychology, and because of this it is easy for psychologists to misunderstand his questions and so to be dissatisfied with his answers. To understand Piaget "from within" we need to know more about the questions that motivated his work, the problems he was concerned with, including the context in which his questions arose. This is more than just of historical interest. Some psychologists acknowledge that Piaget was a pioneer, but claim that he has long since been bypassed by modern methods and so he is irrelevant except as a historical footnote. But we are not dwelling on Piaget merely as a lesson in history. The problems he pointed out have not disappeared in the meantime, in spite of having been swept under the carpet for decades. They are just as relevant today, and the general approach taken by Piaget is still highly fruitful, although, of course, much can be added to and modified about his theory. In this book we build on other scholars as well, which allows us to develop potential avenues that Piaget did not expand on, given that he only had one lifetime.

Jean Piaget is generally acknowledged to be the greatest child psychologist. His influence on developmental psychology has been compared to the influence of Shakespeare on English. He published some 100 books and 600 articles; the number of experiments he and his collaborators conducted has never been counted but greatly exceeds any other psychologist.[42] But, critically, Piaget was more than a child psychologist. He described his own work as "genetic epistemology." "Genetic" does not refer to the current meaning of the word in terms of genes, but rather comes from the Greek *genno*, to give birth. Piaget used it to refer to the origin and development of knowledge. Piaget was concerned with how knowledge, especially scientific knowledge, develops. He considered this to be an interdisciplinary goal and he included logicians and mathematicians as well as psychologists in his center in Geneva.[43] Piaget's goal was to explain both the invention of new knowledge as well as the rigor of knowledge, that is, the understanding that an answer must necessarily be so and could not be otherwise, and that any reasonable person would see that.

To understand the questions that motivated Piaget's work we need to take a step back to see the context in which they arose. Piaget was born in 1896 in Neuchâtel, Switzerland. As a boy he had a strong interest in natural history, particularly birds and mollusks. When he was 10 he published a short article on an albino sparrow he had seen, and he helped the director of the Museum of Natural History in Neuchâtel. Through his adolescence, his interest in science was also coupled with an awareness of the conflict between science and religion. He was not able to overlook this and perhaps it was made personal by the nature of his home life in which his mother was devoutly religious whereas his father was a religious skeptic who emphasized the importance of critical thinking. The young Piaget also saw this conflict between truth and values as a cause of the world's problems.[44]

Piaget experienced a personality crisis between the ages of 15 and 17—what would now be described as an identity crisis. He spent a year in the mountains during this time because of his health and he wrote an auto-biographical novel about the feelings he was experiencing.[45] In this book the protagonist grapples with the conflict between truth and values, and the question of how to find value in science. His intuition was to approach this problem through studying the origin and development of knowledge, both in history and child development. This was a resolution to Piaget's crisis because he saw a way forward, a pathway, an intuition he could build on, through research. The general outline of the ideas he developed throughout his career emerged as his way of resolving this crisis. These were the seeds of ideas that he continued to fill in and develop throughout his long career, working until his death in 1980 at the age of 84. Piaget studied the development of children's thinking as a means to the end of understanding the origins of knowledge in general. He was concerned with valid knowledge, that is, knowledge that is agreed upon, not just personal opinion.[46]

So, Piaget was concerned with questions at a different level from most psychologists, although his approach was more common in the European tradition in which he was educated. To grasp these issues we need to see assumptions about knowledge as problems rather than just the world as it is. Perhaps because they involve philosophical issues, the questions concerning knowledge that Piaget was grappling with have not always been recognized.[47] Psychologists may, for example, study how children learn to do arithmetic and solve problems such as 2 plus 2. And they might be interested in finding the best way to teach preschoolers about numbers and why certain children may have difficulties with arithmetic. But they rarely ask the more fundamental questions that Piaget was concerned with regarding what numbers *are* and how children learn their nature. Understanding number involves understanding a system. For example, Jeremy's son, Max's understanding of infinity at age 6 was that, "numbers never stop." The understanding that 2 plus 2 just *has* to be 4, it is necessarily so, is based on an understanding of numbers. It is not like knowing the answer is 4 in the way we memorize a phone number that can be forgotten. A further principle is the understanding that number is constant. You can take ten pebbles and count them, and then count them backwards and you still get ten in the set. You can even rearrange them and you still get ten when you count them! This is obvious to adults, but this knowledge has nothing to do with the pebbles. It is not about their color, or size, or weight. The knowledge is not from the pebbles but rather it is from our actions—what we do with them. It was this sort of knowledge that Piaget was interested in.

In studying the development of knowledge and asking questions about how it develops, the approach that follows is to describe a sequence of forms of knowledge, or patterns of the child's interaction with the world. These can be described as stages, which are for Piaget the first descriptive step, but the more important next phase is to address the question of how children progress through the forms of knowledge in developing more complete understanding. Unfortunately, most textbooks simply describe Piaget's stages. In taking a developmental approach he described a sequence of forms of babies' understanding of objects, not just one understanding. This contrasts with Baillargeon's research, which comes down to the dichotomy of having or not having knowledge of objects. But taking a developmental approach should not result in just looking for the first glimmer of an ability and jumping to the conclusion that it is all there. At a baby's first step parents shouldn't rush out to sign them up for a 10-kilometer run.

In fact, Piaget did write that even at 2 months, at sub-stage two, babies have some understanding of objects as continuing to exist because they continue to look for them at the place where they vanished behind a barrier. This may well be the form of knowledge assessed with Baillargeon's research method, in her claim that babies have a much earlier understanding of objects. But according to Piaget this is just the first step in the forms of knowledge babies develop about objects, and they still have much to learn before developing full knowledge of objects. Those babies who pass Baillargeon's tests by looking longer at the impossible event of a drawbridge passing through a box still, months later, make curious errors about objects, such as continuing to look for an object where they last found it, even if they see if put in a different location (the "A not B error"). They even do this if the object is visible behind a Perspex barrier or obviously (to us) under the cloth.[48] So perhaps we should not attribute full knowledge of objects to these young infants who can pass Baillargeon's tests. And, instead, we should chart the gradual process through which babies develop skills in interacting with their world.

Concluding thoughts: Thinking and the social process

One of our goals in this chapter was to evaluate the claim that the computer makes a good model for the mind and that human thinking is computation. This computational theory of mind is a competing approach to explaining thinking and how it develops that contrasts with the theory we present in this book. We have reviewed many criticisms, however, that have been leveled against this assumption, showing that it is based on flawed conceptions of meaning and information. These arguments also undermine what are referred to as "information processing" approaches.

We started this chapter by highlighting concerns about the possible negative outcomes of building artificial intelligence. We did so because most current work in AI shares assumptions with the computational theory of mind that thinking is mechanical. Therefore a question that arises is what are the implications of the discussions in this chapter for AI? As we noted, AI can be grouped into two approaches. What is sometimes referred to as narrow AI involves building useful tools that perform particular tasks more efficiently than humans, such as cars that drive themselves. It is claimed that these autonomous vehicles will result in far fewer accidents and so fewer lives will be lost. However, there will still be unavoidable accidents and therefore the cars need to be pre-programmed for what action to take if there are options that vary in harm to the car's occupants, people in other vehicles or pedestrians.[49] For example, the software could be designed with the decision "If there is a choice between steering the car off the road (even if this is into a wall, or off a cliff) and killing the occupants or hitting a group of people then avoid the pedestrians," but this would be a programmer's decision. The car would simply do what it is programed to do. These are moral decisions, but they are not reached by the car through moral reasoning. Instead, they are predetermined by the programmers who formulate the pre-programmed algorithms that determine the choice. This is narrow AI because it is designed to function in a limited context and cannot go beyond that to solve problems in other situations.

We also noted a second area of AI, referred to as general AI, that is meant to be like human intelligence and do anything a human can do so that the computer can understand and reason like a human. This, of course, does not exist, even though we are constantly told it is just around the corner. There are impressive achievements like computers that can play chess and Go and beat world champions. It is somewhat ironic that this seems to be considered in work towards general AI but it is just as narrow as narrow AI, if not narrower. Furthermore, narrow AI involves building machines to do things that we don't want to do. So computers now exist that can play chess for us, if we needed such a machine. Generally, people choose to play chess because they enjoy it. Would we build machines to eat cake for us or go for walks for us, or go dancing for us?

Only if we did not want to do those things. In fact, the goal is not just to win chess, but to try to convince others that the machine is intelligent. There is no question that computers can do some things better than us, even calculators can.

It might seem that computers must be very smart if they can beat world champions at chess and Go, but they don't know anything about winning or losing, or even that they are in fact doing anything. It is a mechanical process. It is different from human intelligence. In Peter Hobson's words, "only humans, and not computers "themselves," make sense of the input and output data. Computers don't understand anything, nor do they care. They do not find meaning, because they do not have the necessary kinds of linkage with the world that surrounds them."[50] In fact, perhaps they don't understand because they don't care. The world cannot become meaningful or significant for computers because their connection to the world is just passive and mechanical, unlike infants who are actively engaged and interested in the world.

As an alternative to the computational theory of mind we have explicitly discussed the approach to knowledge on which our views in this book are based. We have used Piaget's work on child development as an example of this approach. And, in order to better understand his theory, we have examined criticism of it. Although development in science does involve criticism and improvement, common criticisms of Piaget are, unfortunately, often based on misunderstandings. Contrasting these misconceptions with Piaget's theory provides a way to further understand a constructivist approach in which we study the process through which knowledge develops.

Throughout this book we have argued that minds emerge within the social process as communication becomes more complex. In this chapter we have taken a closer look at views regarding the nature of knowledge and how it develops. Much of this discussion has focused on babies' knowledge of the physical world, but the same principles apply to our concern regarding how babies learn about other people. Human infants develop within a social environment that responds differently to their actions compared to the physical environment. Babies learn about the interactive potential of their world, both its physical and social aspects. Here we must think about more than just the individual brain to explain development. Babies, obviously, also have a body. Indeed this is a body that is relatively helpless compared to other species; however, babies can express their needs. And they have arms for reaching and hands for grasping. This makes their interests and desires obvious to others. Their attitudes are clear to parents and other caregivers in their directedness toward aspects of the world. We can see what they are directed toward, what they want or are afraid of, what they like or dislike. The social environment—usually a parent—responds to the infant's attitudes interests and desires as evident in their actions. This is an interactive environment that is contingent on the infant's actions and attitudes. It is here that babies develop and master human forms of communication and thinking. This is the process of becoming a person. We have presented this account to contrast with the way humans develop knowledge according to the computational and representational view of the mind. Humans learn through interaction and this is fundamental to what makes us human.

Suggested further reading

Bibok, M. B., Carpendale, J. I. M., & Lewis, C. (2008). Social knowledge as social skill: An action based view of social understanding. In U. Müller, J. I. M. Carpendale, N. Budwig, & B. Sokol (Eds.), *Social life and social knowledge: Toward a process account of development* (pp. 145–169). New York: Taylor & Francis.

Chapman, M. (1991). The epistemic triangle: Operative and communicative components of cognitive development. In M. Chandler & M. Chapman (Eds.), *Criteria for competence: Controversies in the conceptualization and assessment of children's abilities* (pp. 209–228). Hillsdale, NJ: Erlbaum.

Heil, J. (1981). Does cognitive psychology rest on a mistake? *Mind*, 90, 321–342.

Notes

1 Turing (1951).
2 Rawlinson (2015).
3 McFarland (2014).
4 Cellan-Jones (2014).
5 Friend (2018); Khatchadourian (2015).
6 Russell (1992).
7 Humpty Dumpty in Lewis Carroll's *Through the Looking-Glass* claimed that he could mean anything he wanted when he used a word (he just had to pay extra on Saturday night!).
8 Heil (1998).
9 Bickhard and Terveen (1995).
10 Chapman (1988, p. 414); Müller, Carpendale, and Smith (2009); Piaget (1970).
11 This example was used by Wittgenstein (1968) to demonstrate the problem.
12 Bickhard (2001, 2009).
13 Piaget (1972, p. 66).

14 Heil (1998).
15 Heil (1981).
16 Kenny (1991); Müller, Sokol, and Overton (1998a, 1998b).
17 Kenny (1991).
18 For example, Perner (1991, p. 41).
19 Putnam (1988).
20 If the computational view of the mind fails to explain how the symbols claimed to be used in thought are actually linked to the world, then how is our thinking linked to the world? As an alternative, in this book we suggest a constructivist view of knowledge according to which infants come to understand the world of objects as well as other people in terms of what they can do with it.
21 Pinker (1997, p. 21).
22 Heil (1981).
23 Wittgenstein (1972, §287).
24 Adams (1982).
25 We approach knowledge of the world as a limit. A limit is a mathematical concept concerning how a curve can get closer and closer to a line without ever actually touching it. This concept can also be illustrated in everyday life. Think of the example of a party with polite friends and one piece of cake left. Someone might cut it in half and take half. The next person might cut the remaining piece in half, and this could go on and on, so that although practically you would end up with no cake, theoretically it would never be completely gone.
26 Müller (2009); Müller, Carpendale, and Smith (2009); Piaget (1952, 1954, 1970).
27 An infant's interaction with the world is not sharply divided between emotions and intelligence. Interest and value are interlinked with intelligence. In a baby's activity, we see interest, motivation, emotion, as well as understanding and cognition; they are interrelated, not separate. As infants construct knowledge of their physical and social world they develop ways of interacting with this world. These ways will differ in how the infant interacts with the social and the physical aspects of her world. And these ways of acting on the world, involve both emotions and thinking (Piaget, 1962, p. 207: "personal schemas, like all others, are both intellectual and effective").
28 In Smith (1996, p. vi).
29 For example, Baillargeon (1987, 2005).
30 Baillargeon (1987, 2004, 2008).
31 See Hirsh-Pasek et al. (2004).
32 Wynn (1992).
33 There have been both interpretative (Bremner, 1988) and methodological (Bogartz et al., 1997) analyses of this work since the 1980s.
34 For reviews see Allen and Bickhard (2013); Müller and Overton (1998).
35 Alexander Pope, *From an Essay on Criticism*, pt II.
36 Chapman (1988).
37 Piaget (1970).
38 Chapman (1988).
39 Smith (2009).
40 Bringuier (1980, p. 54).
41 Piaget in Chapman (1988, p. 1).
42 Smith (2009).

43 Chapman (1988); Carpendale, Lewis, and Müller (2018, 2019).
44 Chapman (1988); Müller, Carpendale, and Smith (2009); Bennour and Vonèche (2009).
45 Chapman (1988); Müller, Carpendale, and Smith (2009).
46 Chapman (1988); Müller, Carpendale, and Smith (2009).
47 Although psychology has split from philosophy, psychologists may have wanted to keep philosophy out of psychology—to maintain the division of work. But, unfortunately, it hasn't worked. The philosophy is still there, it is just invisible, so the assumptions on which the theories are based are not examined, they are not questioned, just taken for granted.
48 Infants' experience seems to be crucial here. If they have no familiarity with the Perspex screen then they do not search behind it (Butterworth, 1977). Interestingly if they are allowed to play with the screen before the experiment, infants do search behind it (Yates & Bremner, 1988). This underscores the role of experience in the infant's acquisition of knowledge.
49 Greene (2016); Rhim et al. (2020).
50 See Hobson (2002, p. xiv).

Chapter 10

Social relations and reason
What are the implications of self-awareness?

In which we explore the implications of the perspective we have outlined, and discuss the role of culture in human development.

What is the nature of human thinking?

We started this book with a puzzle: How can we explain the evolution and development of human thinking. We have grappled with questions such as: How do we transform from a bunch of cells to something that thinks?; How did things start thinking?; How do minds emerge from nature? Ravens, crows, and many other animals can be very smart. They are skilled in negotiating their world in a flexible, intelligent manner, even bending a pipe cleaner to hook a reward out of a test tube. Humans, however, are able to engage in reflective thought, which adds another level of complexity. Other animals interact successfully in the world, but knowing they are alive in the way humans do requires another form of thinking, of awareness. We are self-aware in a myriad of ways. Not only do we reflect upon our immediate interactions with others, we can appreciate or regret the past and look forward to or fear the future. If we wish to remind ourselves of this we have a range of symbolic systems (spoken and written language, photograph and film). These abilities can have positive or negative effects. We can plan ahead, imagine possible future outcomes, and we can consciously draw on the past in making decisions about the future. Even if we do not always use such abilities wisely humans do have the potential to do so.

These are the questions we have addressed in this book. Although they have been debated by scholars for centuries, they have only more recently entered popular discussion. There is a widespread interest in physics because it seems to address fundamental issues about the nature and origin of our universe: including whether there is life at all in other parts of the universe. But in this book we have focused on the simple fact that we can even *ask* and attempt to answer questions such as how did the universe begin and will it end. How is that we, and not other species, can worry about the future, regret the past, and reflect upon ourselves? There are many additional problems to address within psychology that we have not touched on in this book, such as how emotional and family problems arise, but these at least partially, presuppose and derive from human forms of thinking. It is that more fundamental question of the origin of human intelligence that we have been concerned with. Our goal, which we revisit here, is to consider explanations of the nature, development and evolution of human intelligence, and to do so by rooting this development in a process of interaction.

How does human thinking develop?

Where do human forms of thinking come from? We have built on the idea from George Herbert Mead and others suggesting that self-awareness and an ability to reflect are acquired through becoming aware of others' perspectives on ourselves. Accordingly, thinking is acquired socially. Children need to grow up with others in order to develop the ability to think in this reflective way. Therefore, human forms of thinking are necessarily social; we can take a perspective on ourselves only because we have experienced others' perspectives on us. This way of thinking emerges first as a way of interacting with others, and once it is mastered as a social process, individuals can then take it on, and think and act by themselves, as individuals.

Language is an important medium through which human thinking takes place. Thinking involves a system of meaning; it allows us to consider, and imagine, what is not actually right there in front of us. Other forms of thinking draw on systems such as music and symbolic media such as diagrams and organizing systems. But a primary mode for reflective thought is grounded in language. And this is what we focus on. The debate about the role of language in thought has been continuing for centuries. It can be traced back to Plato's view that thinking is a form of conversation we have with ourselves. This idea is now more generally attributed to the soviet psychologist Lev Vygotsky, although many other philosophers have also discussed it. The analysis that we have put forward has referred, implicitly or explicitly, to the traditions of thought that have developed this perspective.

Copernican revolutions

This book turns on two Copernican revolutions. The first is from the perspective of the reader. As adults we have the experience of having our own individual, private, minds, separate from others. Our total immersion in these daily activities makes it hard for us to think that it could ever have been otherwise. When this preconception of the mind as simply given becomes built into and taken for granted in psychological theories there can be no explanation given for how the mind comes to be—how it develops. This fits with a long tradition in philosophy. It was perhaps most famously articulated by René Descartes, but has much earlier sources. At the beginning of the book we pointed out that this way of thinking was already evident in Saint Augustine's *Confessions* from 1500 years ago. But, in contrast to this tradition in philosophy, there is also another strand of thinking beginning about 150 years ago that reverses this way of thinking. Instead of assuming that our minds already pre-exist, consider that they develop through social experience. This way of thinking has been traced to Charles Sanders Peirce and other American philosophers taking a perspective known as *pragmatism* or *pragmaticism*. We have drawn on G. H. Mead from this tradition of thought. Similar strands have also emerged, apparently independently, in other thinkers as diverse as Wittgenstein and Heidegger, and more recently by Jürgen Habermas and others.[1] The Copernican revolution we ask readers to make is that instead of thinking of the mind as given—as always there—think of human minds as developing, and this development is occurring within social relations. We have argued throughout this book that taking a developmental perspective is essential for understanding what makes us human.

One demonstration of how adults are orientated towards social interaction can be seen in a recent manipulation of an old task (Figure 10.1). Imagine sitting at a table upon which I place a capital letter like an "R." This could be the right way up or inverted so it's back to front. The letter is presented to you anywhere along a 360° orientation to you. The original study 50 years ago shows that the time taken to make a decision about whether the letter is correct or its mirror image is directly related to its orientation to yourself. As a result this has been known as the mental rotation task, as we are supposed to rotate the object in our mind's eye to identify what it looks like.[2] However, recently is has been found that performing the task with someone else looking at the same object reduces our decision time if the letter is oriented towards them. There is no such advantage if a lamp is oriented towards the object. This both throws into question how "mental rotation" works and provides clear evidence of how influential upon us are our "interactions," or orientations, towards others in how we process the world. Our minds do not originate from our ability to reflect inwards: they are grounded in social processes, some of which are as basic as watching an object with another person and therefore having different perspectives.[3]

Figure 10.1 The letter orientation task

This brings us to the second, and related, Copernican revolution, which is from the perspective of the developing baby. If, instead of starting with the mind, we want to explain how minds develop, then we have to start from a different beginning point. We have to take a leap of imagination. Physicists in trying to understand the nature of the universe must attempt to imagine a world that is vastly different from our immediate experience, and they think that if it is not strange enough then it cannot be right. Why should understanding the mind be any different? Rather than assuming that newborns' perceptions of the world are like ours, that is, in terms of ourselves as distinct from others, think of babies as being immersed in a sea of experience, while not yet clearly differentiating the self as separate from this ocean of people and objects. This is what Donald Winnicott was trying to get across with his bold statement that "there is no such thing as a baby." In psychology we see this way of thinking as most well known in Piaget but also in Pierre Janet and James Mark Baldwin.[4] And in philosophy in the work of George Herbert Mead. So embedded are they in experience, that babies have not yet learned where they stop and others begin. Infants can tell the difference between, for example, their own fingers touching their cheek or someone else's finger.[5] This ability is needed in the process of learning about themselves and others through their actions on the world. Our adult experience of self and others is a long developmental achievement, the outcome of a great deal of learning. The distinctions between inner and outer, self and objects, and self and others are gradually constructed by the infant through activity with others and the world of objects. Early forms of communication and then language are extensions of everyday life. They are built onto typical patterns of interaction. As it gets more complex, communication is then the source of human minds.

We add a caveat concerning how much of human experience we are attempting to explain. We have talked about becoming self-aware in the process of developing human forms of thinking. However, we do not claim that individuals become aware of all aspects of how they respond emotionally in particular situations. That is, we are not always completely aware of who we are in the sense of repeated immature emotional reactions in particular situations. The study of how emotional reactions from infancy can continue to be an obstacle to further development and enjoyment of life was explored by Sigmund Freud[6] and since by his many followers. Immature emotional reactions can continue to reemerge and disrupt further development. We have presented a view of the development of human forms of thinking, but we must acknowledge the important areas of human experience that we have not touched on.

The consequences of self-awareness

We will expand here on the view of how human thinking and self-awareness develops within the experience of social relations. With such development there are a series of further consequences. Our sense of self develops as a result of this self-awareness. Young children *are* selves in the sense of having characteristic ways of acting and reacting, but this does not require an awareness of this self. A more complex understanding of *having* a self requires developing this awareness through experiencing how others react to us. This seeing ourselves through others' eyes and reactions emerges within social relations.[7] In George Herbert Mead's words, a self is "an eddy in the social current and so still a part of the current."[8] It emerges in the process of social relations just as an eddy forms in the flow of a liquid such as water in a stream or river, and its existence depends on that flow, yet it has some stability in itself. Clearly our sense of ourselves requires this feeling of continuity, but can also be threatened by negating experiences, like a child brought up in social isolation or an adult placed in a concentration camp. A further development in self-understanding is an *identity*—a conception of ourselves in relation to social systems through which we derive a sense of meaning, of purpose and significance. We have a feeling of ourselves as individuals separate from others and of course we are in one sense separate persons, but this is a developmental outcome. We have developed, and most of us still live, within webs of interpersonal relationships. Although individuals develop in this way they may later choose to live isolated from others, even hermits grew up within such webs. Furthermore, reasoning emerges through social relations, through developing in a social world in which reasons are expected—a space of justifications.[9]

The ability to engage in such forms of thinking results in us becoming aware of our own inevitable deaths. Woody Allen was 5 years old he first became aware that he, like everyone else, was going to die, and he thought it was "a bad idea." He says that his position hasn't changed since then—he is still "against it."[10] Such awareness of our own inevitable mortality has further implications regarding our sense of purpose in life. Nature has created an animal that is not at ease living in the environment resulting from our ability to think about ourselves. Thus, humans seek to generate more comfortable worlds in terms of belief systems. We are a story-telling species. In the face of the realization of our own insignificance in the universe we must construct some sense of purpose for our lives to gain significance.[11]

It is the ability to take others' perspectives on the self—as well as valuing these attitudes—that is not only the strength of humanity, making human forms of thinking possible, but it is also the curse because of the suffering that can be felt due to this experience. We are not just aware of our mortality, we agonize over evaluations from others and our regret over past misdeeds. Humans, unlike other animals, are aware that we are alive, and that knowledge means the loss of Eden.[12] We are a species that has created an environment that is too uncomfortable for us to live in—in becoming aware of the future and our death we need to find some source of meaning for our lives—so we must change this environment; that is, we construct belief systems that provide meaning, or significance in our lives.

As Douglas Adams has noted in *The Restaurant at the End of the Universe*,

> The Universe, as has been observed before, is an unsettlingly big place, a fact which for the sake of a quiet life most people tend to ignore. Many would happily move to somewhere rather smaller of their own devising, and this is what most beings in fact do.[13]

Kurt Vonnegut also observed that, "The universe is a big place, perhaps the biggest."[14] In response to this realization, people develop and buy into belief systems that provide a more comfortable life.

Critical theorists such as Ernest Becker and David Sprintzen have explored the ways in which humans attempt to find purpose in their lives. Sprintzen draws the point from Becker that, "We need to feel that we are a locus of value in a world of meaning."[15] And he extends it to elaborate that, "We need to feel that we are a meaningful center of activity and value in a socially rooted cosmic drama."[16] Certainly, some people attempt to gain a sense of significance and purpose for their lives through trying to play heroic roles within cultural belief systems such as working toward high status positions and winning prizes. But this may not be so important for other people. There are diverse ways of achieving a sense of place in our social world. For some people caring for others, looking after and enjoying children or grandchildren, growing a garden, building things or fixing things, cooking food that others enjoy and watching their enjoyment may be equally important. These are the everyday facts of social or family life that are all around us, but it is still hard to notice their significance because such actions are always right in front of us. We may not notice these social and emotional interconnections—unless we lose them. Carl Sagan famously pointed out that there is nothing like a brush with a terminal disease to set one's priorities.[17] The same applies to disruptions in our relationships. For some people their pets play an important role in such sustaining relationships. The potential loss of our relationships reminds us of their central importance in our lives. As we have argued, we develop as persons embedded within relationships. Most of us live supported by webs of interpersonal relationships. There is extensive research showing the crucial importance of social relations for our health.[18] This applies to both close interpersonal relationships as well as just everyday interaction with the people we meet in our daily lives.

An implication of the role of social relationships is the importance of communities. Kurt Vonnegut suggested that the most daring thing that young people could do with their lives is to "create stable communities in which the terrible disease of loneliness can be cured."[19] And that this, even more than curing cancer or getting to Mars will make people happier.

Individualism is at the heart of the computational and representational perspectives that we discussed in Chapter 9. It is a theory of human development that focuses only on individuals. As a political ideology it is flawed because it does not explain the development of individuals, as we have discussed throughout this book. Furthermore, there are economic and political implications of the theory. If we are simply isolated individuals then we can just move around from place to place wherever there is work or an opportunity for a good time. But this disrupts social networks and communities and results in social isolation and problems for individuals' physical and mental health. This mobility can also result in less concern about places, because it is assumed that we can always move on to destroy another environment.

Individualism is also linked to justification from one popular approach to evolutionary theory. It is sometimes argued that humans have evolved to be selfish, and it is just a part of our "human nature." First, this view of nature, famously portrayed in Tennyson's words as "red in tooth and claw," is endorsed in Thomas Henry Huxley's interpretation of evolutionary theory, where the survival of the fittest rules.[20] However, in contrast to this view of selfish competition developed in a highly populated, industrialized England, Peter Kropotkin emphasized cooperation and "mutual aid" based on his experience as a young naturalist working in northern Russia where he viewed survival as dependent on cooperation among species rather than competition.[21] Following Kropotkin, recent theories have also argued for a more cooperative view of humans and other primates.[22] If our communicative development occurs within the context of helplessness and caring, then human intelligence depends on development within our cooperative social and emotional developmental system.

As a second reaction against individualism, this book has been an extended argument that the nature of being human is not fixed in biology and instead is constructed within a human developmental system. Obviously, human biological characteristics create the developmental system in which children grow up, but that is only a start. To think about such a system it is important to consider the biological characteristics as well as the cultural context of development, to which we turn next.

Humans as cultural creatures

> Culture makes humans as much as the reverse.
> —Paul Griffiths and Karola Stotz[23]

Human development is, not uniquely but certainly outstandingly, reliant on external scaffolding. This scaffolding is commonly referred to as culture. Part of the rationale of the traditional idea of human nature was to isolate features that do not depend on culture. These "biological" features represent our true nature—the naked ape stripped of its cultural clothes. It seems to us that this traditional project is as misguided as seeking to investigate the true nature of an ant by removing the distorting influence of the nest! Human beings and their cultures have co-evolved as surely as ants and hives or dogs and packs. Human nature must inevitably be a product of a developmental matrix which includes a great deal of cultural scaffolding.

> —Paul Griffiths and Karola Stotz[24]

Just as it would make no sense to study ants separate from their nests and the influences on one another through their pheromones (see Chapter 1), it would not be appropriate to study human development in isolation because culture is such a central aspect of a children's and adults' environment. When we think about this developmental niche an important influence is, of course, the specific beliefs and practices adopted by each baby's parents. Yet, as cultural creatures, developing humans also change their cultures. This is a reciprocal process through which cultures and persons create each other.

Humans have evolved as cultural creatures. Our biology makes this possible, and culture is necessary for child development. Thus, we grapple with the questions posed by the German sociologist, Norbert Elias, namely:

> "Which biological characteristics of man make history possible?"
> Or, to phrase it in sociologically more precise terms: "which

biological characteristics are prerequisites for the changeability, and particularly for the capacity for development, shown by human societies?"[25]

This has been one of our tasks. In one respect we have explored the evolution of those biological characteristics that make human forms of living possible. Yet, we have largely been preoccupied with the social-emotional developmental systems in which babies develop into persons. These systems are set in cultural and historical processes. In the words of the influential American anthropologist Clifford Geertz (writing at a time when gendered statements were often overlooked), "Man is an animal suspended in webs of significance he himself has spun. I take culture to be those webs ..."[26] Chapter 1 made the point that humans are a story telling species. Those stories form the psychological cradle in which persons develop, but they are also transformed by new generations as they are passed on. The structure of these groups continually changes over historical time, unlike the social structure of ant colonies, within which changes have been hard won through millions of years of evolution. These webs of significance, spun by ourselves, support human lives by providing complex meanings for individuals.

The study of cultures is a vast field with much debate about how the key term should be defined. One way of conceptualizing it is as a set of traditions that endure but also change and are passed on across generations. This is what Michael Tomasello, Ann Cale Kruger, and Hilary Horn Ratner referred to as a "ratchet effect" because particular ways of doing things are preserved and are passed on to the following generations, but they are also changed in this process.[27] This can be seen in some subtle differences between different societies which stress compliance for the general good, and individualism, as is promoted by several Western cultures. For example, in a more collectivist culture, India, mothers make more directive comments to their 6-month-olds than mothers in an individualist culture, England. By 8 months Indian children respond more to such instructions.[28] Similarly Canadian 24-month-olds are more likely than Indian children of the same age spontaneously to help an adult who has dropped something or cannot reach it.[29]

The vast diversity of cultures might give the impression that human forms of living are free to vary without limit. But this is not so. Although there can be cultural differences in how social interactions take place, we can also think about forms of interaction that may be universal due to being rooted in our embodied interaction with others. These are common parts of human ways of life. For example, as discussed in Chapter 1, making requests might be expected to emerge in all cultures because of the problem space encountered by human infants.[30] Such acts may be accomplished in different ways across cultures but it seems that any form of human society would need at least requests as well as other acts such as greeting, directing attention and ending an interaction. Communication can be possible because ways of living can be similar across cultures. For example, how can we share a joke across a cultural gap without a single word in common? Well, some years ago, Jeremy was walking quickly to catch the only train that day from Mandalay to Rangoon, Burma, and his partner was on the train, so he was hurrying. The Burmese people, being very friendly and laid back, don't hurry very much. One young fellow walking on the other side of the street made a joke by smiling at Jeremy and copying the way he was walking fast. It was the shared human way of life concerning walking and hurrying that made it possible to communicate in this way—and to impress upon a Westerner that rushing may not be a good idea.

Culture provides a complex social environment which is both re-created by members of a social group, and is also enduring, in that knowledge is shared and negotiated across families, local communities and more widely. The process of a child's development is stable but is not simply encoded in her or his genes. Indeed it is the sum of experiences that individuals are exposed to that constitutes their participation in culture. If an aspect of the environment is consistently present it can be relied on in the developmental process. Development is due to bi-directional interactions among many levels of factors from genetic to societal processes, so there is nothing fixed about being human. Ways of living vary across cultures and history, and assumptions about the nature of human nature change over history.[31] Cultures within particular historical periods provide distinctive ways of being.[32]

While we do not assume an essential human nature rooted in biology, we suggest that human biological characteristics do set up potential patterns of interaction leading to common outcomes. For example, typically developing humans learn to walk on two legs given the typical circumstances of growing up on a planet with the gravitational force of the Earth. The outcome could be different developing without gravity on a space station or on a much larger planet like Jupiter. Within our shared gravitational environment, most babies learn to crawl before they walk, but some learn to scoot around on their bottom, and others skip crawling and go straight from sitting to walking. Aspects of development that are more social will be even more complex. For example, we expect that some way of coordinating attention would be important across human cultures. It seems that pointing with an extended index finger is a common way of doing this, as we discussed in Chapter 4. Perhaps this is because of the musculature of the index finger, due to the evolution of the pincer grip, and the use of this finger for exploration in the social context of development in which adults may respond to the infant's actions. However, there are also many other ways of pointing in various cultures with one's lips or even nose.

Organisms adapt to their environment in many ways; one way is through intelligence. As Jean Piaget wrote, "Intelligence is a particular instance of biological adaptation."[33] The ability to develop intelligence depends on biology, but there are different ways to think about the role of biology in development. The two frameworks we described in Chapter 1 are linked to contrasting ways of thinking about the role of biology and evolution in explanations of human thinking. In Chapter 8 we discussed approaches that use terms like "genetically determined" or "hard-wired" based on the assumption that the mind is a product of "genetic information." We point out a series of problems in leaping from genes to minds, and in assumptions about how the organism and environment are conceptualized. Instead, we suggested that it is necessary to consider many more levels of interacting factors in the complex developmental systems that influence human learning and experience. What has evolved are the interactive conditions, the developmental niche, in which humans develop. The nature of our thinking is an outcome of that social interaction and it involves the ability to enact cultural practices as individuals.

Conclusion

We started with the problem of how we can explain the nature of human thought. Proposed solutions from contemporary psychology tend to home in on the individual, and reduce thinking to computation or the manipulation of internal "representations"—pictures in the mind. We have discussed criticism of such approaches, and if this is the contemporary account of human nature it cannot actually explain knowledge. Skeptical concerns about the circularity of these accounts have been around for a very long time. The usual approach is just to ignore such criticism even though it is so obvious that we do develop an understanding of the world and other people. If the representational explanation for how we acquire knowledge of the world fails is there an alternative?

Some researchers get into even deeper trouble by wedding this problematic view with evolutionary theory. We outlined a number of fundamental flaws with these assumptions in Chapters 8 and 9. Instead we need another way of conceptualizing the nature of human thought. We have to build an alternative view from the ground up, based on children's activity with their physical and social worlds. Indeed the same applies to us as adults.

Ironically, even the way the problems to be solved are raised often assumes particular stances that include assumptions about the nature of the solution. That is, answers can be smuggled in with the way the question is framed. Our starting point follows us right to the end.[34] For the American philosopher Susanne Langer part of the job is in recognizing that the assumptions we hold are themselves the problems that we need to address. Questions contain answers, so to reach new answers we have to come up with new questions, new problems. All this means that it is important to examine our starting assumptions carefully. For example, we could ask how it is possible that we as individuals are able to communicate with others at all. But this way of framing the question already seems to presuppose the self as the starting point with communication based on this. As George Herbert Mead and others have pointed out this leads us into a theoretical quagmire. His alternative is that communication develops first and "selves" arise out of this social process.

The alternative that we propose is that it is relations between people that are primary. And knowledge of the world is rooted in successful action on the world. For us all, thinking emerges within social interaction, and this involves emotional engagement, not an abstract and detached set of inferences. In her poem entitled "First Weeks," Sharon Olds[35] describes her difficulties as a new mother in engaging with her newborn baby, but she ends with the lines: "When she smiled at me, … I fell in love, I became human." We would add that her young baby took an important step in the process of developing as a person. There is something about the kinds of relationships that are possible for humans that makes human forms of thinking possible. Human infant–parent interaction is an evolved system—babies are cute and we like to play with them. It is this interaction in which human development begins, and in which thinking emerges.

Suggested further reading

Carpendale J. I. M., & C. Lewis, C. (2011). Self constructed in culture. In K. J. de López & T. G. B. Hansen (Eds.), *Development of self in culture* (pp. 25–40). Denmark: Aalborg University Press.

Carpendale, J. I. M., Lewis, C. & Müller, U. (2018). *The development of children's thinking: Its social and communicative foundations*. London: Sage.

Notes

1 Bernstein (2010).
2 Shepard and Metzler (1971).
3 Ward, Ganis, and Bach (2019).
4 For example, Piaget (1972, p. 21); Baldwin (1906); Hobson (2002); Merleau-Ponty (1962); Piaget (1954); Werner and Kaplan (1963).
5 Rochat and Hespos (1997).
6 Lear (2005).
7 Carpendale and Lewis (2011).
8 Mead (1934, p. 182).
9 Forst (2005).
10 *Woody Allen: A Documentary* (2011), directed by Robert B. Weide.
11 Becker (1973).
12 Cf. Canfield (2007).
13 Adams (1980, pp. 58–59).
14 From the fictional character Kilgore Trout, created by Kurt Vonnegut, in the novel *Venus on the Half-shell*, pseudonymously written by Philip José Farmer.
15 Sprintzen (2009, p. 26).
16 Sprintzen (2009, p. 26).
17 This statement was cited widely and taken up by Neil Dagnall and Ken Drinkwater (2018) in an article titled "What happens to your brain when you die?"
18 See, for example, Cohen (2004).
19 Vonnegut (1981, p. 144).
20 Gould, 1992).
21 Glassman (2000); Kropotkin (1989).
22 See de Waal (2006); Meloni (2013).
23 Griffiths and Stotz (2000, p. 45).
24 Griffiths and Stotz (2000, p. 44–45).
25 Elias (1978, p. 107).
26 Geertz (1973, p. 5).
27 Tomasello, Kruger, and Ratner (1993).
28 Liebal et al. (2011).
29 Callaghan et al. (2011).
30 For example, Canfield (2007).
31 Smith (2007).
32 Sugarman (2015).
33 Piaget (1952, pp. 3–4).
34 Jopling (1993).
35 Olds (2002, pp. 40–41).

References

Adams, D. (1980). *The restaurant at the end of the universe: The hitchhiker's guide to the galaxy 2.* London: Pan Books.

Adams, D. (1982). *Life, the universe and everything: The hitchhiker's guide to the galaxy 3.* London: Pan Books.

Adolph, K. E. (2000). Specificity of learning: Why infants fall over a veritable cliff. *Psychological Science,* 11(4), 290–295.

Adolph, K. E., Robinson, S. R., Young, J. W., & Gill-Alvarez, F. (2008). What is the shape of developmental change? *Psychological Review,* 115, 527–543.

Aldwin, C. M. (2014). Rethinking developmental science. *Research in Human Development,* 11, 247–254.

Allen, J. W. P., & Bickhard, M. H. (2013). Stepping off the pendulum: Why only an action-based approach can transcend the nativist-empiricist debate. *Cognitive Development,* 28, 96–133.

Ambrosini, E., Reddy, V., de Looper, A., Constantini, M., Lopez, B., & Sinigaglia, C. (2013). Looking ahead: Anticipatory gaze and motor ability in infancy. *PLOS One,* 8, 1–9.

Anisfeld, M. (1996). Only tongue protrusion modeling is matched by neonates. *Developmental Review,* 16, 149–161.

Anisfeld, M., Turkewitz, G., & Rose, S. (2001). No compelling evidence that newborns imitate oral gestures. *Infancy,* 2, 111–122.

Archer, J. (2000). Sex differences in aggression between heterosexual partners: A meta-analytic review. *Psychological Bulletin,* 126, No. 5, 651–680.

Astington, J. W., & Baird, J. A. (Eds.) (2005). *Why language matters for theory of mind.* New York: Oxford University Press.

Augustine (1923). *The confessions of St Augustine.* Translated by T. Matthew. London: Fontana Books.

Augustine (2001). *Saint Augustine's childhood: Confessions book one.* Translated by G. Wills. New York: Viking.

Avinun, R., & Knafo, A. (2014). Parenting as a reaction evoked by children's genotype: A meta-analysis of children-as-twins studies. *Personality and Social Psychology Review,* 18(1), 87–102.

Baillargeon, R. (1987). Object permanence in 3 1/2- and 4 1/2-month old infants. *Developmental Psychology*, 23, 655–664.

Baillargeon, R. (2004). Infants' reasoning about hidden objects: Evidence for event-general and event-specific expectation. *Developmental Science*, 7, 391–414.

Baillargeon, R. (2008). Innate ideas revisited: For a principle of persistence in infants' physical reasoning. *Perspectives on Psychological Science*, 3, 2–12.

Bakermans-Kranenburg, M. J., & Van IJzendoorn, M. H. (2007). Genetic vulnerability or differential susceptibility in child development: The case of attachment. *Journal of Child Psychology and Psychiatry*, 48, 1160–1173.

Bakermans-Kranenburg, M. J., & Van IJzendoorn, M. H. (2011). Differential susceptibility to rearing environment depending on dopamine-related genes: New evidence and a meta-analysis. *Development and Psychopathology*, 23(1), 39–52.

Bakermans-Kranenburg, M. J., & Van IJzendoorn, M. H. (2015). The Hidden Efficacy of Interventions: Gene × Environment Experiments from a Differential Susceptibility Perspective. *Annual Review of Psychology*, 66, 381–409.

Baldwin, J. M. (1906). *Thoughts and things, vol. 1: Functional logic*. New York: The MacMillan Company.

Bartal, I. B.-A., Decety, J., & Mason, P. (2011). Empathy and pro-social behavior in rats. *Science*, 334(6061), 1427–1430.

Bates, E. (1976). *Language and context*. New York: Academic Press.

Bates, E. (1979). *The emergence of symbols: Cognition and communication in infancy*. New York: Academic Press.

Bates, E. (1984). Bioprograms and the innateness hypothesis. *Behavioral and Brain Sciences*, 7(2), 188–190.

Bates, E. (1999). Plasticity, localization and language development. In S. H. Broman & J. M. Fletcher (Eds.), *The changing nervous system: Neurobehavioral consequences of early brain disorders* (pp. 214–253). New York: Oxford University Press.

Bates, E. (2005). Plasticity, localization, and language development. In S. T. Taylor, J. Langer, & C. Milbrath (Eds.), *Biology and knowledge revisited: From neurogenesis to psychogenesis* (pp. 205–253). Mahwah, NJ: Erlbaum.

Bates, E., Camaioni, L., & Volterra, V. (1975). The acquisition of performatives prior to speech. *Merrill-Palmer Quarterly*, 21, 205–226.

Bateson, G. (1979). *Mind and nature: A necessary unity*. New York: Bantam Books.

Beach, F. A. (1955). The descent of instinct. *Psychological Review*, 62, 401–410.

Beck, D. M. (2010). The appeal of the brain in the poplar press. *Perspectives on Psychological Science*, 5, 762–766.

Becker, E. (1973). *The denial of death*. New York: Free Press.

Bell, R. Q. (1968). A reinterpretation of the direction of effects in studies of socialization. *Psychological Review*, 75(2), 81–96.

Bennett, M. R. & Hacker, P. M. S. (2003). *The philosophical foundations of neuroscience*. Oxford: Blackwell.

Bennour, M., & Vonèche, J. (2009). The historical context of Piaget's ideas. In U. Müller, J. I. M. Carpendale, & L. Smith (Eds.). *The Cambridge Companion to Piaget* (pp. 45–63). New York: Cambridge University Press.

Bernstein, R. J. (2010). *The pragmatic turn.* Malden, MA: Polity Press.

Bibok, M. B., Carpendale, J. I. M., & Lewis, C. (2008). Social knowledge as social skill: An action based view of social understanding. In U. Müller, J. I. M. Carpendale, N. Budwig, & B. Sokol (Eds.), *Social life and social knowledge: Toward a process account of development* (pp. 145–169). New York: Taylor & Francis.

Bickhard, M. H. (2001). Why children don't have to solve the frame problems: Cognitive representations are not encodings. *Developmental Review, 21,* 224–262.

Bickhard, M. H. (2009). The interactivist model. *Synthese, 166,* 547–591.

Bickhard, M. H., & Terveen, L. (1995). *Foundational issues in artificial intelligence and cognitive science: Impasse and solution.* Oxford: Elsevier Scientific.

Bigelow, A. E. (2003). The development of joint attention in blind infants. *Development and Psychopathology, 15,* 259–275.

Bloom, P. (2010). The moral life of babies. *New York Times,* May 5.

Bogartz, R. S., Shinskey, J. L., & Speaker, C. J. (1997). *Interpreting infant looking: The event set × event set design. Developmental Psychology, 33*(3), 408–422.

Bowlby, J. (1958). The nature of the child's tie to his mother. *The International Journal of Psychoanalysis, 39,* 350–373.

Bowlby, J. (1969). *Attachment.* Harmondsworth: Penguin.

Brandom, R. B. (1994). *Making it explicit: Reasoning, representing and discursive commitment.* Cambridge, MA: Harvard University Press.

Bremner, J. G. (1988). *Infancy.* Oxford: Blackwell.

Bringuier, J.-C. (1980). *Conversations with Jean Piaget.* Chicago, IL: University of Chicago Press. (Original work published 1977)

Brown, D., Lamb, M. E., Lewis, C., Pipe, M, Orbach, Y., & Wolfson, M. (2013). The NICHD Investigative Interview Protocol: An analogue study. *Journal of Experimental Psychology: Applied, 19,* 367–382.

Bruck, M., & Ceci, S. J. (1997). The suggestibility of young children. *Current Directions in Psychological Science, 6*(3), 75–79.

Bruder, C. E. G. *et al.* (2008). Phenotypically concordant and discordant monozygotic twins display different DNA copy-number-variation profiles. *The American Journal of Human Genetics, 82,* 763–771.

Bruner, J. S. (1972). Nature and uses of immaturity. *American Psychologist, 27,* 687–708.

Bryson, B. (1996). *Notes on a small island.* London: Penguin.

Bryson, B. (2015). *The road to Little Dribbling: More notes from a small island.* London: Penguin.

Butterworth, G. (1977). Object disappearance and error in Piaget's stage IV task. *Journal of Experimental Child Psychology, 23*(3), 391–401.

Butterworth, G. (2003). Pointing is the royal road to language for babies. In S. Kita (Ed.), *Pointing: Where language, culture, and cognition meet* (pp. 9–33). Mahwah, NJ: Lawrence Erlbaum.

Caballero-Gaudes, C., & Reynolds, R. C. (2017). *Methods for cleaning the BOLD fMRI signal.* NeuroImage, 154, 128–149.

Callaghan, T., Moll, H., Rakoczy, H., Warneken, F., Liszkowski, U., Behne, T., ... & Collins, W. A. (2011). Early social cognition in three cultural contexts. *Monographs of the Society for Research in Child Development*, 76(2), i–142.

Callahan, M. (2014). Twins separated at birth reveal their incredible reunion story. *New York Post*, October 19. Retrieved from https://nypost.com/2014/10/19/twins-separated-at-birth-reveal-their-incredible-reunion-story.

Campbell, R. L., & Bickhard, M. H. (1993). Knowing levels and the child's understanding of mind. *Behavioral and Brain Sciences*, 16, 33–34.

Campos, J. J., Anderson, D. I., Barbu-Roth, M. A., Hubbard, E. M., Hertenstein, M. J., & Witherington, D. (2000). Travel broadens the mind. *Infancy*, 1, 149–219.

Campos, J. J., Anderson, D. I., Barbu-Roth, M. A., Hubbard, M., Hertenstein, M. J., Witherington, D. (2000). Travel broadens the mind. *Infancy*, 1, 149–219.

Canfield, J. V. (1995). The rudiments of language. *Language and Communication*, 15, 195–211.

Canfield, J. V. (1999). Folk psychology versus philosophical anthropology. *Idealistic Studies*, 29, 153–171.

Canfield, J. V. (2007). *Becoming human: The development of language, self, and self-consciousness*. New York: Palgrave Macmillan.

Carpendale, J. I. M. (2009). Piaget's theory of moral development. In U. Müller, J. I. M. Carpendale, & L. Smith (Eds.), *The Cambridge companion to Piaget* (pp. 270–286). Cambridge: Cambridge University Press.

Carpendale, J. I. M., & Carpendale, A. B. (2010). The development of pointing: From personal directedness to interpersonal direction. *Human Development*, 53, 110–126.

Carpendale, J. I. M., & Chandler, M. J. (1996). On the distinction between false belief understanding and subscribing to an interpretive theory of mind. *Child Development*, 67, 1686–1706.

Carpendale, J. I. M., & Hammond, S. I. (2016). The development of moral sense and moral thinking. *Current Opinion in Pediatrics*, 28, 743–747.

Carpendale, J. I. M., Hammond, S. I., & Atwood, S. (2013). A relational developmental systems approach to moral development. *Advances in Child Development and Behavior*, 45, 125–153.

Carpendale, J. I. M, Kettner, V. A., & Audet, K. N. (2015). On the nature of toddlers' helping: Helping or interest in others' activity? *Social Development*, 24, 357–366.

Carpendale, J. I. M., & Lewis, C. (2004). Constructing an understanding of mind: The development of children's social understanding within social interaction. *Behavioral and Brain Sciences*, 27, 79–151.

Carpendale, J. I. M., & Lewis, C. (2006). *How children develop social understanding*. Oxford: Blackwell Publishers.

Carpendale J. I. M., & C. Lewis, C. (2011). Self constructed in culture. In K. J. de López, & T. G. B. Hansen (Eds.), *Development of self in culture* (pp. 25–40). Aalborg: Aalborg University Press.

Carpendale, J. I. M., & Lewis, C. (2015). The development of social understanding. In L. Liben & U. Müller (Eds.), *Handbook of child psychology and developmental science vol. 2: Cognitive processes*, 7th edition. New York: Wiley Blackwell.

Carpendale, J. I. M., Lewis, C., & Müller, U. (2018). *The development of children's thinking: Its social and communicative foundations*. London: Sage.

Carpendale, J. I. M., Lewis, C., & Müller, U. (2019). Piaget's theory. In S. Hupp & J. Jewell (eds.), *Encyclopedia of child and adolescent development*. New York: Wiley.

Carpendale, J. I. M., & Racine, T. P. (2011). Intersubjectivity and egocentrism: Insights from the relational perspectives of Piaget, Mead, and Wittgenstein. *New Ideas in Psychology*, 29, 346–354.

Carpendale, J. I. M., & Ten Eycke, K. (in press). From reflex to meaning via shared routines. In M. F.Mascolo & T. Bidell (Eds.) *Handbook of integrative psychological development: Essays in honor of Kurt W. Fischer*. Abingdon: Routledge.

Carpendale, J. I. M., & Wereha, T. J. (2013). Understanding common developmental timetables across cultures from a developmental systems perspective. *Human Development*, 56, 207–212.

Carruthers, P. (2006). *The architecture of mind*. Oxford: Oxford University Press.

Carruthers, P., & Smith, P. K. (Eds.) (1996). *Theories of theories of mind*. Cambridge: Cambridge University Press.

Cellan-Jones, R. (2014). Stephen Hawking warns artificial intelligence could end mankind. BBC News, December 2.

Chandler, M. J. (1973). Egocentrism and antisocial behavior: The assessment and training of social perspective-taking skills. *Developmental Psychology*, 9, 326–332.

Chapman, M. (1988). *Constructive evolution: Origins and development of Piaget's thought*. New York: Cambridge University Press.

Chapman, M. (1991a). Self-organization as developmental process: Beyond the organismic and mechanistic models? In P. Van Geert & L. P. Mos (Eds.), *Annals of theoretical psychology, vol. 7* (pp. 335–348). New York: Plenum Press.

Chapman, M. (1991b). The epistemic triangle: Operative and communicative components of cognitive development. In M. Chandler & M. Chapman (Eds.), *Criteria for competence: Controversies in the conceptualization and assessment of children's abilities* (pp. 209–228). Hillsdale, NJ: Erlbaum.

Chapman, M. (1999). Constructivism and the problem of reality. *Journal of Applied Development Psychology*, 20, 31–43.

Cheney, D. L., & Seyfarth, R. M. (2005). Constraints and preadaptations in the earliest stages of language evolution. *The Linguistic Review*, 22, 135–159.

Chomsky, N. (2007). Biolinguistic explorations: Design, development, evolution. *International Journal of Philosophical Studies*, 15, 1–21.

Chong, S., & Whitelaw, E. (2004). Epigenetic germline inheritance. *Current opinion in genetics & development*, 14(6), 692–696.

Christiansen, M. H., & Kirby, S. (2003). Language evolution: Consensus and controversies. *Trends in Cognitive Sciences*, 7(7), 300–307.

Churchland, P. (2004). How do neurons know? *Daedalus*, 133(1), 42–50.

Clark, R. A. (1978). The transition from action to gesture. In A. Lock (Ed.), *Action, gesture and symbol: The emergence of language* (pp. 231–257). New York: Academic Press.

Cobb, M. (2020). *The idea of the brain*. London: Profile.

Cohen, S. (2004). Social relationships and health. *American Psychologist*, 59(8), 676.

Colbourne, J. K. *et al.* (2011). The ecoresponsive genome *Daphnia pulex. Science*, 331(6017), 555–561.

Coltheart, M. (2006). What has functional neuroimaging told us about the mind (so far)? *Cortex*, 42, 323–331.

Coltheart, M. (2013). How can functional neuroimaging inform cognitive theories? *Perspectives on Psychological Science*, 8(1), 98–103.

Cooperrider, K., & Núñez, R. (2012). Nose-pointing: Notes on a facial gesture of Papua New Guinea. *Gesture*, 12, 103–129.

Cosmides, L., & Tooby, J. (2013). Evolutionary psychology: New Perspectives on cognition and motivation. *Annual Review of Psychology*, 64, 201–229.

Coulter, J. (2010). Reflections on the "Darwin–Descartes" problem. *Journal for the Theory of Social Behaviour*, 40(3), 274–288.

Cowell, J. M., & Decety J. (2015). Precursors to morality in development as a complex interplay between neural, socioenvironmental, and behavioral facets. *Proceedings of the National Academy of Sciences USA*, 112(41), 12657–12662.

Crawford, M. B. (2008). The limits of neuro-talk. *The New Atlantis*, Winter, 65–78.

Cumming, G. (2013). *Understanding the new statistics: Effect sizes, confidence intervals, and meta-analysis*. London: Routledge.

Dagnall, N., & Drinkwater, K. (2018). What happens to your brain when you die? Near-death experiences explained by scientists. *Newsweek*, December 12. Retrieved from www.newsweek.com/what-happens-your-brain-when-you-die-near-death-experiences-explained-1243305.

Dahl, A., Campos, J. J., & Witherington, D. C. (2011). Emotional action and communication in early moral development. *Emotion Review*, 3(2), 147–157.

Darwin, C. (1872). *The expression of the emotions in man and animals*. London: John Murray.

Darwin, C. (1877). A biographical sketch of an infant. *Mind*, 2, 285–294.

Darwin, E. (1978). *Progress of the mind, in the Temple of nature; or, The origin of society: A poem with some philosophical notes*. New York: Garland Publishing. (Original work published 1803)

Deary, T. (2014). *Groovy Greeks*. London: Scholastic.

de Barbaro, K., Johnson, C. M., & Deák G. O. (2013). Twelve-month "social revolution" emerges from mother-infant sensorimotor coordination: A longitudinal investigation. *Human Development*, 56, 223–248.

Decety, J., Bartal, I. B.-A., Uzefovsky, F., & Knafo-Noam, A. (2016). Empathy as a driver of prosocial behaviour: Highly conserved neurobehavioural mechanisms across species. *Philosophical Transactions of the Royal Society B*, 371(1686), 20150077.

Devine, R. T., & Hughes, C. (2017). Let's talk: Parents' mental talk (not mind-mindedness or mindreading capacity) predicts children's false belief understanding. *Child Development*, 90(4), 1236–1253.

Devine, R. T., & Hughes, C. (2018). Family correlates of false belief understanding in early childhood: A meta-analysis. *Child Development*, 89, 971–987.

de Waal, F. (2006). *Primates and philosophers: How morality evolved*. Princeton, NJ: Princeton University Press.

Doguoglu, U. (2004). Naturalism and rule-following practices: Finding fault with Kripke's notion objectivity. In P. Schaber (Ed.), *Normativity and naturalism* (pp. 151–173). Frankfurt: Ontos Verlag.

Dunn, J. (1996). Children's relationships: Bridging the divide between cognitive and social development. *Child Psychology and Psychiatry*, 37, 507–518.

Dunn, J., Brown, J., Slomkowki, C., Tesla, C., & Youngblade, L. (1991). Young children's understanding of other people's feelings and beliefs: Individual differences and their antecedents. *Child Development*, 62, 1352–1366.

Dyer, G. (2008). *Climate wars*. Toronto: Random House.

Eagleman, D. (2007). 10 unsolved mysteries of the brain: What we know—and don't know—about how we think. *Discover*, July 30.

Edmonds, D., & Eidinow, J. (2001). *Wittgenstein's poker: The story of a ten-minute argument between two great philosophers*. London: Faber & Faber.

Elias, N. (1978). *What is sociology?* New York: Columbia University Press. (Original work published in 1970)

Farroni, T., Massaccesi, S., Pividori, D., & Johnson, M. H. (2004). Gaze following in newborns. *Infancy*, 5, 39–60.

Filippova, E., & Astington, J. W. (2008). Further development in social reasoning revealed in discourse irony understanding. *Child Development*, 79(1), 126–138.

Filippova, E., & Astington, J. W. (2010). Children's understanding of social-cognitive and social-communicative aspects of discourse irony. *Child Development*, 81(3), 913–928.

Finlay, B. L. (2007). Endless minds most beautiful. *Developmental Science*, 10, 30–34.

Fisher, S. E. (2006). Tangled webs: Tracing the connections between genes and cognition. *Cognition*, 101, 270–297.

Fitch, W. T. (2005). The evolution of language: A comparative review. *Biology and Philosophy*, 20, 193–230.

Fitch, W. T. (2010). *The evolution of language*. Cambridge: Cambridge University Press.

Fogel, A., & Hannan, T. E. (1985). Manual actions of nine- to fifteen-week-old human infants during face-to-face interaction with their mothers. *Child Development*, 56, 1271–1279.

Forst, R. (2005). Moral autonomy and the autonomy of morality: Toward a theory of normativity after Kant. *Graduate Faculty Philosophy Journal*, 26, 65–88.

Franco, F., & Butterworth, G. E. (1996). Pointing and social awareness: Declaring and requesting in the second year. *Journal of Child Language*, 23, 307–336.

Freedman, D. D. (1964). Smiling in blind infants and the issue of innate vs. acquired. *Journal of Child Psychology and Psychiatry*, 5(3–4), 171–184.

Freud, S. (1954). *Project for a scientific psychology. In: The Origins of psychoanalysis* (pp. 347–445). New York: Basic Books. (Original work published 1895)

Friend, T. (2018). How frightened should we be of AI? Thinking about artificial intelligence can help clarify what makes us human—for better and for worse. *The New Yorker*, May 14.

Frisch, K. von. (1966). *The dancing bees: An account of the life and senses of the honey bee.* London: Methuen & Co. (Original work published 1927)

Frisch, K. von. (1967). *The dance language and orientation of bees.* Cambridge, MA: The Belknap Press of Harvard University Press.

Frodi, A. M., Lamb, M. E., Leavitt, L. A., & Donovan, W. L. (1978). Fathers' and mothers' responses to infant smiles and cries. *Infant Behavior and Development*, 1, 187–198.

Fuchs, T. (2011). The brain—a mediating organ. *Journal of Consciousness Studies*, 18, 196–221.

Geertz, C. (1973). *The interpretation of cultures.* New York: Basic Books.

German, T. P., & Leslie, A. M. (2004). No (social) construction without (meta) representation: Modular mechanisms as a *basis* for the capacity to acquire an understanding of mind. *Behavioral and Brain Sciences*, 27, 106–107.

Glassman, M. (2000). Mutual aid theory and human development: Sociability as primary. *Journal for the Theory of Social Behaviour*, 30, 391–412.

Goldberg, B. (1991). Mechanism and meaning. In J. Hyman (Ed.), *Investigating psychology: Sciences of the mind after Wittgenstein* (pp. 48–66). New York: Routledge.

Gopnik, A., & Wellman, H. M. (1992). Why the child's theory of mind really is a theory. *Mind & Language*, 7(1-2), 145–171.

Gordon, R. M. (1986). Folk psychology as simulation. *Mind and Language*, 1, 156–171.

Gottlieb, G. (1991). Epigenetic systems view of human development. *Developmental Psychology* 27, 33–34.

Gottlieb, G. (2007). Probablistic epigenesis. *Developmental Science*, 10, 1–11.

Gould, S. J. (1977). Human babies as embryos. In S. J. Gould, *Ever since Darwin: Reflections in natural history* (pp. 70–75). New York: W. W. Norton.

Gould, S. J. (1992). Red in tooth and claw. *Natural History*, 101(11), 14.

Greenberg, G., & Partridge, T. (2010). Biology, evolution, and psychological development. In W. F. Overton (Ed.), *Handbook of life-span development, vol. 1: Cognition, biology, and methods across the lifespan* (pp. 115–148). Hoboken, NJ: Wiley.

Greene, J. (2003). From neural 'is' to moral 'ought': What are the moral implications of neuroscientific moral psychology? *Nature Reviews Neuroscience*, 4, 847–850.

Greene, J. D. (2016). Our driverless dilemma. *Science, 325(6293)*, 1514–1515.

Greene, J., & Haidt, J. (2002). How (and where) does moral judgment work? *Trends in Cognitive Sciences*, 6(12), 517–523.

Greene, J. D., Sommerville, R. B., Nystrom, L. E., Darley, J. M., & Cohen, J. D. (2001). An fMRI investigation of emotional engagement in moral judgment. *Science*, 293, 2105–2107.

Griffiths, P. E. (2009). The distinction between innate and acquired characteristics. In E. N. Zalta (Ed.), *The Stanford encyclopedia of philosophy*. Retrieved from https://plato.stanford.edu/entries/innate-acquired

Griffiths, P. E. (in press). Evo-devo meets the mind: Towards a developmental evolutionary psychology. In R. Brandon & R. Sansom (Eds.), *Integrating evolution and development*. Cambridge: Cambridge University Press.

Griffiths, P. E., & Gray, R. D. (2004). The developmental systems perspective: Organism-environment systems as units of evolution. In M. Pigliucci & K. Preston, *Studying the ecology and evolution of complex phenotypes* (pp. 409–431). New York: Oxford University Press.

Griffiths, P. E., & Machery, E. (2008). *Innateness, canalization, and 'biologicizing the mind.'* Philosophical Psychology, 21, 397–414.

Griffiths, P. E., & Stotz, K. (2000). How the mind grows: A developmental perspective on the biology of cognition. *Synthese*, 122, 29–51.

Habermas, J. (1990). *Moral consciousness and communicative action*. Cambridge, MA: MIT Press. (Original work published 1983)

Haidt, J. (2001). The emotional dog and its rational tail: A social intuitionist approach to moral judgment. *Psychological Review*, 108, 814–834.

Haidt, J., & Bjorklund, F. (2008). Social intuitionists answer six questions about moral psychology. In W. Sinnott-Armstrong (Ed.), *Moral psychology, vol. 2: The cognitive science of morality: Intuition and diversity*. Cambridge, MA: MIT Press.

Hamlin, J. K. (2015). The case for social evaluation in preverbal infants: Gazing toward one's goal drives infants' preferences for helpers over hinders in the hill paradigm. *Frontiers in Psychology*, 5, article 1563.

Hamlin, J. K., & Wynn, K. (2011). Young infants prefer prosocial to antisocial others. *Cognitive Development*, 26, 30–39.

Hamlin, J. K., Wynn, K., & Bloom, P. (2007). Social evaluation by preverbal infants. *Nature*, 450, 557–559.

Hamlin, J. K., Wynn, K., & Bloom, P. (2010). Three-month-olds show a negativity bias in their social evaluations. *Developmental Science*, 13, 923–929.

Harris, P. L. (1991). The work of the imagination. In A. Whiten (Ed.) *Natural theories of mind* (pp. 283–304). Oxford: Blackwell.

Hauser, M. D. (2006a). *Moral minds: How nature designed our universal sense of right and wrong*. New York: HarperCollins.

Hauser, M. D. (2006b). The liver and the moral organ. *Scan*, 1, 214–220.

Hay, D. (2009). The roots and branches of human altruism. *British Journal of Psychology*, 100, 473–479.

Hay, D., & Murray, P. (1982). Giving and requesting: Social facilitation of infants' offers to adults. *Infant Behavior and Development*, 5, 301–310.

Heal, J. (1996). Simulation, theory, and content. In P. Carruthers & P. K. Smith (Eds.), *Theories of theories of mind* (pp. 75–89). Cambridge: Cambridge University Press.

Heath, S. B. (1983). *Ways with words: Language, life and work in communities and classrooms*. New York: Cambridge University Press.

Heaton, J., & Groves, J. (1999). *Introducing Wittgenstein*. Cambridge: Totem Books.

Hebb, D. O., Lambert, W. E., & Tucker, G. R. (1971). Language, thought and experience. *Modern Language Journal*, *55*, 212–222.

Hegi, U. (1994). *Stones from the river*. New York: Poseidon.

Heil, J. (1981). Does cognitive psychology rest on a mistake? *Mind*, *90*, 321–342.

Heil, J. (1998). *Philosophy of mind: A contemporary introduction*. London: Routledge.

Hendriks-Jansen, H. (1996). *Catching ourselves in the act*. Cambridge, MA: MIT Press.

Herculano-Houzel S. (2012). The remarkable, yet not extraordinary, human brain as a scaled-up primate brain and its associated cost. *Proceedings of the National Academy of Sciences USA* 109 (Suppl 1), 10661–10668.

Heritage, J. (1984). *Garfinkel and ethnomethodology*. Cambridge: Polity Press.

Hirsh-Pasek, K., Golinkoff, R. M., & Eyer, D. (2004). *Einstein never used flash cards: How our children really learn—and why they need to play more and memorize less*. New York: Rodale Books.

Hobbes, T. (1988). *The leviathan*. New York: Prometheus Books. (Original work published 1651)

Hobson, P. (2002). *The cradle of thought: Exploring the origins of thinking*. London: Macmillan.

Hölldobler, B., & Wilson, E. O. (1994). *Journey to the ants: A story of scientific exploration*. Cambridge, MA: The Belknap Press of the Harvard University Press.

Hölldobler, B., & Wilson, E. O. (2011). *The leafcutter ants: Civilization by instinct*. New York: W. W. Norton & Company.

Hume, D. (1751). *An enquiry concerning the principles of morals*. London: A. Millar.

Huurneman, B., & Boonstra, F. N. (2016). Assessment of near visual acuity in 0–13 year olds with normal and low vision: a systematic review. *BMC Ophthalmology*, *16*(1), 215.

Hutto, D. D. (2013). Psychology unified: From folk psychology to radical enactivism. *Review of General Psychology*, *17*, 174–178.

Itkonen, E. (2008). The central role of normativity for language and linguistics. In J. Zlatev, T. Racine, C. Sinha, & E. Itkonen (Eds.), *The shared mind: Perspectives on intersubjectivity* (279–305). Amsterdam: John Benjamins Publishing Company.

Jablonka, E., & Lamb, M. (2005). *Evolution in four dimensions: Genetics, epigenetics, behavioral, and symbolic variation in the history of life*. Cambridge, MA: MIT Press.

Jablonka, E., & Lamb, M. (2007). Precis of: Evolution in four dimensions. *Behavioral and Brain Sciences*, *30*, 378–392.

James, W. (1890). *Principles of psychology*. New York: H. Holt.

Jaswal, V. K., & Akhtar, N. (2019). Being versus appearing socially uninterested: Challenging assumptions about social motivation in autism. *Behavioral and Brain Sciences*, 42, e82.

Jayaraman, S., Fausey, C. M., & Smith, L. B. (2017). Why are faces denser in the visual experiences of younger than older infants? *Developmental Psychology*, 53(1), 38–49.

Jonas, H. (1984). *The imperative of responsibility: In search of an ethics for the technological age*. Chicago, IL: University of Chicago Press. (Original work published 1979)

Jones, S. (2008). Nature and nurture in the development of social smiling. *Philosophical Psychology*, 21, 349–357.

Jones, S. S. (1996). Imitation or exploration? Young infants' matching of adults' oral gestures. *Child Development*, 67, 1952–1969.

Jones, S. S. (2006). Exploration or imitation? The effect of music on 4-week-olds' tongue protrusions. *Infant Behavior & Development*, 29, 126–130.

Jones, S. S. (2007). Imitation in infancy: The development of mimicry. *Psychological Science*, 18, 593–599.

Jones, S. S. (2009). The development of imitation in infancy. *Philosophical Transactions of the Royal Society, B*, 364, 2325–2335.

Jones, W., & Klin, A. (2013). Attention to eyes is present but in decline in 2–6-month-old infants later diagnosed with autism. *Nature*, 504, 427–431.

Jopling, D. (1993). Cognitive science, other minds, and the philosophy of dialogue. In U. Neisser (Ed.), *The perceived self* (pp. 290–309). Cambridge, MA: MIT Press.

Joseph, J. (2001). Separated twins and the genetics of personality differences: A critique. *American Journal of Psychology*, 114, 1–30.

Kachel, G., Moore, R., & Tomasello, M. (2018). Two-year-olds use adults' but not peers' points. *Developmental Science*, 21(5), e12660.

Kaminski, J., Riedel, J., Call, J., & Tomasello, M. (2004). Domestic goats, Capra hircus, follow gaze direction and use social cues in an object choice task. *Animal Behaviour*, 69, 11–18.

Kant, I. (2015). *Critique of practical reason*. Translated by M. Gregor. Cambridge: Cambridge University Press. (Original work published 1788)

Kanakri, S. M., Shepley, M., Varni, J. W., & Tassinary, L. G. (2017). Noise and autism spectrum disorder in children: An exploratory survey. *Research in Developmental Disabilities*, 63, 85–94.

Karasik, L. B., Tamis-LeMonda, C. S., & Adolph, K. E. (2011). Transition from crawling to walking and infants' actions with objects and people. *Child Development*, 82(4), 1199–1209.

Kaye, K. (1982). *The mental and social life of babies*. Hemel Hempstead: Harvester Wheatsheaf.

Kenny, A. (1991). The homunculus fallacy. In J. Hyman (Ed.), *Investigating psychology: Sciences of the mind after Wittgenstein* (pp. 155–165). London: Routledge. (Original work published 1971)

Kettner, V., & Carpendale, J. I. M. (2013). Developing gestures for no and yes: Head shaking and nodding in infancy. *Gesture*, 13, 193–209.

Kettner, V., & Carpendale, J. I. M. (2018). From touching to communicating: Forms of index finger use in the development of pointing. *Gesture*, 17(2), 245–268.

Khatchadourian, R. (2015). The doomsday invention: Will artificial intelligence bring us utopia or destruction? *The New Yorker*, November 23.

Kinsbourne, M., & Jordan, J. S. (2009). Embodied anticipation: A neurodevelopmental interpretation. *Discourse Processes*, 46, 103–126.

Klin, A., Gorrindo, P., Ramsay, G., & Jones, W. (2009). Two-year-olds with autism orient to non-social contingencies rather than biological motion. *Nature*, 459, 257–261.

Knecht, S., Dräger, B., Deppe, M., Bobe, L., Lohmann, H., Flöel, A., Ringelstein, E.-B., & Henningsen, H. (2000). Handedness and hemispheric language dominance in healthy humans. *Brain*, 123, 2512–2518.

Knight, C., Studdert-Kennedy, M., & Hurford, J. (2000). Language: A Darwinian adaptation. In C. Knight, M. Studdert-Kennedy, & J. Hurford (Eds.), *The evolutionary emergence of language: Social function and the origins of linguistic form* (pp. 1–16). Cambridge: Cambridge University Press.

Kobayashi, H., & Kohshima, S. (1997). Unique morphology of the human eye. *Nature*, 387, 767–768.

Kobayashi, H., & Kohshima, S. (2001). Unique morphology of the human eye and its adaptive meaning: Comparative studies of external morphology of the primate eye. *Journal of Human Evolution*, 40, 419–435.

Koegel, R. L., & Mentis, M. (1985). Motivation in childhood autism: Can they or won't they? *Journal of Child Psychology and Psychiatry*, 26(2), 185–191.

Krause, M. A., Udell, M. A. R., Leavens, D. A., & Skopos, L. (2018). Animal pointing: Changing trends and findings from 30 years of research. *Journal of Comparative Psychology*, 132, 326–345.

Krebs, D. L. (2011). *The origins of morality: An evolutionary account*. New York: Oxford University Press.

Kropotkin, P. (1989). *Mutual aid: A factor in evolution*. Montreal: Black Rose Books. (Original work published 1902)

Langer, S. K. (1942). *Philosophy in a new key: A study in the symbolism of reason, rite and art*. Cambridge, MA: Harvard University Press.

Lawson, D. F., Stevenson, K. T., Peterson, M. N., Carrie, S. J., Strnad, R. L., & Seekamp, E. (2019). Children can foster climate change concern among their parents. *Nature: Climate Change*, 9, 458–462.

Lear, J. (2005). *Freud*. New York: Routledge.

Leavens, D. A. (2011). Joint attention: Twelve myths. In A. Seemann (Ed.), *Joint attention: New developments in psychology, philosophy of mind, and social neuroscience* (pp. 43–72). Cambridge, MA: MIT Press.

Lehrman, D. S. (1953). Problems raised by instinct theories. *Quarterly Review of Biology*, 28, 337–365.

Levinson, S. C. (1995). Interactional biases in human thinking. In E. N. Goody (Ed.), *Social intelligence and interaction* (pp. 221–260). Cambridge: Cambridge University Press.

Lewis, T. (2014). Twin brothers separated at birth reveal striking genetic similarities. Retrieved from www.cbsnews.com/news/twin-brothers-separated-at-birth-reveal-striking-genetic-similarities.

Lewis, C., & Lamb, M. E. (2003). Fathers' influences on children's development: The evidence from two-parent families. *European Journal of Psychology of Education*, 18(2), 211–228.

Lewontin, R. (2000). *The triple helix: Gene, organism, and environment.* Cambridge, MA: Harvard University Press.

Lewontin, R. C. (2001). Gene, organism and environment. In S. Oyama, P. E. Griffiths, & R. D. Gray (Eds.), *Cycles of contingency: Developmental systems and evolution* (pp. 55–66). Cambridge, MA: The MIT Press. (Original work published 1983)

Lickliter, R., & Honeycutt, H. (2009). Rethinking epigenesis and evolution in light of developmental science. In M. Blumberg, J. Freeman, S. Robinson (Eds.), *Developmental and comparative neuroscience: Epigenetics, evolution, and behavior.* Oxford University Press.

Liebal, K., Reddy, V., Hicks, K., Jonnalagadda, S., & Chintalapuri, B. (2011). Socialization goals and parental directives in infancy: The theory and the practice. *Journal of Cognitive Education and Psychology*, 10(1), 113–131.

Lillard, A. (1998). Ethnopsychologies: Cultural variations in theories of mind. *Psychological Bulletin*, 123, 3–32.

Liszkowski, U., Carpenter, M., & Tomasello, M. (2007). Reference and attitude in infant pointing. *Journal of Child Language*, 34, 1–20.

Liszkowski, U., Carpenter, M., Henning, A., Striano, T., & Tomasello, M. (2004). Twelve-month-olds point to share attention and interest. *Developmental Science*, 7, 297–307.

Liszkowski, U., Carpenter, M., Striano, T., & Tomasello, M. (2006). Twelve- and 18-month-olds point to provide information for others. *Journal of Cognition and Development*, 7, 173–187.

Liszkowski, U., & Tomasello, M. (2011). Individual differences in social, cognitive, and morphological aspects of infant pointing. *Cognitive Development*, 26, 16–29.

Lock, A. (1978). The emergence of language. In A. Lock (Ed.), *Action, gesture and symbol* (pp. 3–18). New York: Academic Press.

Loftus, E. F., Miller, D. G., & Burns, H. J. (1978). Semantic integration of verbal information into a visual memory. *Journal of Experimental Psychology: Human Learning and Memory*, 4(1), 19–31.

Lucker, J. R. (2013). Auditory hypersensitivity in children with autism spectrum disorders. *Focus on Autism and Other Developmental Disabilities*, 28(3), 184–191.

Mackes, N. K., *et al.* (2020). Early childhood deprivation is associated with alterations in adult brain structure despite subsequent environmental enrichment. *Proceedings of the National Academy of Sciences*, 117(1), 641–649.

Macmillan, M. (2008). Phineas Gage: Unravelling the myth. *The Psychologist*, 21: 828–839.

Mameli, M., & Bateson, P. (2006). Innateness and the sciences. *Biology and Philosophy*, 21, 155–188.

Mameli, M., & Bateson, P. (2011). An evaluation of the concept of innateness. *Philosophical Transactions of the Royal Society B*, 366, 436–443.

Mann, C. C. (2011). The dawn of the homogenocene. *Orion*, May/June, 16–25.

Mareschal, D., Johnson, M. H., Sirois, S., Spratling, M. W., Thomas, M. S. C., & Westermann, G. (2007). *Neuroconstructivism: How the brain constructs cognition, vol. 1*. New York: Oxford University Press.

Margoni, F., & Surian, L. (2018). Infants' evaluation of prosocial and antisocial agents: A meta-analysis. *Developmental Psychology*, 54, 1445–1455.

Markham, B. (1983). *West with the night*. San Francisco, CA: North Point Press. (Original work published 1942)

Mauss, M. (1967). *The gift: Forms and functions of exchange in archaic societies*. New York: W. W. Norton & Co. (Original work published 1925)

McCabe, D. P., & Castel, A. D. (2008). Seeing is believing: The effect of brain images on judgments of scientific reasoning. *Cognition*, 107, 343–352.

McDonough, R. (1989). Toward a non-mechanistic theory of meaning. *Mind*, 98, 1–21.

McDonough, R. (2004). Wittgenstein, German organicism, chaos, and the center of life. *Journal of the History of Philosophy*, 42, 297–326.

McFarland, M. (2014). Elon Musk: "With artificial intelligence we are summoning the demon." *Washington Post*, October 24.

Mcquaid, N., Bibok, M., & Carpendale, J. I. M. (2009). Relationship between maternal contingent responsiveness and infant social expectation. *Infancy*, 14, 390–401.

Mead, G. H. (1922). A behavioristic account of the significant symbol. *The Journal of Philosophy*, 19(6), 157–163.

Mead, G. H. (1934). *Mind, self and society*. Chicago, IL: University of Chicago Press.

Mead, G. H. (1977). *George Herbert Mead on social psychology: Selected papers*. Edited by A. Strauss. Chicago, IL: The University of Chicago Press.

Meaney, M. J. (2010). Epigenetics and the biological definition of gene x environment interactions. *Child Development*, 81, 41–79.

Meins, E., Fernyhough, C., Wainwright, R., Das Gupta, M., Fradley, E., & Tuckey, M. (2002). Maternal mind-mindedness and attachment security as predictors of theory of mind understanding. *Child Development*, 73, 1715–1726.

Meloni, M. (2013). Moralizing biology: The appeal and limits of the new compassionate view of nature. *History of the Human Sciences*, 26(3), 82–106.

Meltzoff, A. N. (2011). Social cognition and the origin of imitation, empathy, and theory of mind. In U. Goswami (Ed.), *Wiley-Blackwell handbook of childhood cognitive development* (2nd ed., pp. 49–75). Malden, MA: Wiley-Blackwell.

Meltzoff, A. N., & Brooks, R. (2007). Eyes wide shut: The importance of eyes in infant gaze-following and understanding other minds. In R. Flom, K. Lee, &

D. Muir (Eds.), *Gaze-following: Its development and significance* (pp. 217–241). Mahwah, NJ: Erlbaum.

Meltzoff, A. N., & Moore, M. K. (1977). Imitation of facial and manual gestures by human neonates. *Science*, 198, 75–78.

Meltzoff, A. N., Gopnik, A., & Repacholi, B. M. (1999). Toddlers' understanding of intentions, desires, and emotions: Explorations of the dark ages. In P. D. Zelazo, J. W. Astington & D. R. Olson (Eds.), *Developing theories of intention* (pp. 17–41). Mahwah, NJ: Erlbaum.

Merleau-Ponty, M. (1962). *Phenomenology of perception*. London: Routledge & Kegan Paul. (Original work published 1945)

Messinger, D., & Fogel, A. (2007). The interactive development of social smiling. *Advances in Child Development and Behavior*, 35, 327–366.

Mikhail, J. (2007). Universal moral grammar: theory, evidence, and future. *Trends in Cognitive Sciences*, 11, 143–152.

Miller, G. (2008). Growing pains for fMRI. *Science*, 320, 1412–1414.

Moll, J., de Oliveira-Souza, R. & Zahn, R. (2008). The neural basis of moral cognition: Sentiments, concepts, and values. *Annals of the New York Academy of Sciences*, 1124, 161–180.

Moll, H., & Tomasello, M. (2004). 12- and 18-month-old infants follow gaze to spaces behind barriers. *Developmental Science*, 7, F1–F9.

Moll, J., Zahn, R., de Oliveira-Souza, R., Krueger, F., & Grafman, J. (2005). The neural basis of human moral cognition. *Neuroscience*, 6, 799–809.

Monk, R. (1990). *Ludwig Wittgenstein: The duty of genius*. London: Jonathan Cape.

Moore, C. (1996). Evolution and the modularity of mindreading. *Cognitive Development*, 11, 605–621.

Müller, U. (2009). Infancy. In U. Müller, J. I. M. Carpendale, & L. Smith (eds). *The Cambridge Companion to Piaget* (pp. 200–228). New York: Cambridge University Press.

Müller, U., Carpendale, J. I. M., & Smith, L. (2009). Introduction. In U. Müller, J. I. M., Carpendale, & L. Smith (Eds.), *The Cambridge companion to Piaget* (pp. 1–44). New York: Cambridge University Press.

Müller, U., & Overton, W. F. (1998). How to grow a baby: A reevaluation of image-schema and Piagetian action approaches to representation. *Human Development*, 41, 71–111.

Müller, U., & Racine, T. P. (2010). The development of representation and concepts. In W. F. Overton (Ed.), *Handbook of life-span development, vol. 1: Cognition, biology, and methods across the lifespan* (pp. 346–390). Hoboken, NJ: Wiley.

Müller, U., Sokol, B., & Overton, W. F. (1998a). Constructivism and development: Reply to Smith's commentary. *Developmental Review*, 18, 228–236.

Müller, U., Sokol, B., & Overton, W. F. (1998b). Reframing a constructivist model of the development of mental representations: The role of higher-order operations. *Developmental Review*, 18, 155–201.

Murphy, C. M., & Messer, D. J. (1977). Mothers, infants and pointing: A study of gesture. In H. R. Schaffer (Ed.), *Studies in mother–infant interaction* (pp. 325–354). London: Academic Press.

Ochs, E., & Schieffelin, B. B. (1982). *Acquiring conversational competence*. New York: Routledge.

Odling-Smee, F. J., Laland, K. N., & Feldman, M. W. (2003). *Niche construction: The neglected process in evolution*. Princeton, NJ: Princeton University Press.

Olds, S. (2002). *The unswept room*. New York: Alfred A. Knopf.

Osterling, J., & Dawson, G. (1994). Early recognition of children with autism: A study of first birthday home videotapes. *Journal of Autism and Developmental Disorders*, 24(3), 247–257.

Overton, W. F. (2006). Developmental psychology: Philosophy, concepts, methodology. In R. M. Lerner (Ed.), *Handbook of child psychology, vol. 1: Theoretical models of human development* (6th ed., pp. 18–88). Hoboken, NJ: John Wiley & Sons.

Overton, W. F. (2010). Life-span development: Concepts and issues. In W. F. Overton (Ed.), *Handbook of life-span development, vol. 1: Cognition, biology, and methods across the lifespan* (pp. 1–29). Hoboken, NJ: Wiley.

Overton, W. F. (2013). Relationism and relational developmental systems: A paradigm for developmental science in the post-Cartesian era. *Advances in Child Development and Behavior*, 44, 21–64.

Oyama, S., Griffiths, P. E., & Gray, R. D. (Eds.) (2001). *Cycles of contingency: Developmental systems and evolution*. Cambridge, MA: MIT Press.

Papoušek, H., & Papoušek, M. (1977). Mothering and the cognitive head-start: Psychobiological considerations. In H. R. Schaffer (Ed.), *Studies in mother–infant interaction* (pp. 63–85). London: Academic Press.

Perner, J. (1991). *Understanding the representational mind*. Cambridge, MA: MIT Press.

Perner, J., Ruffman, T., & Leekam, S. R. (1994). Theory of mind is contagious: You catch it from your sibs. *Child Development*, 65, 1228–1238.

Piaget, J. (1928). *Judgment and reasoning in the child*. London: Kegan. (Original work published 1924)

Piaget, J. (1952). *The origins of intelligence in the child*. London: Routledge & Kegan Paul. (Original work published 1936)

Piaget, J. (1954). *The construction of reality in the child*. New York: Basic Books. (Original work published in 1937)

Piaget, J. (1959). *The language and thought of the child*. New York: Meridian Books.

Piaget, J. (1962). *Play, dreams and imitation in childhood*. New York: W. W. Norton & Co. (Original work published in 1945)

Piaget, J. (1965). *The moral judgment of the child*. New York: Free Press. (Original work published 1932)

Piaget, J. (1970). Piaget's theory. In P. H. Mussen (ed.), *Carmichael's manual of child psychology*, 3rd edn, vol. 1 (pp. 703–732). New York: Wiley.

Piaget, J. (1972). *Psychology and epistemology: Towards a theory of knowledge*. (trans. A. Rosin) New York: Penguin Books. (Original work published 1970)

Pika, S. (2008). Gestures of apes and pre-linguistic human children: Similar or different? *First Language*, 28, 116–140.

Pika, S., & Bugnyar, T. (2011). The use of referential gestures in ravens (*Corvus corax*) in the wild. *Nature Communications*, 2, 560.

Pimm, S. L., Jenkins, C. N., Abell, R., Brooks, T. M., Gittleman, J. L., Joppa, L. N., Raven, P. H., Roberts, C. M. & Sexton, J. O. (2014). The biodiversity of species and their rates of extinction, distribution, and protection. *Science*, 344, 1246752.

Pinker, S. (1994). *The language instinct.*

Pinker, S. (1997). *How the mind works.* New York: W. W. Norton & Co.

Plato (1973). *Theaetetus.* Translated by J. McDowell. Oxford: Oxford University Press.

Pope, A. (1967). *Alexander Pope: selected poetry and prose.* New York: Holt, Rinehart and Winston. (Original work published 1733–1734)

Portmann, A. (1990). *A zoologist looks at humankind.* New York: Columbia University Press. (Original work published 1944)

Putnam, H. (1988). *Representation and reality.* Cambridge, MA: MIT Press.

Railton, P. (2000). Normative force and normative freedom: Hume and Kant, but not Hume versus Kant. In J. Dancy (Ed.), *Normativity* (pp. 1–33). Oxford: Blackwell.

Rawlinson, K. (2015). Microsoft's Bill Gates insists AI is a threat. BBC News, January 29.

Ray, E., & Heyes, C. (2011). Imitation in infancy: The wealth of the stimulus. *Developmental Science*, 14, 92–105.

Reddy, V. (2008). *How infants know minds.* Cambridge, MA: Harvard University Press.

Reddy, V., Markova, G., & Wallot, S. (2013). Aniticipatory adjustments to being picked up in infancy. *PLOS One*, 8, 1–9.

Reid, V. M., & Striano, T. (2005). Adult gaze influences infant attention and object processing: implications for cognitive neuroscience. *European Journal of Neuroscience*, 21(6), 1763–1766.

Rheingold, H. L. (1982). Little children's participation in the work of adults, a nascent prosocial behavior. *Child Development*, 53, 114–125.

Rheingold, H. L., Hay, D. F., & West, M. J. (1976). Sharing in the second year of life. *Child Development*, 47, 1148–1158.

Rhim, J., Lee, G.-B., & Lee, J.-H. (2020). Human moral reasoning types in autonomous vehicle moral dilemma: A cross-cultural comparison of Korea and Canada. *Computers in Human Behavior*, 102, 39–56.

Rigato, S., Menon, E., Johnson, M. H., Faraguna, D., & Farroni, T. (2011). Direct gaze may modulate face recognition in newborns. *Infant and Child Development*, 20, 20–34.

Robinson, I. (1975). *The new grammarian's funeral: A critique of Noam Chomsky's linguistics.* Cambridge: Cambridge University Press.

Rochat, P. (2014). *Origins of possession: Owning and sharing in development.* Cambridge: Cambridge University Press.

Rochat, P., & Hespos, S. J. (1997). Differential rooting response by neonates: Evidence of an early sense of self. *Early Development and Parenting*, 6(3–4), 105–112.

Ross, R. (2006). *Returning to the Teachings: Exploring Aboriginal Justice.* Toronto: Penguin Canada.

Rosenblueth, A., & Weiner, N. (1951). Purposeful and non-purposeful behavior. *Philosophy of Science*, 18.

Rossmanith, N., Costall, A., Reichelt, A. F., López, B., & Reddy, V. (2014). Jointly structuring triadic spaces of meaning and action: Book sharing from 3 months on. *Frontiers in Psychology*, 5, December.

Russell, J. (1992). The theory theory: So good they named it twice? *Cognitive Development*, 7, 485–519.

Russell, J. (1996). *Agency: Its role in mental development.* Hove: Erlbaum.

Ryle, G. (1949). *The concept of mind.* Harmondsworth: Penguin Books.

Saari, H. (2004). Wittgenstein on understanding other cultures. *Grazer Philosophische Studien*, 68, 139–161.

Saffran, J. R., Aslin, R. N., & Newport, E. L. (1996). Statistical learning by 8-month-old infants. *Science*, 274(5294), 1926–1928.

Salmond, A. (2003). *The trial of the cannibal dog: Captain Cook in the South Seas.* New York: Penguin.

Salvadori, E., Biazsekova, T., Volein, A., Karap, Z., Tatone, D., Mascaro, O., & Csibra, G. (2011). Probing the strength of infants' preference for helpers over hinders: Two replication attempts of Hamlin and Wynn *PLoS One*, 10(11), e0140570.

Sameroff, A. J., & Chandler, M. J. (1975). Reproductive risk and the continuum of caretaking casualty. In F. D. Horowitz, M. Hetherington, S. Scarr-Salapatek, & G. Seigel (Eds.), *Review of child development research, vol. 4.* Chicago, IL: University of Chicago Press.

Sandburg, C. (1916). *Chicago poems.* New York: Holt, Rinehart, & Winston.

Savage-Rumbaugh, E. S., & Fields, W. M. (2011). The evolution and the rise of human language: Carry the baby. In C. S. Henshilwood & F. d'Errico (Eds.), *Homo symbolicus: The dawn of language, imagination and spirituality* (pp. 13–47). Amsterdam: John Benjamins Publishing Company.

Savage-Rumbaugh, S., Fields, W. M., Segerdahl, P., & Rumbaugh, D. (2005). Culture prefigures cognition in *Pan/Homo* Bonobos. *Theoria*, 20, 311–328.

Scaife, M., & Bruner, J. (1975). Capacity for joint visual attention in infant. *Nature*, 253, 256–266.

Scarf, D., Imuta, K., Colombo, M., & Hayne, H. (2012). Social evaluation of simple association? Simple associations may explain moral reasoning in infants. *PLoS One*, 7(8), e42698.

Schaffer, H. R. (1977). *Studies of mother–infant interaction.* London: Academic Press.

Schaffer, H. R., & Emerson, P. E. (1964). The development of social attachments in infancy. *Monographs of the Society for Research in Child Development*, 29(3), 1–77.

Schel, A. M., Candiotti, A., & Zuberbühler, K. (2010). Predator-deterring alarm call sequences in Guereza colobus monkeys are meaningful to conspecifics. *Animal Behaviour*, 80, 799–808.

Schulte, J. (1996). *Experience and expression: Wittgenstein's philosophy of psychology*. Oxford: Oxford University Press.

Scola, C., Holvoet, C., Arciszewski, T., & Picard, D. (2016). Further evidence for infants' preference for prosocial over antisocial behaviors. *Infancy*, 20(6), 684–692.

Seyfarth, R. M., & Cheney, D. L. (2003). Signalers and receivers in animal communication. *Annual Review of Psychology*, 54, 145–173.

Shanker, S. (1998). *Wittgenstein's remarks on the foundations of AI*. New York: Routledge.

Shanker, S. G. (2004). Autism and the dynamic developmental model of emotions. *Philosophy, Psychiatry & Psychology*, 11, 219–233.

Shepard, R. N., & Metzler, J. (1971). Mental rotation of three-dimensional objects. *Science*, 171, 701–703.

Shinn, M. W. (1900). *The biography of a baby*. Boston, MA: Mifflin Company.

Shotter, J. (1984). *Social accountability and selfhood*. Oxford: Blackwell.

Shweder, R. A., Mahapatra, M., & Miller, J. G. (1987). Culture and moral development. In J. Kagan & S. Lamb (Eds.), *The emergence of morality in young children* (pp. 1–83). Chicago, IL: University of Chicago Press.

Slaughter, V., Peterson, C. C., & Carpenter, M. (2009). Maternal mental state talk and infants' early gestural communication. *Journal of Child Language*, 36, 1053–1074.

Sleigh, C. (2003). *Ant*. London: Reaktion.

Slocombe, K. E., Kaller, T., Turman, L., Townsend, S. W., Papworth, S., Squibbs, P., & Zuberbühler, K. (2010). Production of food-associated calls in wild male chimpanzees is dependent on the composition of the audience. *Behavior, Ecology & Sociobiology*, 64, 1959–1966.

Smith, L. (Ed.) (1996). *Critical readings on Piaget*. London: Routledge.

Smith. L. (2009). Introduction III: Reading Piaget in English. In U. Müller, J. I. M. Carpendale, & L. Smith (Eds). *The Cambridge Companion to Piaget* (pp. 28–44). New York: Cambridge University Press.

Smith, L., & Vonèche, J. (2006). *Norms in human development*. Cambridge: Cambridge University Press.

Smith, R. (2007). *Being human: Historical knowledge and the creation of human nature*. New York: Columbia University Press.

Sokolov, A. N. (1972). *Inner speech and thought*. New York: Plenum Press.

Spaemann, R. (2006). *Persons: The difference between 'someone' and 'something'*. New York: Oxford University Press. (Original work published 1996)

Spencer, J. P., Blumberg, M. S., McMurray, B., Robinson, S. R., Samuelson, L. K., & Tomblin, J. B. (2009). Short arms and talking eggs: Why we should no longer abide the nativist-empiricist debate. *Child Development Perspectives*, 3, 79–87.

Sprintzen, D. (2009). *Critique of Western philosophy and social theory*. New York: Palgrave Macmillan.

Stephen Lewis Foundation (2012). World AIDS Day message from Stephen Lewis. Retrieved from www.stephenlewisfoundation.org/blog/?m=201211.

Stiles, J. (2009). On genes, brains, and behavior: Why should developmental psychologists care about brain development? *Child Development Perspectives*, 3, 196–202.

Stiles, J., Brown, T. T., Haist, F., & Jernigan, T. L. (2015). Brain and cognitive development. In L. Liben & U. Müller (Eds.), *Handbook of child psychology and developmental science vol. 2: Cognitive processes*, 7th edition (pp. 9–62). New York: Wiley Blackwell.

Stotz, K. (2008). The ingredients for a postgenomic synthesis of nature and nurture. *Philosophical Psychology*, 21(3), 359–381.

Sugarman, J. (2015). Historical ontology. In J. Martin, J. Sugarman, & K. L. Slaney (Eds.), *The Wiley Handbook of theoretical and philosophical psychology: Methods, approaches, and new directions for social sciences* (pp. 166–182). New York: Wiley Blackwell.

Suomi, S. J. (2006). Risk, resilience, and gene x environment interactions in rhesus monkeys. *Annals of the New York Academy of Sciences*, 1094, 52–62.

Suttie, I. D. (1935). *The origins of love and hate*. Harmondsworth: Penguin Books.

Tafreshi, D., Thompson, J., & Racine, T. (2014). An analysis of the conceptual foundations of the infant preferential looking paradigm. *Human Development*, 57(4), 222–240.

Tallis, R. (2011). *Aping mankind: Neuromania, Darwinitis and the misrepresentation of humanity*. Durham: Acumen.

Tamis-LeMonda, C. S., Kuchirko, Y., & Song, L. (2014). Why is infant language learning facilitated by parental responsiveness? *Current Directions in Psychological Science*, 23(2), 121–126.

Tancredi, L. (2005). *Hardwired behavior: What neuroscience reveals about morality*. Cambridge: Cambridge University Press.

Tesson, G., & Youniss, J. (1995). Micro-sociology and psychological development: A sociological interpretation of Piaget's theory. In N. Mandell (Ed.), *Sociological studies of children*, vol. 7 (pp. 101–126). Greenwich, CN: JAI Press.

Tomasello, M. (1995). Joint attention as social cognition. In C. Moore & P. J. Dunham (Eds.), *Joint attention: Its origins and role in development* (pp. 103–130). Hillsdale, NJ: Lawrence Erlbaum Associates.

Tomasello, M. (2003). *Constructing a language: A usage-based theory of language acquisition*. Cambridge, MA: Harvard University Press.

Tomasello, M. (2014). *A natural history of human thinking*. Cambridge, MA: Harvard University Press.

Tomasello, M., Carpenter, M., & Liszkowski, U. (2007). A new look at infant pointing. *Child Development*, 78, 705–722.

Tomasello, M., Hare, B., Lehmann, H., & Call, J. (2007). Reliance on head versus eyes in the gaze following of great apes and human infants: The cooperative eye hypothesis. *Journal of Human Evolution*, 52, 314–320.

Tomasello, M., Kruger, A. C., & Ratner, H. H. (1993). Cultural learning. *Behavioral and Brain Sciences*, 16, 495–552.

Tugwell, S. (1982). *Early Dominicans*. Mahwah, NJ: Paulist Press.

Turing, A. (1951). Intelligent machinery, a heretical theory. Lecture given to 51 Society, Manchester. (Two versions, one TS numbered 1–10, the other CTS numbered 96–101, in the Turning Digital Archive.)

Turnbull, W. (2003). *Language in action: Psychological models of conversation.* Hove: Psychology Press.

Turkewitz, G., & Kenny, P. A. (1982). Limitations on input as a basis for neural organization and perceptual development: A preliminary theoretical statement, *Developmental Psychobiology*, 15, 357–368.

Vaillant, J. (2005). *The golden spruce: A true story of myth, madness and greed.* Toronto: Vintage Canada.

Valsiner, J., & van der Veer, R. (2000). *The social mind: Construction of the idea.* New York: Cambridge University Press.

Van de Veer, R., & Valsiner, J. (1988a). Lev Vygotsky and Pierre Janet: On the origin of the concept of sociogenesis. *Developmental Review*, 8, 52–65.

Van de Veer, R., & Valsiner, J. (1988b). On the social nature of human cognition: An analysis of the shared intellectual roots of George Herbert Mead and Lev Vygotsky. *Journal for the Theory of Social Behaviour*, 18, 117–136.

Vonnegut, K. (1997). *Timequake.* New York: G. P. Putnam's Sons.

Vonnegut, K. (1981). *Palm Sunday: An autobiographical collage.* New York: Delacorte Press.

von Uexküll, J. (1934). A stroll through the worlds of animals and men: A picture book of invisible worlds. In C. H. Schiller (Ed.), *Instinctive behavior— the development of a modern concept* (pp. 5–80). New York: International Press.

von Wright, G. H. (1963). *Norm and action.* London: Routledge & Kegan Paul.

Vukasović, T., & Bratko, D. (2015). Heritability of personality: a meta-analysis of behavior genetic studies. *Psychological Bulletin*, 141(4), 769.

Vygotsky, L. S. (1978). *Mind in society: The development of higher psychological processes.* Cambridge, MA: Harvard University Press.

Vygotsky, L. (1986). *Thought and language.* Cambridge, MA: MIT Press. (Original work published 1934).

Ward, C. V., Kimbel, W. H., & Johanson, D. C. (2011). Complete fourth metatarsal and arches in the foot of Australopithecus afarensis . *Science*, 331, 750–753.

Ward, E., Ganis, G., & Bach, P. (2019). Spontaneous vicarious perception of the content of another's visual perspective, *Current Biology*, 29(5), 874–880.

Warneken, F. (2015). Precocious prosociality: Why do young children help? *Child Development Perspectives*, 9, 1–6.

Warneken, F. (2016). Insights into the biological foundation of human altruistic sentiments. *Current Opinion in Psychology*, 7, 51–56.

Warneken, F., Hare, B., Melis A. P., Hanus, D., & Tomasello, M. (2007). Spontaneous altruism by chimpanzees and young children. *PLoS Biology*, 5(7), 1414–1420.

Warneken, F., & Tomasello, M. (2006). Altruistic helping in human infants and young chimpanzees. *Science*, 311(5765), 1301–1303.

Warneken, F., & Tomasello, M. (2009). The roots of human altruism. *British Journal of Psychology*, 100, 455–471.

Warneken, F., & Tomasello, M. (2013). Parental presence and encouragement do not influence helping in young children. *Infancy*, 18(3), 345–368.

Warneken, F., & Tomasello, M. (2014). Extrinsic rewards undermine altruistic tendencies in 20-month-olds. *Motivational Science*, 1, 43–48.

Watson, N. V., & Breedlove, S. M. (2016). *The mind's machine: Foundations of brain and behavior* (2nd edn). Sunderland, MA: Sinauer Associates.

Weisberg, D., S., Keil, F. C., Goodstein, J., Rawson, E., & Gray, J. R. (2008). The seductive allure of neuroscience explanations. *Journal of Cognitive Neuroscience*, 20, 470–477.

Weisberg, D. S., Taylor, J. C. V., & Hopkins, E. J. (2015). Deconstructing the seductive allure of neuroscience explanations. *Judgment and Decision Making*, 10, 429–441.

Wereha, T. J., & Racine, T. P. (2012). Evolutionary developmental systems theory and human social cognition. *Review of Philosophy & Psychology*, 3, 559–579.

Werner, H., & Kaplan, B. (1963). *Symbol formation*. New York: Wiley.

West, M. J., & King, A. P. (1987). Settling nature and nurture into an ontogenetic niche. *Developmental Psychobiology*, 20, 549–562.

West, M. J., & King, A. P. (2008). Deconstructing innate illusions: Reflections on Nature-Nurture-Niche from an unlikely source. *Philosophical Psychology*, 21, 383–395.

Westermann, G., Marechal, D., Johnson, M. H., Sirois, S., Spratling, M. W., & Thomas, M. S. C. (2007). Neuroconstructivism. *Developmental Science*, 10, 75–83.

Wikan, U. (2008). Honor, truth, and justice. In C. Wainryb, J. G. Smetana, & E. Turiel (Eds.), *Social development, social inequalities, and social justice* (pp. 185–208). Mahwah, NJ: Lawrence Erlbaum Associates.

Wilkins, D. (2003). Why pointing with the index finger is not a universal (in sociocultural and semiotic terms). In S. Kita (Ed.), *Pointing: Where language, culture, and cognition meet* (pp. 171–215). Mahwah, NJ: Lawrence Erlbaum Associates.

Willems, Y. E., Boesen, N., Li, J., Finkenauer, C., & Bartels, M. (2019). The heritability of self-control: A meta-analysis. *Neuroscience & Biobehavioral Reviews*, 100, 324–334.

Winch, P. (1958). *The idea of a social science and its relation to philosophy*. London: Routledge and Kegan Paul.

Wimmer, H., & Perner, J. (1983). Beliefs about beliefs: Representation and constraining function of wrong beliefs in young children's understanding of deception. *Cognition*, 13, 103–128.

Winnicott, D. W. (1964). *The child, the family, and the outside world*. Harmondsworth: Penguin Books.

Wittgenstein, L. (1968). *Philosophical investigations*. Oxford: Blackwell. (Original work published 1953)

Wittgenstein, L. (1972). *On certainty*. New York: Harper & Row. (Original work published 1969)

Wittgenstein, L. (1976). Cause and effect: Intuitive awareness. Translated by P. Winch. *Philosophia*, 6(3–4), 409–425.

Wittgenstein, L. (1980). *Culture and value*. Chicago, IL: The University of Chicago Press. (Original work published 1977)

Wittgenstein, L. (1983). *Remarks on the philosophy of psychology, vol. 2*. Oxford: Blackwell.

Wittgenstein, L. (1991). *Remarks on the philosophy of psychology, vol. 1*. Oxford: Blackwell.

Woolfe, T., Want, S. C., & Siegal, M. (2002). Signposts to development: Theory of mind in deaf children. *Child Development*, 73, 768–778.

Wright, R. (2004). *A short history of progress*. Toronto: House of Anansi Press.

Wynn, K. (1992). Addition and subtraction by human infants. *Nature*, 358, 749–750.

Yates, D. J., & Bremner, J. G. (1988). Conditions for Piagetian stage IV search errors in a task using transparent occluders. *Infant Behavior and Development*, 11(4), 411–417.

Zeveloff, S. I., & Boyce, M. S. (1982). Why human neonates are so altricial. *The American Naturalist*, 120, 537–542.

Zwaigenbaum, L., Bryson, S., Rogers, T., Roberts, W., Brian, J., & Szatmari, P. (2005). Behavioral manifestations of autism in the first year of life. *International Journal of Developmental Neuroscience*, 23, 143–152.

Index

For Product Safety Concerns and Information please contact our EU
representative GPSR@taylorandfrancis.com
Taylor & Francis Verlag GmbH, Kaufingerstraße 24, 80331 München, Germany